'We are Lovers of the Qalandar'

Piety, Pilgrimage, and Ritual in Pakistani Sufi Islam

Jürgen Wasim Frembgen

'We are Lovers of the Qalandar'

Piety, Pilgrimage, and Ritual in
Pakistani Sufi Islam

Foreword by
MICHEL BOIVIN

OXFORD
UNIVERSITY PRESS

OXFORD
UNIVERSITY PRESS

Oxford University Press is a department of the University of Oxford.
It furthers the University's objective of excellence in research, scholarship,
and education by publishing worldwide. Oxford is a registered trade mark of
Oxford University Press in the UK and in certain other countries

Published in Pakistan by
Oxford University Press
No. 38, Sector 15, Korangi Industrial Area,
PO Box 8214, Karachi-74900, Pakistan

ISBN 978-969-734015-6

Typeset in Times New Roman
Printed on 55gsm Book Paper

Printed by The Times Press (Pvt.) Ltd., Karachi

*To my dear friend and teacher
Ashfaq Ahmad Khan (1951–2018)
with affection and gratitude*

CONTENTS

FOREWORD

Located in central Sindh, not far from the banks of the River Indus, Sehwan Sharif is home to one of the most popular Sufi shrines in Pakistan and arguably South Asia. It houses the tomb of the Sufi saint Lal Shahbaz Qalandar (d. 1274 CE), which attracts a continuous pilgrimage year-round, with a peak in attendance that coincides with the annual feast of 18–19 and 20 Shaban. The figure of Lal Shahbaz Qalandar is very difficult to establish historically, given the small number of sources available. In addition, like all popular saints, he was the victim of his success insofar as he is claimed by several different religious communities as one of their own.

Nor are there many sources to know when the pilgrimage to his tomb (*mazār*) really began. In any case, it is likely that the mass pilgrimage is quite recent and may have commenced during Partition. Among other obscure areas relating to the Sufi we have the nickname Jhule Lal. No doubt that its origin can be found in the famous *damā dam mast Qalandar* song but its reference to swing, through a cradle (*jhūla*) in motion or a dance, is not enough to explain why this title was given to him whereas initially it was that of the Hindu divinity of the River Indus, also known as Uderolal or Zinda Pir. This symbolic interweaving of Islam and Hinduism perfectly reflects the circulation of models between the two chief religions in Sindh.

Moreover, it is true that before Partition, the city of Sehwan was half Hindu. The district to the north of the current *mazār* was called Thakur paro, or the Thakur's district, the latter being the hereditary priests of Udero Lal, whose temple was next to the *dargah* of Bodlah Bahar, the most important disciple of Lal Shahbaz Qalandar. The distribution of ritual roles in the *mazār* can undoubtedly be seen as a vestige of this religious interweaving. Indeed, one of the most decisive ritual moments is constituted by the three processions of the *mendī* (henna) organized each day of the annual festival (*'urs*). This procession is led by Sayyids on the first day, a Hindu on the second, and another Hindu on the third.

The preceding lines not only highlight the richness but also the complexity of Sehwan as a field of study. It is for this reason that we decided in 2007, not only to devote an in-depth study to the site, but also to give it a collective and multidisciplinary form. Academic interest in Sehwan is not new. For a few years, the city had been occupied by a team of French archaeologists led by Monique Kervran. Indeed, to the north of the city is Purana Qilla, or Kafir Qilla, i.e., the ruins of a fort said to have been built by Alexander the Great. Our team was composed of geographers, topographers, architects, historians, sociologists, and anthropologists.

It was under these circumstances that we were fortunate to be able to benefit from the knowledge of one of the best specialists in popular religion in Pakistan: Jürgen Wasim Frembgen. His training in Islamic studies and anthropology made him an ideal collaborator for our study group named the French Interdisciplinary Study Group on Sindh/Mission Interdisciplinaire Française du Sindh (MIFS). This volume is a vivid testimony to his deep knowledge of Sufism and Pakistan. It can be said that it reveals, among other things, two aspects that have been neglected by research on these issues: material culture and pilgrim networks outside the pilgrimage city.

Furthermore, through this study, he addresses unavoidable issues that may have recently emerged in the social sciences, such as the role of women in devotion, or that allow him to reconnect with more classical anthropological issues such as the famous question of this famous trance dance known as the *dhamāl*. Frembgen is a recognized specialist in material religious culture in Pakistan but his pioneering interest in popular Sufi iconography and its use is of note too.

His ethnography is always accurate, reflecting a true gift for observation and understanding, and his analyses draw on a solid knowledge of linguistics, ethnology, and religious sciences. For these reasons, it can be predicted without an iota of doubt that this book will constitute a watershed in Sufi, Islamic, and South Asian studies.

Michel Boivin
Director of the Centre for South Asian Studies
National Center of Scientific Research (CNRS) &
School of Advanced Studies in Social Sciences (EHESS)
Paris Research University

PREFACE

From 2003 to 2015, in the course of nineteen fieldtrips to Sindh and Punjab, I regularly conducted ethnographic research on the veneration of Lal Shahbaz Qalandar. In 2009, I had been a member of a French study group, the Mission Interdisciplinaire Française du Sindh (MIFS) headed by Dr Michel Boivin in which I collaborated in a programme focused on multiple expressions of devotion. I investigated the networks of Punjabi devotees of the Qalandar and studied the ritual spaces in the context of their pilgrimage. From 2010 to 2013, I participated in a multidisciplinary project on 'Muslim devotional practices and aesthetics', headed by Dr Ingvild Flaskerud funded by the Research Council of Norway. My own focus was on the visual culture related to Lal Shahbaz Qalandar. I wish to thank both research teams, the French and the Norwegian, for their cooperation and the respective research councils for funding my fieldwork. Further periods of participant observation were part of the research conducted in my capacity as Senior Curator (Hauptkonservator) of the Museum Fünf Kontinente in Munich (formerly Staatliches Museum für Völkerkunde München) whose Oriental Department I headed throughout my professional life from 1987 till my retirement in 2016.

It is my pleasure to acknowledge the help and support of several dear friends without whom the book in hand about the universe of the Qalandar would not have seen the light of the day. I would like to express my deepest respect and sincere thanks to Dr Ashfaq Ahmad Khan (d. 2018) of Lahore with whom I participated in rituals at Sufi shrines and experienced events of nocturnal Sufi music in Punjab over 20 years. He was the one with whom I regularly discussed my encounters with the living legacy of Sufism and Sufi-inspired folk Islam in Pakistan. I owe to him as much as to my academic teachers in anthropology and Islamic studies. It is to him whom I dedicate this book. Sayyid Asif Ali Zaidi (d. 2017) of Lahore for his long-lasting friendship since 1983 and masterful location managing for the documentary *The Red Sufi* for a German TV channel. I am indebted to him for his sincere commitment and warmheartedness. Shahana Burghri and her husband Aly Philippe Bossin of Hyderabad for being able to join them on several excursions through Sindh to Sehwan Sharif and Lahut Lamakan. Atiya Khan for many insightful conversations and fresh perspectives about the Qalandar and for hosting me in Karachi. Sayyid Mehdi Raza Shah Sabzwari for his continuous support and hosting me on many an occasion in Sehwan. Professor Neelam Hussain, Executive Director of Simorgh–Women's Resource & Publication Centre (Lahore), for her kind permission to use the Urdu booklet '*Ashiqān-e Qalandar* (compiled in 2010 for Simorgh) and to publish its English translation in Chapter IV in the present book. The text (pp. 79-105) was translated by Asif Jehangir, my friend and Urdu conversation partner who always helped me as far as Urdu or Punjabi were concerned. Final thanks to the late Baba Arif Sain (d. 2012) who hosted me on my first visit to Sehwan among his dervishes amidst of hundreds of thousands of pilgrims.

NOTE ON PRESENTATION

Most Urdu, Arabic, Persian, Punjabi, and Sindhi terms, marked in italics, are transliterated in a simplified from. The transliteration system used is mainly that of the *Encyclopaedia of Islam*, with my own modifications as well as those customary for works published in English, but consciously avoiding the 'English-ized' spelling which coming from journalism has today, unfortunately, sometimes even seeped into academic works. As an anthropologist, I have attempted to stay as close to colloquial pronunciation as is feasible. Other terms, names, and words which have found their way from Oriental languages as loan-words into most Western languages have been rendered without diacritics in their by now accepted transcriptions.

Throughout this volume, dates are given in the Common Era (CE), if not specified otherwise.

INTRODUCTION

Sayyid Usman Marwandi, better known by his honorific title Lal Shahbaz Qalandar, is the pivotal figure of the Qalandariyyah: a brotherhood of mystics and ascetics originating in the early thirteenth century in Eastern Iran and Central Asia.[1] The path taken by Qalandar dervishes is based on world-renunciation, antinomianism, and a peripatetic lifestyle. It is a radical, provocative, but also ascetic way of life which rejects the social values and the formalism of the external world and instead strives for states of religious rapture, abandonment, and ecstasy.

Lal Shahbaz Qalandar was born in Marwand or Marand, northwest of Tabriz in 1177 CE. His family traced its ancestry to the sixth Shia Imam, Ja'far as-Sadiq (d. 765), through his son Isma'il. His ancestors migrated from Iraq first to Mashhad in Khorasan and then turned to Marwand. Historical sources depict Lal Shahbaz as a young man with a strong religious inclination who made the pilgrimage to Makkah and was then initiated into the Qalandariyyah in Karbala. In the turmoil brought about by the Mongol invasion, he left Marwand and, following the order of his spiritual guide, moved eastwards together with a group of companions. He reached the subcontinent via the Makran coast and first went to the city of Multan in south Punjab where the famous Sufi Shaikh Baha'uddin Zakariya (d.1267) initiated him into the Suhrawardi order and is also supposed to have given him the honorific name Shahbaz— royal falcon.[2] According to legend, the wandering dervish, poet, and dancer, who carried a begging bowl and a wooden staff, donned a red robe till the end of his life.[3] After travelling to Multan and to other parts of northwest India where he met a number of famous Sufi saints of the Suhrawardi and Chishti orders, he did not choose an imperial city such as Lahore or Delhi to settle but moved to Sehwan in 1251, reaching the small town with a large following of Qalandar dervishes. Here he built his abode in the ancient trading city at the bank of the River Indus in central Sindh, today the southernmost province of Pakistan (Figs. 1–2). He passed away in 1274 CE. Out of veneration for the saint, the town is called since long Sehwan Sharif—the 'noble' Sehwan.

As far as the saint's religious affiliation is concerned, Isma'ilis in Sindh and elsewhere claim him to be one of them because of his descent from Isma'il, the eldest son of Imam Ja'far as-Sadiq, but this is disputed by most local authors as well as devotees who consider him an adherent of the Twelver Shia or a Sunni because of his name.[4] Other sources point out that Lal Shahbaz Qalandar was related to the *bī-shar'* branch of the Suhrawardi Sufi order—*bī-shar'* ('without the religious law') being a simplistic label often used as a reproach of heresy and non-belief by orthodox representatives of Islamic mysticism, and especially ascribed to the Qalandar movement.[5] Louis Massignon, however, emphasized that a Qalandar dervish was not *bī-shar'*, but a staunch ascetic practicing celibacy and living like a hermit.[6] With regard to the local perception of the saint, Michel Boivin argues:

> … evidence indicates that the Sayyid lineages of Sehwan have cleansed the figure of La'l Shahbāz Qalandar of unorthodox features. Mostly attached to the Qādiriyyah, and moreover to their very respectable status in the Sindhi Muslim society, they could have imposed a 'purified' tradition of La'l Shahbāz, although one part was impossible to remove, the *dhamāl'* or trance dance.[7]

Lal Shahbaz became the most well-known master of the Qalandar movement. He is in short 'the Qalandar', the most popular Sufi saint of Pakistan with the largest following of devotees. His adherents transcend all barriers of community and creed and include Muslims as well as Hindus. Christians and Sikhs frequent his tomb too, although in small numbers. People from all walks of life but especially the underprivileged, come to his shrine for solace, peace of mind, and refuge. They venerate him as a charismatic protector, healer, saviour, and a miracle-worker wielding great spiritual power. His devotees adore him as a towering figure among Sufi saints (*kull walīoñ kā sarkār*) and a unifying force beyond all religious denominations in Pakistan. His shrine in Sehwan, 'one of the most fascinating sanctuaries of the subcontinent',[8] is the focus of pilgrimage year-round, but in particular during the annual *'urs* festival (literally 'marriage'), a series of rituals marking the saint's death and his mystic union respectively nuptial with God (Fig. 3). At this time, the flourishing cult centre becomes a vibrant place of ecstatic religiosity marked by intense forms of devotion such as prayers of supplication, processions, trance dance, flagellations by Shias, and musical gatherings celebrated in a spirit of enthusiasm and joyousness. These local folk practices of the contemporary Qalandar tradition belong to popular Sufi Islam or informal Sufism centring at shrines of the 'Friends of God'.

The present volume is organized around three themes: piety, pilgrimage, and ritual. Lal Shahbaz Qalandar has become the focus of immense visual piety firmly embedded in popular imagistic shrine Islam in Pakistan. This visual culture is described and analyzed in detail in the first theme of this volume devoted to exuberant expressions of piety. Chapters I and II investigate memorial images and various aspects of religious aesthetics which also highlight how sacred spaces are constructed and shaped. This volume is thus an ethnographic study of aesthetic and devotional forms of expression deliberately examining the sphere of everyday life. In this context, pictures depicting the Qalandar have become powerful icons of love and devotion cherished by his followers.

The second theme deals with pilgrimage to Sehwan which is deeply embedded in the rhythm of local culture. Thus, Chapters III and IV discuss religious life of devotional communities from Punjab whose members passionately venerate the 'Red Sufi'. Most predominantly these communities consist of men, but, as the exceptional case of the circle of Mai Kausar shows, it can also be a female domain where women take the lead in such Sufi networks since generations. The history of this chain of saintly women or Sufi lineage covers the period from 1910 to 2010. Chapter V, which focuses on three remarkable liminal figures and ritual agents in the cult of Lal Shahbaz Qalandar, is intended to augment the thematical complex of pilgrimage.[9]

Spectacular trance dance known as *dhamāl* is the third and final theme examined in Chapter VI.[10] Swinging and whirling the body to the beat of drums represents essential ritual practice of pilgrims in Sehwan (Fig. 4). This sacred ritual is a characteristic feature of the devotional and ecstatic religiosity embedded in local societies of Sindh and Punjab. It is, in fact, a multisensory performing art and a 'field of aesthetics' on the borderline between religion and drama. With dismay the world came to know that on February 16, 2017 a suicide bomber and member of the self-styled Islamic State (IS) perpetrated a massacre when people assembled to perform *dhamāl* at the shrine.

Based on dense ethnographic description in combination with the analysis of piety, pilgrimage, and ritual related to Lal Shahbaz Qalandar, the present volume aims to contribute to a 'Sufism observed' which often seems to be neglected in mainly text-based Sufi studies.

Notes

1. A monograph by Michel Boivin [*Le soufisme antinomien dans le sous-continent indien. La'l Shahbāz Qalandar et son heritage XIIIe—XXe siècle* (Paris: Les Éditions du Cerf, 2012)] on Lal Shahbaz Qalandar and the Qalandar movement in the subcontinent is highly recommended for reading. For further information on the Qalandariyyah with rich bibliographical references, see Ahmet T. Karamustafa, *God's Unruly Friends: Dervish Groups in the Islamic Later Middle Period 1200-1550* (Salt Lake City: University of Utah Press, 1994), Jürgen Wasim Frembgen, *Journey to God: Sufis and Dervishes in Islam* (Karachi: Oxford University Press, 2008a), 66–127, and Alexandre Papas, *Mystiques et vagabonds en Islam. Portraits de trois soufis qalandar* (Paris: Les Éditions du Cerf, 2010).
2. Anna Suvorova, *Muslim Saints of South Asia: The eleventh to fifteenth centuries* (London and New York: RoutledgeCurzon, 2004), 186–7; and Jürgen Wasim Frembgen, *At the Shrine of the Red Sufi: Five Days and Nights on Pilgrimage in Pakistan* (Karachi: Oxford University Press, 2011a), 47–8.
3. See anonymous, 'Qalandar Lal Shahbaz' (Karachi: Department of Public Relations, Government of Sind, n. d.), 11; and Jethmal Parsram Gulraj, *Sind and its Sufis* (1924; reprint, Karachi: Culture & Tourism Department, Government of Sindh, 2016), 57.
4. See Michel Boivin, 'Reflections on La'l Shahbāz Qalandar and the Management of his Spiritual Authority in Sehwan Sharif,' *Pakistan Historical Society* 61/4 (2003): 42; and *Le soufisme antinomien dans le sous-continent indien*, 93–7.

5. Inam Mohammad, *Hazrat Lal Shahbaz Qalandar of Sehwan-Sharif* (Karachi: Royal Book Company, 1978), 70; cf. Frembgen, *Journey to God*, 44, 66–127 (in this study the term *bī-shar'* is used descriptively to structure diverse religious types).

6. Louis Massignon, *Essai sur les origines du lexique technique de la mystique musulmane* (Paris: Edition du Cerf, 1922), 147.

7. Michel Boivin, 'Note sur la danse dans les cultes musulman du domaine Sindhī,' *Journal of the History of Sufism* 4 (2004): 46–7.

8. Suvorova, *Muslim Saints of South Asia*, 186.

9. The text of this chapter represents a revised and updated version of an article published earlier [Frembgen, 'Betwixt and between: Figures of ambiguity in the Sufi cult of Lāl Shāhbāz Qalandar (Pakistan),' in *Pilgrimage and Ambiguity: Sharing the Sacred*, eds. by Angela Hobart and Thierry Zarcone (Canon Pyon: Sean Kingston Publishing, 2017a), 119–29]. I thank the editors and publisher for their kind permission to publish this revised version. Some names have been changed to protect anonymity.

10. The text of this chapter represents a revised and updated version of an article published earlier [Frembgen, '*Dhamāl* and the Performing Body: Trance Dance in the Devotional Sufi Practice of Pakistan,' *Journal of Sufi Studies* 1 (2012a): 77–113]. I thank the editors for their kind permission to publish the revised version.

I VISUAL PIETY
The Iconic Presence of Lal Shahbaz Qalandar

Introduction

Devotion to Lal Shahbaz Qalandar is the dominant idiom of ritual engagement during the pilgrimage to the saint's shrine in Sehwan in particular during the time of the *'urs*. This religious attitude, mostly called *'aqīdat*, *bandagī*, or *bhaktī* in South Asia, also characterizes the commemorative ritual events (*shām-e Qalandar*) celebrated by Punjabi devotees before the actual pilgrimage. In general, it pervades all places where the memory of the saint is celebrated. This devotion is, in fact, the main stimulus in the creation of aesthetic spaces (Fig. 5).

His ardent followers express their devotion by putting up iconic portraits of the Qalandar at home or workplace, watching pilgrimage footage, and bedecking vehicles with portraits, inscriptions, and stickers. Displayed also across shops, restaurants, hair salons, offices, and shrines, these images create a sacred space, making the saint's power both visible and explicit. In their extraordinary variety, comparable they are to devotional items used to venerate similarly popular saints such as the Hindu-Muslim saint Sai Baba of Shirdi (1838–1918) in India, the Sufi saint Amadu Bamba (c. 1850–1927) in Senegal, or the Catholic priest and Capuchin monk Padre Pio (1887–1968) in Italy. In this way, aesthetic objects related to the Qalandar and his shrine constitute a rich contemporary 'material religion' which I documented over a series of annual research trips (2003–15). My focus has been on common figurative and calligraphic artefacts as well as aesthetic expressions from the world of the pilgrims and not on the saint's relics kept by some of his shrine's custodians or dervishes' equipment.[1] Many of these representational objects are in fact mass-produced commodities used as cheap portable religious souvenirs, while others are individually hand-made by devotees themselves, carried in processions or carefully arranged in ritual context. Each absorbs the *barakat* (divine grace) of Lal Shahbaz Qalandar, considered to reside at his shrine, and henceforward serves as respected *tabarruk* to transfer his spiritual prowess.

In this chapter, I examine pictures from an archive of around 250 object-related photographs taken in the field,[2] of 93 artefacts and prints kept in the collection of Munich's Museum Fünf Kontinente, and from a private collection of audio-cassettes and DVDs of devotional documentary films. After addressing the question of the popularity and 'success' of the Qalandar cult, the visual culture of the veneration of Lal Shahbaz Qalandar will be discussed in the main chapter. The latter will be structured according to the pictorial content of different devotional media, such as portraits, pictorial emblems, and calligraphy. These figurative as well as non-figurative images, both iconic in nature, are not only interpreted with respect to their visual vocabulary and meaning but also explored in context of the following questions:

- How do these images become icons? By icon I mean an authoritative presence and imagination shared by the devotees of the saint.
- In what contexts do these icons appear?
- Other than being religious souvenirs, in which way do these sensory, tangible objects become essential elements of aesthetic spaces encouraging devotional practices?
- What is their performative dimension within imagistic devotion?
- What kind of response do these materialized memories initiate?

Drawing on approaches from visual studies, the anthropology of the senses, and performance theory as well as on the concept of 'visual literacy',[3] this chapter seeks to analyze the Qalandar as a visual icon and religious hero in personal, connective, and collective memory.

From Popularity to Iconicity: The Visual and Oral Culture of Lal Shahbaz Qalandar

Historical sources suggest the posthumous development of the Qalandar cult persisted down the centuries and his fame extended beyond Sindh into Balochistan, Punjab, the Northwest Frontier Province (now Khyber Pakhtunkhwa), and adjacent regions of Afghanistan, Iran, and India. Nevertheless, according to the findings of Michel Boivin, before the twentieth century, the saint's shrine, his *darbār*, had yet to become the centre of the town of Sehwan, as we know it today, but was located on its southern periphery.[4] In those days the shrine was situated, so-to-speak, right on the threshold of human habitation on one hand and graveyards and the wilderness on the other. Thus, in the early twentieth century, his cult was apparently still a more modest affair in comparison with the number of pilgrims in recent times. In those days the average attendance at the annual *'urs* was reported around 30,000–40,000. Similar numbers were recorded across other major shrines in Sindh.[5] A century later, this number has increased to about 500,000, even up to 1.2 million according to news and official press releases. Of course, the population of what was to become Pakistan had been much smaller before Partition in 1947, but the question of why the saint rose to such prominence in the second half of the twentieth century, particularly since the 1970s, remains. It seems that the major reason for this enormous drive in popular Qalandar piety, a popularity bordering on fandom, had been the music and film industry of Lahore.[6]

Songs and hymns paying homage to the Qalandar which invoke his 'absent presence', to quote an expression coined by Pierre Centlivres and Micheline Centlivres-Demont,[7] is a way to gain access to his *barakat*, his sacred power.[8] They had apparently already been popular among devotees in the first half of the twentieth century. In the 1950s, the emerging Pakistani middle class started to support musical performances other than the spiritual music which had always been part of traditional shrine culture. Thus, in the course of the 1960s, new urban venues and platforms for music were opened, the newly established National Institute of Folk Heritage recorded traditional folk music and commercial companies started the production and sale of audio-cassettes. Songs hitherto performed locally could now be purchased across bazaars and heard nationwide on radio. Even *qalandarī gīt* and *qasīdaiñ* performed by various folk singers became part of Punjabi films produced by Lollywood as the Lahore-based film industry is known. In musical gatherings at shrines noted artists, such as the nomad singer Reshma, Rubina Qureshi from Hyderabad, and the *malang*[9] and musician Sain Akhtar Husain from Lahore were regularly performing Qalandar songs in the 1960s. The real breakthrough for this evocative devotional poetry came through Noor Jahan, the legendary melody queen of Pakistan, who popularized the Punjabi (but originally Sindhi) folk song, *Lāl mērī pat rakhīo*.[10] In the hymn, the anonymous poet praises the superior status of his beloved saint:

> *Lāl mērī pat rakhīo bhalā Jhūle Lālan*
> *Sindhrī dā, Sehwan dā, Shāhbāz Qalandar*
> *Damā dam mast Qalandar, 'Alī dam dam dē andar,*
> *Sākhī Shāhbāz Qalandar*
> *Pīrān meñ mērā pīr sab dā wālī āe*
> *Laqab Asadullāh tē nām 'Alī āe*
> *Nām 'Alī sōe bhāg jagāe Jhūle Lālan*
> *Sindhrī dā, Sehwan dā, Shāhbāz Qalandar*
> *'Alī dam dam dē andar*
> *Maiñ dhukhīārī mardī jāwāñ, nazar karo tē kardī jāwāñ*
> *Koī nahīñ mērā tērē sewā Jhūle Lālan*
> *Sindhrī dā, Sehwan dā, Shāhbāz Qalandar, damā dam mast Qalandar*[11]

Oh Lal, keep my honour safe. Oh 'thou ruby who rocks himself in a cradle' [or simply 'the Red swinging'; sobriquet of the saint].
Oh thou of Sindh, oh thou of Sehwan, Shahbaz Qalandar.
Through your breath, oh Qalandar. In every breath resides (the saint) Ali.
Oh bounteous Shahbaz Qalandar.
Among all saints, my saint (Lal Shahbaz Qalandar) is the highest 'Friend of God'.
Your epithet is 'Lion of God' whilst your real name is Ali.
By chanting Ali's name my dormant good fortune comes back to life, oh Jhule Lal.
Oh thou of Sindh, of thou of Sehwan, Shahbaz Qalandar.
Ali is present in each breath of mine.
Full of agonies, I am slowly dying. If you cast your kind eyes on me, I shall keep on chanting.

There is no helper other than you, oh Jhule Lal.
Oh thou of Sindh, of thou of Sehwan, Shahbaz Qalandar. Through your breath, oh Qalandar.

In 1968, renowned music composer Nazir Ali collaborating with Noor Jahan[12] arranged this traditional song for the Punjabi film, *Dilan de Soudey* (Deal of Hearts), directed by S. A. Bukhari. A variation of this ode of intoxicated abandonment and ecstatic experience is *Damā dam mast Qalandar*, later made world famous by Nusrat Fateh Ali Khan, an outstanding exponent of mystical *qawwālī* music, and is also the title of a Bollywood movie. In 1971/72, Nazir Ali composed the Qalandar song, *Shāhbāz kare Parwāz*, for the Punjabi movie, *Ma te Mama* (Mother and her Brother), and other songs of the popular genre of devotional *qalandarī dhamālaiñ*. The latter are sung to enhance the longing for visiting the saint and to accompany ecstatic dance (Fig. 6). From the 1970s onwards, Sufi chants of the *qawwālī* genre, which were spectacularly performed in public, were further popularized and turned into media commodities. Musicologist Jean During notes in this context:

With radio, record, and then the recovery by World Music, the *qawwālī* has become an international commercial product. Many of these hymns can be heard in every disco club in India and Pakistan, arranged in diverse ways. These include the pop style of the famous Sindhi hymn *Jhūle La'l*, whose adaptations are innumerable, as well as variations of *damā dam mast Qalandar*.[13]

In fact, the original Sindhi hymn *Jhūle La'l* as well as its later derived Punjabi song *Lāl mērī pat rakhīo*, and its variation *damā dam mast Qalandar* often get mixed.[14] Also, beyond the domain of profane entertainment, mentioned by During, namely in popular piety, songs, and hymns praising the Qalandar play a similar important role like, for instance, the Sufi poetry of the famous Sindhi saint Shah Latif. An outstanding exponent of Qalandar songs is Abida Parveen, the queen of mystical music in Pakistan. This popular genre of devotional *qalandarī dhamālaiñ* belongs to the repertoire of many renowned Pakistani musicians (Fig. 7).[15]

Although its affinity with music contributed decisively to the success of the Qalandar cult in reaching out to a far greater audience, the saint's popularity in the modern media is complemented by other important determinants of his durable fame. Thus, the Qalandar is attractive for devotees because he appears as a major miracle-working and healing saint and, of course, because of the ecstatic dance (*dhamāl*) said to be introduced by him. In addition, he is respected as a learned Sufi and preacher, particularly by the local population. Due to the lack of reliable historical sources, the saint's genealogy is contested and remains plurivocal so-to-speak. Although the saint bears the name of the Sunni caliph Harat Usman RA, he has, as the descendant of Isma'il, an Isma'ili predigree. According to Isma'ili tradition, Usman Marwandi/Lal Shahbaz Qalandar was the son of a preacher (*da'ī*, known in South Asia as *pīr*) and helped his brother Pir Tajuddin, the Isma'ili Imam's deputy, in spreading the Isma'ili faith on the subcontinent.[16] Twelver Shias, on the other hand, emphasize his descent from Hazrat Imam Husain RA and fervently venerate him at the time of his *'urs* through public flagellation. Competitive traditions thus link him to both, Sunni and, genealogically, to Shia Islam (Twelver Shia and Isma'iliyyah) cutting thus across sectarian denominations. The Qalandar is likewise worshipped as Raja Bharthari, a Shivaite ascetic considered to be an incarnation of Lord Shiva, by his many Hindu followers. The name Sehwan and its older form Sewestan is, in fact, derived from *shīv astāno* (the place of Shiva).[17] Thereby, Lal Shahbaz Qalandar himself appears as an incarnation of the Hindu God Shiva. Hindus also simply call the Qalandar 'The Red Lord', Lal Sain.[18]

In tandem with the boom in media promoting passionate love for the Qalandar, the small town of Sehwan, with a mere 10,000–12,000 inhabitants in the mid-1970s, suddenly found itself in national limelight. Zulfikar Ali Bhutto, born into a prominent Sindhi Muslim feudal family, who served as president of Pakistan from 1971–3 and prime minister from 1973–7, promoted the Qalandar cult and ordered the town's development among other things to increase his popularity. In the mid-1970s, Sehwan, which had only had electricity for some 10 years, was connected by metalled road with Jamshoro/Hyderabad in the south and Dadu in the north. In addition to the renovation of the shrine by the Auqaf Department,[19] rest houses, lodges for pilgrims, restaurants, shops, banks, and schools were also built.[20] Furthermore, Sehwan benefitted from improvements in rail and better air connectivity to Hyderabad. The underprivileged, from the countryside as well as the cities, were able to travel more easily to Sehwan. This holds especially true for the Punjabi devotees who started coming en masse in the late 1970s. It is estimated they comprise about 70 per cent of all pilgrims.

The growing popularity of the Qalandar interlinked with the growth of the media has also been the reason for the plenitude of pictures available since the 1970s. Most of the visual and aural media of piety expressing inner attachment to the saint is mass-produced: printed material is primarily produced and distributed from Lahore and secondarily from Faisalabad, Hyderabad, and Karachi. Since the late 1970s and early 1980s, a market for devotional items developed in which commercial artists designed new variations each year to satisfy consumer demand. In this, pictures with benevolent images are sold as commodities which contradict conservative Muslim image anxiety. In the festival period of the 'urs, Sehwan quite literally becomes a 'consumptionscape'[21] with hundreds of stalls around the shrine selling cheap religious articles. As a rule, the barakat of the saint is transferred onto them when the respective devotional object is touched on the grave. It is important to devotees that the image they bring home from the pilgrimage is practically efficient in terms of protecting them and emanating divine energy. Aesthetics are not in the foreground when pilgrims buy posters or other images although they do captivate on account of sensory reality. Instead, as Christopher Pinney aptly emphasized, 'the meaning of images lies in their needs.'[22]

Since the 1970s, first the print industry, followed by companies working with the new digital media such as video from the 1980s onwards, hastened to meet pilgrims' demands by propagating imaginary portraits of the Qalandar. Apart from songs on tape cassettes, which spread an 'aural aura' of the saint, there has been a major shift to the visual through mass-production of lithographs and, since 2005/06, also DVDs and Video-CDs (which have completely replaced video-cassettes). These VCDs are in fact hagiographic movies with music showing popular and current devotional practices at the shrine in Sehwan (Fig. 8). They refer to a Qalandar 'mythscape', that is to say to a memorized history transformed into myth and localized in the commemorative space of Sehwan. Occasionally, these pictures also appear on the Internet, and the Qalandar VCDs even find their way to India. Thus, over the last 40–50 years, the Qalandar has become a veritable visual icon, 'made' popular, so-to-speak, in interaction with the public. Part and parcel of the popular is that it is not legitimized by content but rather by public approval. Such images strengthen devotional fervour and the sense of belonging to the Qalandar. This process of 'iconization' is still ongoing: iconic images are copied again and again and taken as models for conventional paintings as well as for modern stickers and new devotional items such as calligraphic pendants. In the present visual age, there is no other Sufi saint in Pakistan whose image is presented in such number on posters, placards, banners, pendants, stickers, as well as in films. Illustrated articles in the press cover his veneration.[23] Devotion and iconolatry are closely intertwined in his cult.

Before discussing his iconic images, the most basic and essential symbol of devotion to the Qalandar should be explored: the colour red.

Iconic Red

The affectionate *laqab* (descriptive epithet) of the saint is Lal Shahbaz, which means 'red royal falcon', red like a ruby (*la'l*, *lāl*).[24] This is the colour of mystic ardour and passionate love for God. In Sufi poetry, the mystical seekers of God drink wine (referred to as *la'l* in Persian) which is a metaphor for divine love and inspiration. Therefore, *la'l* signifies divine knowledge.[25] Moreover, red is a 'hot colour' which mainly stands for blood and vital energy as well as for the ambiguities of life and death in general. Thus, it is also a metaphor 'for anything that is strident or violent'.[26] These connotations are not only an intrinsic part of Sufism, but the colour red is also similarly important in the Hindu cult of Shiva, who was worshipped in Sehwan before the Qalandar's arrival. In the Shia tradition, red is the symbolic colour of Hazrat Ali RA and the *ahl al-baīt* (family of the Prophet PBUH) but especially associated with the Prophet's grandson, Hazrat Imam Husain RA, who died a martyr in the battle of Karbala. As aforementioned, Shias consider the Qalandar a descendant of Hazrat Imam Husain RA. Boivin points to yet another meaning of red: 'Red is also the symbol of royalty and power, and it is well-known that Sufism borrowed from the lexicon of kingship.'[27] Thus, for instance, among the Mughal dynasty, royal regalia, such as the costume, the canopy of the ruler's tent, the umbrella providing shadow as well as honour, were all red.

According to legend, the Qalandar dressed in a red garment for the duration of his life;[28] consequently he is always depicted wearing the colour in figural imagery. The red robe was probably typical of the saint's hometown Marwand/Marand close to Tabriz in northwest Iran known for the farming of cochineal beetles (*qırmız*) reared to make carmine dye for colouring fabrics.[29] *Qalandarī la'l*, the colour of the Qalandar, is nowadays a specific term for a shade of red-orange. At the time of the *'urs*, this colour is ubiquitous not only in Sehwan, but wherever devotees in Pakistan prepare themselves for pilgrimage. Among the resident dervishes of Sehwan, only those attached to Bodlah Bahar, the beloved disciple of the Qalandar, dress in red.

In short, 'Qalandar red' has become an important visual marker of the cult: triangular or rectangular flags and pennants, the basic artefact of the cult, so-to-speak, are used to decorate the camps and houses of the pilgrims, their buses and vehicles, boats on River Indus (Fig. 9) and, of course, the streets and alleys of Sehwan. The colour of the pilgrims' dress is a shining synthetic red (Fig. 10) as are the inscribed cloths (*chādar*) placed on the saint's tomb. These match with the red rose petals scattered on the grave and the red plume put on the Qalandar's turban. Shia standards (*'alam*) and flag poles are painted red. Red is the background colour of posters, placards, banners, embroideries, stickers, panels, and walls with inscriptions as well as those devotional pendants the pilgrims wear.

Visitors to the shrine tie a red woollen thread (*dhāgo*) around their right wrist, symbolizing their bond with the saint, and many also put on a red woollen necklace (*gāno*). At the southern periphery of Sehwan, there is the ancient Lal Bagh or 'red garden'. In 2001, a Lal Haveli or 'red castle' was built in Sehwan's Khosa Mohalla. Painted completely red, here two wealthy devotees from Lahore and Sukkur maintain a free (day and night) kitchen for the poor during the *'urs*.

Red is clearly the dominant symbolic colour of Sehwan (Fig. 11). Considering its meaning in the Qalandar universe of devotion, red, in fact, acquires an iconic quality. In a model of sensory categories, drawn up by Ernst H. Gombrich to understand emotional expressions, the colour red is an element at a rising scale of sensory experiences associated with brightness and, in sensory terms, with gaiety, warmth, and light as well as with fast, loud, and high sounds.[30] This placement of the sight of red in visual culture perfectly fits with the emotional intensity of the Qalandar cult.

Iconic Images

In this chapter, I mainly describe and analyze industrially-produced religious commodities available from specialized vendors in the bazaar, sold from push-carts or commissioned for advertisement.[31] As pointed out by Marilyn Strathern, these physical things, for instance prints, have the potential for endless dissemination.[32] In addition, I refer to unique hand-painted pictures. Both mass-produced and the individually hand-made subaltern images appeal to the taste of the masses of common devotees. They serve to objectify the Qalandar's charisma and to protect those who keep such an image at their homes. To transfer *barakat* to them, a portable devotional object is either brought into contact with the canopy of the Qalandar's tomb or blessed by a holy man, be it a custodian of a Sufi lodge or a wandering dervish who blows on it. Focussing on the socio-religious context and agency of these Qalandar images in accordance with my initial research questions, I also try to identify zones of convergence between aesthetics and rituals.

Imaginary Portraits

Sensory poster-portraits are a characteristic medium of everyday piety in the veneration of Sufi saints in Pakistan. Because of the Qalandar's popularity he is depicted in multiple ways on a large number of poster prints,[33] devotional paintings, placards, banners, laminated pictures, round plastic pendants with miniature images carried around the neck, and stickers. His imaginary (khayālī) idealized portraits are also printed on the covers of video- and music-cassettes. The saint's representation is 'veristic' or 'mimetic' in the sense that the painter or poster artist tries to depict the saint's physical reality in a natural manner as a corporeal figure.[34] Typical for these posters is a 'perspective of meaning', that is to say not a linear one, but one which instead builds upon polychronic aspects of sacredness. Referring to contemporary popular visual media depicting 'Friends of God', John Renard aptly notes: 'Pictorial images […] can collapse time by including multiple characters and episodes in a single frame. They can distil an entire narrative by juxtaposing key symbols that viewers will readily associate with essential moments in a Friend's life story.'[35] This is also exemplified by the imaginary portraits of the Qalandar discussed below.

The 43 Qalandar posters in the collection of the Museum Fünf Kontinente in Munich all date from the last quarter of the twentieth century and the early twenty-first century. I know of only two earlier miniature-like lithographs: One of them shows the white-bearded Qalandar wearing a gold-embroidered cap and green dress, counting prayer beads in contemplation and sitting in a somewhat cross-legged position (Fig. 12). This depiction, which has been cut out and pasted on contemporary posters, is probably based on a late nineteenth or early twentieth-century painting whose whereabouts are unknown.[36] The second image is a small drawing from the nineteenth century showing the saint in the characteristic

South Asian Sufi position, crouching with drawn-up knees and holding a bowl in his hand.[37] He is shown bald with a black goatee surrounded by ascetic accessories, such as a sturdy wooden stick, a metal pot, an alms bowl as well as a blanket. The inscription 'Lal Shahbaz' is given in Arabic letters as well as in Devanagari. This hastily drawn sketch was a typical product of the bazaar industry in Lahore and, in all likelihood, had been drawn as a religious souvenir by a Hindu painter for a Muslim devotee.

The figural representations of the Qalandar on both of these images bear no resemblance to the variety of depictions on contemporary poster-portraits. The latter are mainly based on figures of Jesus borrowed from Christian devotional posters. In their paintings and montages collage artists, Sarwar Khan and Saeed Khan, placed the long-haired and bearded head of the middle-aged Christ in three-quarter profile on a so-to-speak 'Suficated' torso which then shows the saint in the characteristic ascetic kneeling position counting prayer beads or sitting cross-legged with his hands raised in prayer. There are three other standard forms of representing the saint, namely the red-robed Qalandar flying in the air with wings spread out taken from the model of Icarus; dancing bare-foot in abandonment with both arms raised borrowed from a Christian painting with Jesus Christ on the cross; and finally the Qalandar with his beloved disciple Bodlah Bahar.[38]

The Flying Saint

According to hagiography, the Qalandar once transformed himself into a falcon to travel to Makkah. On another occasion, he went by air to Multan to save his friend Shaikh Sadruddin Arif Shah, son of the famous Suhrawardi saint, Baha'uddin Zakariya, from the hands of a pagan ruler—hence his honorific *laqab* Shahbaz ('royal falcon'). Because the colour of his robe is said to have been *la'l* ('red like a ruby'), he is called the 'red royal falcon' out of devotion. In a mystical sense imagined as flying high in the spiritual domain, the pious mind of devotees turns him into a miracle-working saint with superhuman powers imagined to metamorphose into a man with the wings of a falcon as depicted in popular visual Sufi art.

In fact, his ability to fly marks the most important miracle of Lal Shahbaz Qalandar.[39]

There are posters showing the saint as the figure of Icarus (borrowed by the collage artist from some book) flying above a city which is supposed to represent Makkah.[40] Recently, this depiction of the flying saint became an almost heraldic motif, often appearing smaller in size and sometimes in pairs on Qalandar posters as well as in hagiographic movies (Fig. 13). A fantastic composition is shown on a print with the devotional icons of the saint's figure sitting in prayer, his tomb, and his shrine in the foreground giving ample view of the sky where Garuda—Vishnu's holy mount—carries the Qalandar who is depicted in standing posture (Fig. 14).[41] The king of the birds and demigod of Hindu mythology is wearing a crown and a long garland. In this scenery, borrowed from a Hindu poster, he is accompanied by a female musician (*gandharvī*) in the sky.

The Dancing Qalandar

It is a peculiarity of Qalandar images not found on any other Pakistani Sufi posters that the saint is represented in a single picture by two or even three different figures whereby motifs are fused.[42] Thus, collages from the 1980s show the saint in prayer on the right side and dancing on the left, usually with views of the shrine as a backdrop.[43] Fig. 15 is a triptych from the early twenty-first century which opens a wider space of view, in fact, a 'darshanic' field (derived from the Sanskrit term *darshan*—auspicious sight), denoting the all-pervasive gaze and presence of the Sufi saint.[44] In South Asian religious context (notwithstanding labels such as 'Muslim' or 'Hindu'), *darshan* means to be in the presence of the divine, receiving blessings through visual contemplation, but also through touching, adorning, and verbally addressing the living or figurally represented saint or deity.[45] Unlike other Sufi posters allowing eye-to-eye contact between devotee and saint, it is here the Qalandar's 'gift of appearance' made in different poses, especially in the movement of dance, which confers his blessing and leads to a 'merging of consciousness according to devotionalist interpretation'.[46]

Already in posters discussed above, Lal Shahbaz Qalandar is represented by an enraptured, bare-footed dancing figure in black robe taken from a Christian devotional painting showing Jesus and his apostles (Fig. 16). But to identify this long-haired, bearded figure in a flowing garment with an original image of Jesus is problematic insofar as Christ is always depicted in standing position, sober, asexual, and never in a movement of abandonment like here. Nevertheless, the posture of head, arms, hands, and feet indicates that probably a figure of Jesus Christ on the cross could have been used, retouched, and the partly covered body finally dressed with a black garment. The figure was further, so-to-speak, 'Sufi-cated' or—even more appropriately 'Qalandar-ized'—by placing a small lute and a flower garland in his raised hands and a Sindhi cap on his head.[47] Likewise his disciples are equipped with *chimtā*s (the fire-tongs and rhythm instruments used by Qalandar dervishes and wandering *malang*s), necklaces, bracelets, and embroidered caps. In the background, there is usually the image of a dervish beating a huge *naqqārah* drum (typical for the ritual veneration in Sehwan).

This emblematic image of the dancing Qalandar in frontal, heraldic representation—single or surrounded by his companions—is the focus of compositions in vertical and horizontal format (Figs. 17–18). Pictures of the enraptured Qalandar performing *dhamāl* seem to animate the devotees to go into trance themselves, thus mirroring the action of the saint.[48] In Alfred Gell's words, '[…] the situation is defined in terms of the devotee's own agency and result; the devotee looks and sees. The image-as-mirror is doing what the devotee is doing, therefore, the image also looks and sees.'[49]

Lal Shahbaz Qalandar and his Disciple Bodlah Bahar

The image of the Qalandar together with his closest follower Bodlah Bahar (in Sindhi, Bodlo Bahar) recently has become another popular icon of love and devotion among pilgrims to Sehwan. The disciple's Sindhi name roughly means 'innocent spring';[50] on posters he is also called Bodlah Sikandar. According to hagiography, Bodlah Bahar lived in Sehwan already before the arrival of the Qalandar, cleaning roads with his long beard. He became his disciple and most loyal servant. One day, the Qalandar ordered him to buy some meat in the bazaar. Although Bodlah had no money and things to barter for meat, he went to the butcher, Anud, and commanded his body be slaughtered and the pieces sold. From the proceeds, Anud was to send good lamb to the saint. When Bodlah did not return in time his master went looking for him. Learning his disciple had just been butchered, he became extremely distressed, collected the pieces of Bodlah's body and restored him to life. Such pious tales of obedience and deep affection as well as the shamanistic miracle of reassembling the dead body and bringing it back to life constitute the background for the iconic representation of both ascetics.

Bodlah Bahar is depicted leaning his head against the heart of his master, hands folded in a Christian gesture of prayer with the Qalandar gently touching Bodlah's head with his right hand (Fig. 19). This portrait scene has apparently also been borrowed from Catholic devotional paintings showing the apostle Peter being consoled by Christ.[51] A significant difference is, of course, the fact that Saint Peter is portrayed as a beardless young apostle in the Christian context whereas Bodlah is portrayed as a full-bearded Sufi saint in the Qalandar context.

The three modern depictions discussed afore showing the Qalandar in different poses are usually combined with views of his shrine and tomb and at times with pictorial references to other Sufi saints. With their intense, lush colours and vivid sceneries they became real icons of love and devotion widely disseminated through a multitude of media and easily understood by devotees. Pilgrims, with whom I discussed their pictorial content, spontaneously emphasized that the respective image expressed love, rapture, piety, or miracle. They perceived these not only as visual qualities but also experienced them as equivalents of esteemed moral values. Being obviously 'visually literal', they quickly switched to the non-visual sphere, narrating miracle stories of the saint and their own stories of being successfully healed by the saint's intercession.

It is important to point out that the above-mentioned figural representations from composite Qalandar posters not only appear on printed placards and banners but that they are also occasionally copied, enlarged, and transformed into hand-painted devotional images which also appear on buses (Fig. 20) as well as on the back of trucks, trailers, and oil-tankers (Fig. 21). Thus, a large metal board in vertical format displayed at *kāfī* (lodge) Bukhari-Bodlah, a dervish lodge close to the remnants of the ancient fort in Sehwan, shows the Qalandar dressed in red with Bodlah Bahar dressed in green. A similar board has been installed at the very shrine of Bodlah Bahar in Sehwan; it shows the Qalandar in a long dark green robe dancing. He holds a lute in his left hand and wears a red shawl. In addition, he is adorned with an ornate silver necklace with a pendant. The realistic depiction of the latter has apparently been directly copied from the display of a jeweller's shop by the painter. This derivative image of the dancing Qalandar hardly bears any resemblance to the original Christian model, as for instance exemplified by a beautifully painted image on a tractor-trailer photographed in Baldia on the outskirts of Karachi (Fig. 22). The same holds true for another 'veristic' painting of the dancing Qalandar, executed in oil on canvas by one Shabu Qalandari and displayed at *kāfī* Sayyid Bukhari by the Shia *qalandarī sangat* (that is to say an association of Qalandar devotees) from the district of Jhang in Punjab. In this image, the saint is dressed in black richly garlanded with shining diamond necklaces and holds a garland of white flowers in his right hand and a peaked black club in his left. The latter no longer betrays the original model of the lute.[52] The long flowing garment still resembles the dress of Christ on the poster from the 1960s or 1970s from whence it has been borrowed, but now the figure is depicted in a frontal, standing position in which the raised arms no longer recall that Jesus was nailed to the cross. The standard depictions of the Qalandar in dance and in contemplation counting prayer beads are even executed as large mural paintings, for example at the shrine of Baba Taj Sain (d. 1994) close to the historic Mughal fort in Lahore (Fig. 23).[53]

It should be added that the poster-depiction of the praying Qalandar in three-quarter profile is, for instance, also found on coloured boards mounted on buses as well as on devotional cards issued by *sangat*s (associations of devotees), on images pasted on cheap plastic pendants and on a particular type of sticker alongside a depiction of the shrine and the inscription '*Alī Shahbāz Qalandar*.[54] An unusual image printed on a large scroll was put on a wall opposite the shrine of Shah Jamal in Lahore. Originally hand-painted, the depiction showed the Qalandar sitting on a prayer mat, fully enveloped in a red shawl. His bearded head, surrounded by a jagged red halo, has been borrowed from a poster but the artist lengthened the saint's hair so that it touches the ground in the manner of a dervish of the *malang-sādhu* type. The Qalandar's right hand holds a yellow ball or stone emanating rays of light and energy.

The above-mentioned standard poster-depictions of the Qalandar in poses of contemplation, prayer, flying in the air, dancing, and embracing Bodlah Bahar also appear on the placards advertising the '*urs* and *shām-e Qalandar* events as well as on banners displayed by different *sangat*s during pilgrimage. Thereby, the Qalandar's imaginary portraits usually appear more as an addition to the central motif which is the shrine or the grave. Since the beginning of the twenty-first century, the 'veristic' depiction of the Qalandar embracing his disciple has become the most popular to be printed on these devotional items. The same narrative images are found on small pocket-size plasticized cards which are, in fact, reductions of actual posters, and also on small plastic pendants in the form of round or pentagonal shields or of irregular shapes which follow the contours of the flying and the dancing Qalandar. These pendants, which have been pasted on both sides with a coloured picture, have been sold at stalls in Sehwan since 2009 and are worn by devotees around their neck or suspended from a mirror in a rickshaw (Fig. 24). They can either serve as a mere souvenir or as an amulet with protective power. A particular sort of pendant in the shape of the Qalandar flying like Icarus is simply cut out from thick plastic foil. When these motifs are removed from their pictorial context in posters to fit the small format, their iconic character becomes especially apparent. The same holds true for the depiction of the flying Qalandar on audio-cassette covers and for the popular sticker motif showing the dancing Qalandar prominently displayed by rickshaw drivers on vehicles' windscreens.

This type of bumper sticker (*chamak pattī, stikar*) is always hand-made by specialized sticker vendors whose stalls are situated close to rickshaw workshops (Figs. 25–27). I have seen them particularly in Lahore but also in Karachi and other cities. Usually the Qalandar sticker is pasted right in the middle of the windscreen's lower part, at times flanked by stickers depicting other saints. The clients can select a favourite basic colour for the Qalandar's dress, mostly red, black, or green; otherwise they usually leave it to the sticker-maker to select colours and to apply a more sophisticated or a simpler decoration for the saint's dress and equipment. Thus, stickers of the dancing Qalandar show a considerable variety in the pose of the saint, the shape and colour of his beard and hair, and in the necklaces and the decoration of the robe. In case of the Lahore-made stickers, the Qalandar usually carries one or two flower garlands in his right hand and a lute in his left (the latter is often hardly recognizable as a string musical instrument and resembles a Moroccan Gnawa rattle more). Sometimes, the saint is shown in a swinging posture apparently singing without any paraphernalia in his hands, only a red shawl prominently draped around his body. Such images hardly show any resemblance to the original prototype of the crucified Christ. The ground colour for the dress of the Qalandar is usually red-orange, black, or dark green, at times also turquoise-green. All pieces are cut out with scissors and pasted onto the main shape. In Sindh, the figure of the saint often carries a red cap and a long shawl in red or orange as well as a yellow lute.

The Performative Dimension of Imaginary Portraits

After these introductory notes on the iconography and different media of imaginary Qalandar portraits, I discuss their context and performative dimension and explore the devotees' somatic engagement with these visual images. What do these images 'do', what kind of efficacy do they have in the vernacular contexts analyzed here?[55] Usually, a pilgrim buys an image from a stall in Sehwan to be taken home as a religious memento. Nowadays, posters are often already framed to be reverentially hung on a wall at home as a blessing (in German, a 'Haussegen').[56] Frequently, such an image is affectively activated and enlivened by its owner becoming the focus of domestic rituals:

> In an interview, Omar Kasmani was told that the devotee brought the poster back home, hung it on the wall, arranged a special place for it like a small oratory, and performed some rituals there. The main ritual was the lightning of lamps every evening, given that lamps (*chirāgh*, *charāg* or *dīya*) are one of the significant objects of Lal Shahbaz. However, other informants confessed that they also performed the *dhamāl* in front of the poster, while listening to audio cassettes of drumming.[57]

Yet, already during their stay in Sehwan, the pilgrims are surrounded by posters and paintings which are publicly displayed in dervish lodges, restaurants, tea stalls, shops, etc. Large banners, put up by dervishes and devotees' *sangat*s at their camps, can be seen everywhere; pilgrims, for their part, wear pendants showing imaginary portraits of the Qalandar around their necks. Thus, during the pilgrimage, the saint's iconic portrait is virtually omnipresent in Sehwan. Wherever the devotees look, they have the feeling of being in the presence of the saint, an invisible, but beneficial presence. The image influences and activates them; it intensifies their spirituality and their joyous mood.

Looking at a mimetic picture of the Qalandar appearing in different poses, the devotees get the feeling of receiving the saint's benevolence and might invoke his help and protection. For them, the auspicious portrait of the Qalandar is a sacred object containing *barakat*, bestowing *khaīr* (prosperity) and capable of diverting the 'evil eye' from the house.[58] Blessings are therefore thought to flow from such an image—conveyed through the eyes of the depicted saint and transferred to the recipient. In addition to this auspicious 'darshanic' gaze, so typical for South Asian practiced and lived religion, the devotees will often also touch the picture with their forehead, kiss it, rub their cheeks against it, and garland it with flowers. The portrait's inherent *barakat* and magical potency is transferred to the devotees through such haptic gestures. There is thus a sensory interaction between the saint's image and the devotees. Furthermore, when imaginary Qalandar portraits are grouped together with other pictures of Sufi saints forming a 'sacred assemblage', for instance, in a dervish lodge, they convey *rahmat kā sāyah* (shadow of mercy), which means that the devotees feel themselves sitting at the feet of the 'Friends of God'.[59] As I have witnessed several times, in such a setting devotees are often inspired by these images to extol the virtues of Lal Shahbaz Qalandar and Bodlah Bahar and to narrate their dreams in which these saints appear as well as their own mystical experiences. To quote Bruce Kapferer: 'The aesthetic object frames individual experience, sets it in motion, and establishes the context of his experiencing.'[60] In the context of ecstatic Qalandar religiosity not only individual but also collective forms of devotion are stimulated through images. Thus, poster views of the enraptured Qalandar performing ecstatic *dhamāl* at times animate devotees to sing *qalandarī dhamālaiñ* and to go into a trance themselves, thus mirroring the action of the saint through a full body experience. In Alfred Gell's words, '[...] the situation is defined in terms of the devotee's own agency and result; the devotee looks and sees. The image-as-mirror is doing what the devotee is doing, therefore, the image also looks and sees.'[61] Thus objects operate, so-to-speak, as social agents. The prominent *dhōl* player Mithu Sain told me once that he and his congenial partner, Gunga Sain, would venerate the Qalandar as their benefactor receiving his *barakat* during their performances. Wherever they would perform in the world, they would stick a poster showing Lal Shahbaz Qalandar to the wall.

Aside from this act of looking, another particular performative dimension of imaginary Qalandar portraits is related to the accessories of wandering *malang*s and *malangnī*s. Some individuals among them, who have fully devoted their lives to the veneration of the Qalandar, carry figurative images with them. Whereas the small laminated picture of the dancing Qalandar affixed to the necklace of a green-robed *malang*, whom I happened to meet in Lahore, should probably be read more as the 'identity card' of this dervish, as an emblematic part of his jewellery, there are cases in which images are presented as veritable portable icons which invite people to engage in sensory acts of reverence. For instance, a red-robed *malangnī* praying and circumambulating in the inner sanctum of the main shrine in Sehwan carried a poster of the Qalandar in contemplation along with her. Protected by a plastic foil, she had fixed it to her *'alam*, a standard consisting of metal hands (*panjah*) symbolizing the martyrdom of Hazrat Ghazi Abbas Alamdar in Karbala. In combination with these Shia religious symbols, the Qalandar image took a public life beyond merely stating the *malangnī*'s personal identity. Prominently and clearly visible, it was given equal importance with respect to traditional Shia icons. Within the context of Qalandar piety, this female mystic also acted as a 'holy travelling performer' making her *faqīrī* (dervishdom) quite apparent through visual means and other paraphernalia. This custom of displaying devotional images by itinerant dervishes is actually no new phenomenon; already in the past, Iranian dervishes carried and displayed images of saints—even reverse-glass paintings.[62] Similarly, an old red-robed *malang*, who wandered the streets of Sehwan during the *'urs* in July, 2011, carried two pictures around his neck, both framed and behind glass, one a faded poster of the Qalandar in contemplation and the other an assemblage of hand-painted, photographed, and printed depictions of Baba Nur Shah Wali, a minor saint of the Qalandar tradition. The latter framed picture had the quality of an artefact, put together by the person himself and utilized during his wanderings to attract people to give alms. On the same day of the *'urs*, a Pathan *malang* from Quetta carried a metal staff, the finial of which consisted of a poster-portrait of the Qalandar with Bodlah Bahar (Fig. 28). This picture was charmingly framed with elaborate embroidery of glass beads and decorated with additional wool tassels, larger beads, and triangular amulet pendants also made of glass beads. The dervish staff as image-holder represents a new version of the traditional dervish standard whose finial can be shaped as a *panjah*, a snake, a calligraphed invocation or an ascetic crutch in the form of the letter T.[63] Although both, the picture-garland and the metal staff with picture, are symbols of authority, the image-standard has a distinctly devotional character which serves, in addition, as an advertisement for the veneration of Lal Shahbaz Qalandar.

Pictorial Emblems

Views of the shrine, tomb, and other pictorial emblems such as falcon and boat are either depicted side-by-side with 'veristic' Qalandar portraits or very often also independently. Sharing the same iconic quality, they function as a synecdoche for the saint. Of course, their increasing number over the last years also reflects the preference for non-figurative art in the public sphere in Pakistan which meets the demands of reformist and fundamentalist Islamic movements.

The Shrine

The major non-figurative motif is without doubt the *darbār* or *dargāh*, the monumental domed sanctuary in Sehwan where the saint is said to be buried, a place of prestige and grandeur. In fact, the golden dome is the main visual marker of the mausoleum and a metaphor for outward splendour, divine radiance, and preciousness. First, there are occasionally devotional paintings from the first half of the twentieth century as well as mass-produced posters from the 1970s and 1980s which show the main eastern façade of the Qalandar's mausoleum with the *dhamāl* court in front. In this courtyard, there had been a small domed pavilion containing the *mach* (dervish fire) on the left and a colonnaded hall to the right. During the rebuilding of the shrine in early 1970s, both buildings were unfortunately demolished. The older posters in question, based on hand-painted pictures, still show the previous original setting of the eastern courtyard; I also found this depiction painted on a cloth banner as well as represented in embroidery.[64] Since the 1990s, however, there are depictions of the eastern façade of the shrine often in combination with the famous huge Shia standard devoted to Hazrat Ghazi Abbas Alamdar known as *qadīm 'alam*.[65] The latter is usually shown in the foreground but sometimes the collage artist also takes the liberty to place it further to the right or doubles it to frame the building on both sides. The mausoleum itself has four minarets often topped by red flags. This view of the shrine, actually based on recent photographs, has become a standard depiction appearing most frequently on posters, placards, banners, single page information leaflets for commemorative rites, hagiographic booklets, audio-cassette covers, and the covers of DVDs and VCDs. In a newly designed poster by a Shia Qalandar *sangat* from Chakwal in Punjab, the mausoleum is placed within a dream-like setting right in the middle of a desert. Another pictorial banner shows the saint's *darbār* with former prime minister Benazir Bhutto and local Pakistan Peoples Party (PPP) leaders in the foreground. This hoarding had been placed at the Lal Shahbaz CNG station in Kotri near Hyderabad. Digitally printed posters in similar formats, showing contemporary Qalandar Babas and 'small saints', often have the shrine with its golden dome as a backdrop. Such 'personality banners' which have been installed, for instance, at the residential place of a Baba in Lahore, are taken along on the pilgrimage to Sehwan where they are positioned in his temporary home. They often include the Qalandar's nickname *Jhūle La'l* in writing. Likewise, official brochures, such as the annual *Dam Mast Qalandar ma'gzīn* distributed on the occasion of the *'urs* are closely related to local politicians and dignitaries and include scores of personal welcomes. The magazine issued for the seven hundred fifty-ninth *'urs* (2011) contains no less than 70 depictions of the shrine across 60 pages.

Apart from the posters, the functions of which were discussed in the last section of this chapter, placards showing the motif of the shrine announce and advertise the saint's *'urs* give specific information about a pilgrimage group or announce the ritual event of a *shām-e Qalandar* (Fig. 29). They are pasted on walls, in the street, put up in restaurants and tea houses, fixed on the front of buses and on auto-rickshaws. Unlike placards, which are mostly printed on paper and at times also laminated, banners are much larger and always made of a more durable material. Banners are displayed during *shām-e Qalandar* performances, carried by *sangat* members on their way to Sehwan, and prominently displayed there at their camp, at times even in the form of veritable picture galleries. Apart from the shrine and other religious emblems, they often show portraits of important members of the respective *sangat*. It should be emphasized that views of the shrine found on placards and banners are all copied from posters. Banners are nowadays also used as markers of memorial places, for instance, in the Walled City of Lahore. As far as their performative dimension is concerned, I observed that large banners were ceremoniously spread out on the platform at Lahore's City Railway Station before the *sangat* embarked on the journey to Sehwan (Fig. 30). Out of reverence members of the group touched the banner with their right hand to transfer its blessings to them.

In addition to such printed media, I found colourful mural paintings in typical folk-art style at a small local shrine situated in Sehwan's Makrani Mohallah. The wall behind the tomb of Sayyid Gulshah Bukhari is painted everywhere in red, green, and yellow showing the eastern façade of the domed Qalandar mausoleum with its four minarets topped by red flags including a view of the tomb in the centre (Fig. 31). The *qadīm 'alam* is seen to the right of the building. In the foreground, the artist, Faqir Talib Husain Solangi, has, among other things, painted two large kettle drums and the gong with mallet used to announce the *dhamāl* performed daily in the interior courtyard of the Qalandar's shrine. This mural seems to be inspired by the contemporary standard depictions of the eastern façade of the shrine printed on posters and banners and sometimes also hand-painted on boards. These depictions are all based on photographs. At the small neighbourhood shrine in question, the same view of the domed mausoleum is painted on the wall of an adjacent alcove-like space, but in a less geometrical, more naturalistic way. The model for this devotional painting is, in all likelihood, a glazed piece of brown local pottery in the shape of the eastern façade of the Qalandar shrine with three oil lamps in the foreground. Such small architectural models on sale in the bazaar are used by pilgrims as devotional 'altars' at home. The above-mentioned older poster's views of the southern façade, on the other hand, frequently served as models for hand-painted pictures on trucks (Fig. 32). Nevertheless, sometimes depictions of the shrine, for instance, executed in plastic mosaic work on trucks or painted on tea houses in the slums of Karachi, show little resemblance to the actual building in Sehwan despite captions clearly referring to the Qalandar saint. As far as different media are concerned, it should be mentioned that the view of the eastern façade was even copied by embroiderers to attract customers and sell their products on the streets of Karachi. An exquisitely embroidered votive picture of the shrine had been displayed right at the tomb of Lal Shahbaz Qalandar in Sehwan.[66]

Finally, following the tradition of manufacturing models of a Sufi saint's shrine, known as *dālī* in parts of Punjab, groups of pilgrims carry such models of the Qalandar's shrine in their processions (Fig. 33). These models are, for instance, made of shining golden cardboard and decorated with stickers of religious formulas and small imaginary portraits of the saint.

The Tomb

Views of the richly adorned saint's tomb frequently appear as main motif on *'urs* placards (Fig. 34), posters, banners and, in small size, on posters. They show the canopied cenotaph covered with a pile of *chādar*s (ceremonial tomb covers) and flower garlands as well as the red-plumed turban placed on the tombstone. The latter is placed under a canopy (*kathēro*), made of sandalwood and covered with silver, supported by 12 pillars with multi-cusped arches whose ceiling is decorated with a deep-blue valance. This canopy was donated by the landlord, Mahbub Khan Wagan, in 1939; according to another source, however, it was offered by two Talpur princes, Mir Karam Ali Khan and Mir Ghulam Ali Khan, as early as 1822.[67]

Aside from the earlier painted images, all others are based on photographs and prominently depict the famous heart-shaped stone hanging from the canopy above the cenotaph. There are several mythological narratives explaining the meaning of this heavy stone, commonly known as the *gulūband* and in Sufi language also called *sang-e maftūl* (stone of the belt). According to the Shia version, it originally belonged to Hazrat Imam Zain ul-Abidin, the young fourth Shia Imam, who had to carry it around his neck as a captive on his way by foot from Karbala to Yazid's court in Damascus.[68] On the occasion of the *'urs* in July, 2011, a *sangat* from Punjab publicly displayed a precious, marvellously embroidered *chādar* in one of the lanes in Sehwan. In addition to pious inscriptions (*bāsmalah*, *kālimah*, names of the *panjtān pāk*) as well as the Islamic icons of the Kaaba in Makkah and the Prophet's mosque in Madinah, a large depiction of the stone embroidered in gold and silver occupied the centre of the red-grounded vertical *chādar*. The cloth had been placed on a sloping pedestal to invite people to donate money, which was to be presented as a gift to the Qalandar after the *chādar* had been carried in a procession to the saint's tomb.

The Falcon

According to oral hagiography, 'Lal Shahbaz' ('The Red Royal Falcon') had the miraculous ability to travel to Makkah in shape of a falcon. Typically for a number of saints of the Qalandar movement, they are thought to fly through the air either in the course of a nocturnal journey or the saint could even be transported to the Kaaba in the space of a moment.[69] In Sufi terminology, this shamanistic flight is called 'rolling up the earth' or 'folding space'. Inspired by such miraculous tales about the flying Qalandar and the depiction of the saint as Icarus, pictures of a falcon with outspread wings are synecdochical of the Qalandar. Thus, a falcon is painted on a wall of the above-mentioned shrine in Sehwan's Makrani Mohallah (Fig. 35) and labelled *haq shahbāz* ([oh] truth—royal falcon). Sometimes a depiction of a falcon can be found on *'urs* posters in which the red wings are inscribed with words borrowed from a popular devotional song: *Shahbāz kare Parwāz* (the royal falcon is flying). I saw the same depiction (without inscription) painted on the skin of a drum in Sehwan and on visiting cards. However, the most common depiction of the falcon is a calligram with the name *Sākhī La'l Shahbāz Qalandar* written in Arabic script in the shape of a bird of prey flying with outspread wings. This calligraphed zoomorphic image is a recent development of the early twenty-first century and is mostly seen in the form of a large sticker stuck to the rear window of buses or painted with the help of a stencil onto Qingqi rickshaws or printed on banners (Fig. 36). A Lahori craftsman even copied this shape to manufacture perforated colliers from shining aluminium which are sold to Qalandar devotees during saint's festivals (Fig. 37).[70]

Finally, in this subchapter on visual hagiography, I refer to a specific *'urs* placard issued in the honour of two deceased devotees from Lahore. The major motif set against a red background is a naturalistic depiction of a falcon (apparently based on a photograph) which is superimposed by a calligraphic falcon. This type of calligram in *tughrāh*-script is well-known throughout the Shia world and gives the apotropaic formula *Nādi 'Alīyyan* with which Hazrat Ali RA is frequently invoked by Shias.[71]

The Boat

The rich symbolism concerning the boat and ship in Islam, particularly in Sufi and Shia imagery, is based above all on notions of Prophet Noah's Ark, the 'ship of salvation' of the 'Seven Sleepers', the 'ship of faith' of the Prophet Muhammad PBUH and members of his family (*panjtān pāk*), the 'ship of the Shi'ism' as well as boats associated with Sufi saints.[72] According to legend, Lal Shahbaz Qalandar travelled upstream on the River Indus to Multan in south Punjab in a boat, therefore the *Qalandarī baīrāh* or 'Qalandar boat' represents an important icon in his cult. A saying in Punjabi frequently recited by devotees goes: *Qalandarī baīrāh hoya tēra, a-jāi, bhaīt-jā, lagna-e par* (The Qalandar boat is ready, come and sit if you want to cross [the river]). It suggests that those who join the Qalandar in his boat and are devoted followers, they will be saved and protected throughout their lives. At the afore-mentioned shrine of Sayyid Gulshah Bukhari in Sehwan's Makrani Mohallah we find a lovely folk painting of the *Qalandarī baīrāh* with a small pavilion and two peacocks opposing each other. Close to Lahore's City Railway Station, members of the Qalandari *sangat* of Humayun Khan painted the boat of their patron saint right on a wall (Fig. 38). An exquisitely embroidered picture of a boat, with the names of the *panjtān pāk* written on the five sails, had been displayed right at the tomb of the Qalandar.[73] On the banner of a Punjabi *sangat*, the central image shows the contours of a red-painted boat which carries the saint's mausoleum and has a flame burning at each end, thus also transforming the boat into a giant oil lamp. Another pilgrimage group in Sehwan by the name of *'Alī La'l Sangat* proudly displayed a richly embroidered *chādar* showing a sailing boat with inscriptions (Fig. 39). Said inscriptions not only refer to the Qalandar through his title *Sayyid Sākhī Sardār Qalandar Mast* written below the waves but also to the Prophet Noah, the fourteen *Ma'sūmeh* (the infallible 14)—that is to say the Prophet Muhammad PBUH, his daughter Hazrat Fatima RA, and the 12 Shia Imams whose names are written on the sections of both sails—and to Hazrat Ghazi Abbas Alamdar, the carrier of the banner in the battle of Karbala. As usual in such devotional images, God and the Prophet Muhammad PBUH are invoked through inscriptions in the uppermost right and left corners. The iconic boat is thereby turned into a veritable amalgam of Sufi, Shia, and 'orthodox' Islamic imagery. Finally, during a *shām-e Qalandar* joyously celebrated in Lahore, devotees exhibited a beautifully-crafted replica of a ship decorated with small red flags, garlands of flowers, and bedded on red roses (Fig. 40).

Iconic Vernacular Calligraphy

In the popular Sufi tradition of Sindh and Punjab, Arabic script serves as a prominent manifestation of Islamic spirituality and marks an essential element of the visual programme of shrines.[74] Thus, in the context of the Qalandar cult too, sacred places, posters and placards,[75] devotional objects, walls and signs in the public sphere, and in particular motor vehicles are decorated with printed or hand-written religious calligraphy. In addition to formulas and excerpts taken from the Holy Quran and the poetry of the Qalandar, there are Shia and Qalandari invocations. The latter usually gives the saint's nickname and formula of praise *Jhūle La'l* (the Red One, who rocks himself—like a child in the cradle) which dervishes repeatedly recite and exclaim in ecstasy. This is also the name with which Hindu devotees address the Qalandar. At times, also the saint's full name, an epithet, devotional verse, formula of praise, or evocative statement is written in a declarative mode. Calligraphers commonly use variations of *naskh* and *nasta'līq* script. These calligraphic references to the Qalandar found on various surfaces are a clear mark of his symbolic presence and function as iconic images.[76] They are seen and understood with a 'focused gaze', to use a term coined by Bärbel Beinhauer-Köhler, whereby words are not read as a text, but perceived as signs. The sacred names and formulas in question are substitutes for figural representations and, as such, reflect what could be called the 'absent presence' of the saint.[77]

Calligraphy in Sacred Places

On a wall of the dervish lodge adjacent to the shrine of Bodlah Bahar in Sehwan the saint is invoked in large *naskh* letters painted in red as *Jhūle La'l Qalandar Mast*, which means 'the Red One, who rocks himself, the enraptured Qalandar' (Fig. 41).[78] Another calligraphic wall decoration in the *kāfī* Bukhari Bodlah close by showed the rhyming invocation *haq shahbāz boland parwāz* ('the truthful royal falcon, he flies high') and a famous line from the Punjabi song discussed above: *Alī Alī dam mast Qalandar* ('the highest, the highest, through your breath, oh Qalandar intoxicated'). Next to the entrance of the meeting place of a *Qalandarī sangat* in Lahore's Allama Iqbal Town, in addition to Ali invoking *Jhūle La'l*, there is a niche with oil lamps as well as a red wall with several religious inscriptions. A similar place of veneration dedicated to the martyr Hazrat Ghazi Abbas Alamdar situated in Lahore's Samiana Bazaar (inside Taxali Gate) also has *Jhūle La'l* written on the wall. Summing up, it can be said that calligraphic references to the Qalandar in sacred places address every pilgrim and thus help to deepen the collective memory of the saint.

Calligraphy on Posters and Placards

Of course, printed media related to the veneration of the Qalandar, such as posters and placards, are full of inscriptions. Whereas figural imagery dominates Sufi posters placards announcing the *'urs* of the saint and other congregations tend to be dominated by epigraphy.[79] The Qalandar's honorific titles, pious Islamic formulas, and eulogizing verses are especially calligraphed whereby the saint's name and sobriquets acquire a noticeably iconic quality (see Chapter II). The latter are always placed in the upper or more often central part of the placard. Their Arabic letters form a calligram or scriptural icon easily perceived and recognized as a sign for the Qalandar even by illiterate devotees. This holds true, for instance, for an early *'urs* placard (probably printed in the 1960s or 1970s) which had been framed and displayed on the wall of a Shia assembly hall off Lahore's Mohni Road. The name and title, *Sākhī La'l Shahbāz Qalandar*, written in bold *naskh*, figures prominently in white letters on red ground. Likewise, the name *Jhūle La'l* often appears on printed media, for example, embossed in gold on small black boards which are put up in shops for saintly protection or on stickers.

Calligraphy on Devotional Objects

A precious framed calligraphic embroidery panel, which was donated by a devotee to *kāfi* Sayyid Naban Darya Bukhari in Sehwan, shows the saint's sobriquet *Qalandar kibrīyā* (Fig. 42). His honorific names also appear on all of the inscribed, often richly-decorated, banners and tomb cloths donated to the shrine; usually said names are especially emphasized in this calligraphy. In addition, *La'l Shahbāz Qalandar* is frequently embroidered as the sole calligraphic marker on lavishly decorated garlands (*dastār*) adorning the turbans placed on the headstones of saints' tombs in Sehwan. The custodians of *kāfi* Sayyid Naban Darya Bukhari had *Shahbāz Qalandar La'l* and their own personal names inscribed on round wooden panels mounted on the head of a bed. Embossed and perforated calligraphic panels with *Jhūle La'l* are made of cheap gold-coloured plastic to be hung on the wall. Pilgrims purchase shiny silver aluminium neckpieces with the name *Sākhī La'l Shahbāz Qalandar* in openwork. Simple plastic pendants used as necklaces are pressed with the letters *Jhūle La'l*. The latter is also printed on bands worn by pilgrims around their forehead.

Calligraphy on Walls, Doors, and Signboards in the Public Space

Whereas calligraphic references to the Qalandar on posters and devotional objects help to visualize and memorize the saint collectively as well as in private contexts when displayed at home, other vocative references are clearly used to advertise his cult in the public (Fig. 43). Thus, at times, the Qalandar's popular nickname *Jhūle La'l* is part of graffiti, particularly in the Walled City of Lahore, for instance, when the *'urs* is announced by writing names, dates, etc. on a wall—beside an advertisement for burgers—or when such information is prominently placed among the wall inscriptions belonging to a sweet shop, namely the former *Sābrī-hālwā-pūrī-dukān* inside Lohari Gate. Frequently *Jhūle La'l* is also written in red on a wall inside a shop or restaurant, sometimes close to a poster depicting the Qalandar's shrine. Close to Taxali Gate, I met a devotee who had written *Jhūle La'l House* on the front door of his house and *La'l Saiñ* beside a wall niche with an oil lamp. In the village of Nurpur near Islamabad, I saw *Jhūle La'l barī lajpāl* ('Jhule Lal—great guardian of honour') written on a metal door. To give a few more examples: close to Lahore's central bus stand I found a *Jhūle La'l tī shāp* (tea shop), there are also *Jhūle La'l pān shāp*s in various parts of the city; in Nawabshah there is a Lal Shahbaz Restaurant and at the shrine of Abdullah Shah Ghazi in Karachi a *Jhūle La'l Hotal* as well as the *Qalandarī Dēg House*. A barber in Lyari in Karachi wrote *Jhūle La'l* in black letters under the mirror in his shop. A tailor in Sehwan had it written in red letters on his sewing machine (Fig. 44). Furthermore, the saint's nickname appears on signboards of soft drink stalls and the small cabins used for selling all sorts of sweets and stimulants. There is, just to give a few more examples, the Qalandariyyah Chowk (i.e. a roundabout by the name of the saint) in North Karachi, the Shahbaz Qalandar Flyover in Hyderabad-Qasimabad, Lal Shahbaz Qalandar Motors in Hyderabad, Jhuley Lal CNG (compressed natural gas) in Gharo (Indus delta), Qalandar CNG in Sehwan, Jhuley Lal Communication in Jamshoro, and Jhule Lal Autos in Tando Allahyar. The town of Sehwan itself is, of course, full of hotels and shops which bear the name of the saint. Even a Karachi-based company, selling Waves refrigerators, launched in 1999/2000 an advertisement with the slogan *Murshid La 'l—nām hī kāfī* ('red spiritual guide—only your name is sufficient'). And last but not least there is even a renowned cricket team in the Pakistan Super League called Lahore Qalandars.

Calligraphy on Vehicles

Trucks, buses of all sizes, Qingqi rickshaws and the common auto-rickshaws plying the roads of Sindh and Punjab, as well as, on occasion, also the private car, the motorcycle of a devotee, or even a wedding chariot can be protected from the evil eye, from accidents and other calamities through calligraphed references to the Qalandar. These inscriptions are either written on the vehicle or applied as a sticker to the windscreen, dashboard, or in the cabin above the windscreen; they are often executed in high-quality calligraphy. Drivers decorate their vehicles with a keen sense of personal aesthetics, ingeniously using space available.

In the decorative programme of richly embellished Pakistani trucks, the front and especially the 'crown' above the driver's cabin contain Islamic inscriptions and images, pious slogans, and references to Sufi saints, hence also invocations of Lal Shahbaz Qalandar.[80] Stickers with *Jhūle La 'l* are often found on the front windscreen of large buses, whereas *Murshid La 'l*, *Jhūle La 'l*, *Qalandar La 'l*, or the evocative *Jīwe Murshid La 'l Saiñ* appear on the back, one word set in each of the two screens. Such buses have their terminal at Lea Market in Karachi. The drivers or owners of smaller buses for public transport (such as Toyota Hiace) often protect their vehicle on the single rear windscreen with the saint's name *Jhūle La 'l* or with *Qalandarī kishtī*, *Qalandarī baīrāh*, *Qalandar La 'l*, and *nigāh-e Qalandar* ('vision of the Qalandar'). One particularly conspicuous and impressive example of calligraphy is a sticker with characters in *kūfī* style whereby the letter *lām* appears in the shape of a minaret (Fig. 45). Sometimes the driver or owner also has his own name written below the name of the saint. *Jhūle La 'l* is again the most popular reference to the

Qalandar on the recently introduced Qingqi rickshaws as well as on the *tuk-tuk* rickshaws with two benches which ply the roads of Karachi; I also found *Jhūle La'l Qalandar pāk* and the rickshaw's self-appellation *Qalandar kī dīwānī* ('the Qalandar's madwoman') as well as *Jhūle La'l kī dīwānī* written on the side panels. The covering of a common rickshaw seems the most ideal medium to show one's religious identity and, in our case, the driver's attachment to the Qalandar.

Frequently *Jhūle La'l* is written on the back of the vehicle (Fig. 46), at times also the formulas *Jhūle La'l—Qalandar sarmast* ('the fully enraptured Qalandar'), *Jhūle La'l—sukh nāl nasibāñ de* ('not everybody comes close to him'), *Jhūle La'l—Murshid La'l* ('the red spiritual guide'), *Dam Mast Qalandar—Qalandar La'l*, the full name *Sākhī La'l Shahbāz Qalandar*, *shām-e Qalandar* (referring to the nocturnal festivities honouring the Qalandar in Lahore) or *qalandarī*, obviously referring to the religious affiliation of the driver himself. One rickshaw, which I saw in Karachi, displayed very fine Qalandar-related calligraphy: *Qalandarī baīrāh* ('boat of the Qalandar') and *Jhūle La'l Qalandar* were written prominently on its rear covering (Fig. 47). In addition to iconic references to God and the Prophet Muhammad PBUH, both side panels of the covering were decorated with a red heart and *Jhūle La'l* calligraphed below. On another rickshaw, *Jhūle La'l* had been written in a particularly flowery style, obviously derived from truck painting (Fig. 48). In Lahore, the metropolis with the largest concentration of Qalandar devotees in the country, rickshaw drivers are particularly fond of stickers pasted to the windscreen: apart from the usual *Jhūle La'l* calligram, there are also iconic combinations reflecting the affiliation to Shia Islam, for instance, the name Ali with the shape of a standard inscribed into its last letter which itself is crowned by a red flag bearing the inscription *Shahbāz Qalandar*. Sometimes calligraphy is also found on the chassis above the windscreen.

Finally, I want to emphasize that Qalandar devotees occasionally decorate and protect their car or motorcycle with calligraphic references to their beloved saint. In the case of motorbikes, either stickers are pasted on certain body parts, such as plastic screens,

lights, and speedometers, or inscriptions are handwritten on them
(Figs. 49–50). In combination with the motif of the eye, the name
Jhūle La'l appears very conspicuous. Of course, the short reference
Jhūle La'l is ideal given the limited space available on the body
of a motorbike. In Lahore, I once also saw the formula *Jhūle La'l
baīrāh par* ('Jhule Lal, help my boat to cross safely!') written on
the front of a motor scooter. In exceptional cases, the bonnet of a
car can be decorated with several inscriptions (Fig. 51). On cars
the Qalandar's name is sometimes followed by the emphasis *sirf
tum* ('only you'). To sum up, watching the traffic in Karachi and in
Lahore, I had the impression that hardly a minute passed without
spotting a vehicle which did not bear the name of the Qalandar.

Conclusion

The majority of the Qalandar's 'veristic' portraits, pictorial
emblems, and calligrams are portable devotional items sold as
commodities which come from the world of modern industrial
capitalism. When purchased in the bazaar, and when they enter, in
Appadurai's words, the 'consumption phase of their social life',[81]
they are religious souvenirs foremost which materialize the memory
of a visit to the saint's tomb. As icons, they are markers of personal
identity anchoring the individual 'in the labyrinths of memory'.[82]
Secondly, and even more importantly, they are charged with saintly
charisma and power and are therefore considered to have real
protective value. In this sense they can be understood as tokens
of moral renewal having a bearing on the conduct of devotees in
this mundane world by energizing their lives. Creating such visual
hagiography and using it in devotional practices means that the
spiritual heritage of the Qalandar, handed down from one generation
to the other, is being kept alive through modern iconic signs.

Iconic images, whether mass-produced or hand-made, are
'indicators' of the Qalandar's representational presence which are
not only found at the saint's shrine in Sehwan, at sacred memorial
places dedicated to him in Punjab and Sindh and at various shrines
of other Sufi saints, even at Hindu temples,[83] where he is a key

figure of reference, but also in private homes and in shops, in the context of processions and pilgrimages, and in urban public space more generally. In these contexts, Qalandar-related images are used to create an aesthetic and commemorative framework for rituals. They are often the most prominent images within gallery-like assemblages of devotional pictures, which sacralize the particular space.[84] Be they large banners, medium-sized posters, or pocket-size portable icons, with their magical-realist iconography and their tangibility they allow the devotee not only to visualize the beloved saint, but also to connect with him on personal and pious terms, implying thus a 'corporeality of aesthetics'.[85] They avail of performative and interactive dimensions and provoke active response, devotional acts, and forms of physical intimacy on behalf of the beholder.[86] Through such devotional practices the material world of the objects is connected with the spiritual world, bridging the gap between the human and the divine.[87]

In addition to their spiritual and protective significance as well as the emotional responses they initiate, images of the Qalandar shape the devotee's religiosity and intensify his love for the saint, drawing him even deeper into the symbolic system of Qalandar piety. They represent a constant affirmation of the devotee's religious identity. In the field of collective consumption, figural and calligraphic representations of the Qalandar are markers of difference with regard to other religious objects, for instance, in comparison to more standard and 'orthodox' emblems of Sunni or Shia faith. As such they have a distinctly public character. Their ubiquity is finally a testimony to the attraction of the saint; sacredness by all means needs the public.

Being personifications of Pakistan's most popular Sufi saint, printed or digitalized images as well as Qalandar folk poetry, hymns, and songs on videos exemplify how an age-old esoteric mystical tradition filters through to the masses of common devotees in the twentieth and twenty-first centuries. Mass-produced images condition the world-view of Qalandar devotees and mark their visual piety. Although commoditized, they are, nevertheless, bearers of benevolence and retain their powerful auratic character. Embedded in a universe of holistic and pragmatic devotion they open a wide 'darshanic' space for experiencing the all-pervasive love of this extraordinary Sufi saint, making it both visible and palpable. Iconic images of the Qalandar are thus highly condensed, ritual, and sensuous symbols for his presence and, at the same time, code signs for devotion, particularly for the highly-valued gifts of rapture and ecstasy which are thought to be bestowed upon the devotees by God himself. The same holds true for the placards and banners investigated in the next chapter.

Notes

1. The relics of Lal Shahbaz Qalandar have been studied in depth by Michel Boivin in the fourth chapter of his book, *Artefacts of Devotion: A Sufi Repertoire of the Qalandariyya in Sehwan Sharif, Sindh, Pakistan* (Karachi: Oxford University Press, 2011).
2. Since the year 2003, I regularly conducted ethnographic fieldwork related to the visual culture of Lal Shahbaz Qalandar in Sindh and Punjab: October, 2003, October, 2004, September, 2005, November, 2007, November, 2008, July/August and October, 2009, July/August and November, 2010, February, July and December, 2011, February, 2012, February and October–December, 2013, January, September and November, 2014, and February, 2015. Some images were taken during subsequent fieldtrips to Karachi and Lahore. Pakistani art historian Muhammad Asghar kindly provided me with two photographs taken from his dissertation defended at the Muthesius Kunsthochschule in Kiel, Germany (2016).
3. James Elkins, 'The Concept of Visual Literacy, and its Limitations,' in *Visual Literacy*, ed. James Elkins (New York: Routledge, 2008), 1–9.
4. Boivin, *Artefacts of Devotion*, 135.
5. E. H. Aitken, *Gazetteer of the Province of Sind* (1907; reprint, Karachi: Indus Publications, 1986), 386.
6. On the role of music and film in popularizing the Qalandar cult I have greatly benefitted from conversations with Pakistani scholar Nazir Husain Soomro (Sindhi Adabi Sangat, Sehwan), linguist Fateh Muhammad Malik (Chairman National Language Authority, Islamabad), performers Gogi Nazir Ali and Sajjid Nazir Ali (Lahore), musicologist Salwat Ali (National College of Arts, Lahore), scholar and musicologist Raza Kazim (Lahore), and Ashfaq Ahmad Khan (Lahore).
7. Pierre Centlivres and Micheline Centlivres-Demont, 'Une présence absente: symboles et images populaires du prophète Mahomet,' in *Derrière les images*, eds. Marc-Oliver Gonseth, Jacques Hainard, Roland Kaehr, and François Borel (Neuchatel: Musée d'ethnographie, 1998), 139–70; cf. Frank J. Korom, 'The Presence of Absence: Using Stuff in a South Asian Sufi Movement,'

AAS Working Papers in Social Anthropology/ÖAW Arbeitspapiere zur Sozialanthropologie 23 (2012): 1–19.

8. Uzma Rehman, 'Spiritual Power and "Threshold" Identities: The *Mazārs* of Sayyid Pīr Waris Shāh Abdul Latīf Bhitai,' in *South Asian Sufis: Devotion, Deviation, and Destiny*, eds. Clinton Bennett and Charles M. Ramsey (London et al.: Bloomsbury, 2012), 71.

9. This term means a 'wandering dervish' in South Asia and Afghanistan.

10. This popular Punjabi song is based on an ancient anonymous Sindhi *panjrā* (prayer) to honour Jhule Lal or Udero Lal, the deity of the River Indus, venerated by the people of Sindh [Charu J. Gidwani, 'Three *panjrā*s of Udero Lāl,' *Mission Interdisciplinaire Française du Sindh, Newsletter* 3 (September 2009): 8–9]; see also Dominique-Sila Khan, 'Jhulelal and the Identity of Indian Sindhis,' in *Sindh through History and Representation: French Contributions to Sindhi Studies*, ed. Michel Boivin (Karachi: Oxford University Press, 2008), 72–81; and Lata Parwani, 'Myths of Jhuley Lal: Deconstructing a Sindhi Cultural Icon,' in *Interpreting the Sindhi World: Essays on Society and History*, eds. Michel Boivin and Matthew A. Cook (Karachi: Oxford University Press, 2010), 1–27. It begins with the words: 'Lal, keep my honour safe (which means that the devotee has surrendered to God, that out of humility he pleads with God to keep his name, respect and dignity 'safe' and intact)', goes on with 'mast Qalandar' (the reference to Lal Shahbaz Qalandar) and includes the famous verses 'four lamps always burn at your shrine, the fifth one I have come to light Oh Jhule Lalan, Oh thou of Sindh, of Sehwan [...]' (Gidwani, 'Three *panjrā*s of Udero Lāl,' 9). Later on, in local folk religion, the figures of Jhule Lal and Lal Shahbaz Qalandar merged to a certain extent. Jhule Lal on one hand becoming a Muslim saint and his name, on the other hand becoming associated with the Qalandar (cf. Parwani, 'Myths of Jhuley Lal,' 2, 5–7; Boivin, *Artefacts of Devotion*, 132). Gidwani writes: 'This song is a fine example of how the Sindhi mind is not rigidly fanatic about one religion. Here Jhulelal – a Hindu God – is seen as one with Mast Qalandar – Muslim Peer' ('Three *panjrā*s of Udero Lāl,' 9). The modern mix version of this emblematic Qalandar song probably came into being in the late nineteenth or early twentieth century (personal information by Raza Kazim in Lahore, November 4, 2009). It was first sung by Madam Noor Jahan in the 1950s. Some years ago, this Qalandar hymn was introduced to African musicians in Kenya by the Pakistani music composer, music director, and instrumentalist, Nizar Lalani (personal information by Sohail Bawani in Karachi, October 19, 2009). Recently even a Hip-hop version of the song was performed by the popular Indian singer Mika Singh too.

11. For more information, see the detailed chapter on the *Mast Qalandar* song in Michel Boivin, *Le soufisme antinomien dans le sous-continent indien*, 143–60, which includes several interpretations. In the following, I quote the Punjabi text as published in the work of Hasan Aziz [*Kalaam-e-Aarifaan. Poetry of Sufis and Mystics* (Karachi: Kalaam-e-Aarifaan, 2014), 337] but instead of using an 'English-ized' script for transliteration I prefer a scholarly,

albeit somewhat simplified form throughout this book. The translation of the poem partly relies on Aziz (*Kalaam-e-Aarifaan*, 338) and on Gidwani ('Three *panjrā*s of Udero Lāl,' 9). It is important to emphasize that this is just one version of the song text. For instance, the essential verse: 'your shrine is always lighted with four lamps, and here I come to light a fifth lamp in your honour' is missing here. In fact, one can find several versions of this hymn on the Internet.

12. Kaleem Raza from Lahore, a manager of renowned musicians and a *tablā* player himself, told me in a letter dated February 28, 2011 that Nazir Ali 'had been the hallmark of Punjabi film music' in his time and had produced music for four hundred films and, in particular, 'that he had no one next to him in composing *dhamāl* music'. 'For about 37 years, he produced two or three new *dhamāl* compositions every year.'

13. Jean During, 'Sufi Music and Rites in the Era of Mass Reproduction, Techniques and Culture,' in *Sufism, Music and Society in Turkey and the Middle East*, eds. Anders Hammarlund, Tord Olsson, and Elisabeth Özdalga (Istanbul: Swedish Research Institute in Istanbul, 2001), 158.

14. On the Internet, one finds the title of this mixed song written in 'English-ized' corrupted transliteration as: *jhoole laal jhoole laal dum mast kalander* (really painful to decipher for any philologist, anthropologist, or historian).

15. Among the large number of contemporary Pakistani artists who sing and record Qalandar songs, Naseebo Lal, Shazia Khushk, Sanam Marvi, Sher Miandad Khan, Hasan Sadiq, and Sain Khawar stand out. Others such as Mukhtiar Ali Shidi, Nadeem Abbas, Farzana Parveen, Farah Lal, and Samina Iqbal are also worth mentioning. In the 1960s and 1970s, Suriya Mastani was a well-known singer of *qalandarī dhamālaiñ* too. Today artists like Sami Yusuf sing *Mast Qalandar* too. 'Modern' performances are recorded by Coke Studio in Karachi and can be watched on YouTube. View, for instance, a fascinating version crooned by Quratulain Baloch (featuring Akbar Ali and Arieb Azhar). Here it should be mentioned that songs devoted to Lal Shahbaz Qalandar are not only widespread throughout Balochistan (including Iranian Balochistan, cf. Boivin, *Le soufisme antinomien dans le sous-continent indien*, 142–3) but also among lute players in Khorasan (for instance, in Torbat-e Jam southeast of Mashhad).

16. Boivin, *Artefacts of Devotion*, 16 and 18.

17. Ibid., 13.

18. Zulfiqar Ali Kalhoro, 'Ashram of Ascetics,' *The Friday Times*, December 28, 2018.

19. This department functions under the Ministry of Religious Affairs which took over the organization of the Qalandar shrine in 1960 (Mohammad, *Hazrat Lal Shahbaz Qalandar*, 49 and 58).

20. Ibid., 12, 58–61.

21. Güliz Ger and Russell W. Belk, 'I'd like to buy the World a Coke: Consumption Scenes of the "Less Affluent World",' *Journal of Consumer Policy* 19 (1996): 271–304.

22. Christopher Pinney, 'Piercing the Skin of the Idol,' in *Beyond Aesthetics: Art and the Technologies of Enchantment*, eds. Christopher Pinney and Nicholas Thomas (Oxford and New York: Berg, 2001), 162.

23. See, for instance, Azra Sadiq, 'Hazrat Lal Shahbaz Qalandar,' *Humsafar* (PIA in-flight-magazine) (February 2012): 60–3.

24. On the saint's *laqab*s, see Boivin, *Le soufisme antinomien dans le sous-continent indien*, 110–15.

25. Thus, Boivin emphasizes: 'Le sens premier de ce terme est rubis, ou rouge. Mais par un jeu sémantique et sémiologique, *la'l* désigne finalement la connaissance divine. La connaissance divine est en effet souvent mentionnée par l'expression de *daryā-ye la'l*, la mer de rubis, c'est-à-dire la mer des connaissances divines' (*Le soufisme antinomien dans le sous-continent indien*, 114).

26. Ernst H. Gombrich, 'Expression and Communication,' in *Meditations on a Hobby Horse and other Essays on the Theory of Art*, ed. Ernst H. Gombrich (London and New York: Phaidon Press, 1985), 56–69.

27. Boivin, *Artefacts of Devotion*, 119.

28. Mohammad, *Hazrat Lal Shahbaz Qalandar*, 52.

29. See anonymous 'Qalandar Lal Shahbaz,' 21.

30. Gombrich, 'Expression and Communication,' 58.

31. Their reflection in audio-visual media and on the Internet should be examined too in future.

32. Marilyn Strathern, *Property, Substance, and Effect: Anthropological Essays on Persons and Things* (London: Athlone Press, 1999), 177.

33. For iconography of these devotional images, see the next chapter and Frembgen, *The Friends of God-Sufi Saints in Islam: Popular Poster Art from Pakistan* (Karachi: Oxford University Press, 2006), 62–70.

34. Christiane Gruber, 'Between Logos (*Kalima*) and Light (*Nūr*): Representations of the Prophet Muhammad in Islamic Painting,' *Muqarnas* 26 (2009): 220–30.

35. John Renard, *Friends of God: Islamic Images of Piety, Commitment, and Servanthood* (University of California Press, 2008), 220.

36. Although the caption on the posters say that this *shabīh-e mubarak* is kept in the National Museum of Lahore, my enquiries proved in vain. According to my colleague Kanwal Khalid, who had been in charge of the miniature department, this image is not (or is no longer) in possession of the museum.

37. This drawing is kept in the National Museum of Lahore (Inv. No. A-757).

38. Concerning the following three short sections, see Frembgen, 'Icons of Love and Devotion: Sufi Posters from Pakistan depicting Lal Shahbaz Qalandar,' in *Religiöse Blicke – Blicke auf das Religiöse. Visualität und Religion*, eds. Bärbel Beinhauer-Köhler, Daria Pezzoli-Olgiati, and Joachim Valentin (Zürich: Theologischer Verlag Zürich, 2010b), 232–8.

39. Boivin, 'Reflections on La'l Shahbāz Qalandar,' 47.

40. Sufi posters in the collection of the Museum Fünf Kontinente in Munich (Inv. Nos. 02-323 597, 02-323 594).

41. Museum Fünf Kontinente, Munich (Inv. No. 02-324 097).
42. Frembgen, *The Friends of God-Sufi Saints in Islam*, 65 and 69.
43. Museum Fünf Kontinente, Munich (Inv. Nos. 88-310 816, 02-323 595).
44. Museum Fünf Kontinente, Munich (Inv. Nos. 02-323 596, 04-325 497); see Frembgen, *The Friends of God-Sufi Saints in Islam*, 69 (Fig. 25) and 134.
45. Diana Eck, *Darśan: Seeing the Divine Image in India* (New York: Columbia University Press, 1998); and Alfred Gell, *Art and Agency: An Anthropological Theory* (Oxford: Clarendon Press, 1998), 116.
46. Gell, *Art and Agency*, 120.
47. Frembgen, *The Friends of God-Sufi Saints in Islam*, 66 f.
48. On *dhamāl* in Sehwan and elsewhere in Pakistan, see Frembgen, '*Dhamāl* and the Performing Body,' esp. 83 (Fig. 1).
49. Gell, *Art and Agency*, 120.
50. Boivin, 'Reflections on La'l Shahbāz Qalandar,' 51 f.
51. I guess the montage artist was hardly aware about the fact that Christian saint Simon Peter is favourably regarded in Islam and even considered a prophet [cf. Julian Baldick, *Imaginary Muslims: The Uwaysi Sufis of Central Asia* (New York: New York University Press, 1993), 114].
52. Frembgen, 'Icons of Love and Devotion,' 231 (Fig. 3).
53. Jürgen Wasim Frembgen, '*Rehmat ka Sayah*—The Shadow of Mercy: Glimpses of Muslim Saints' Portraits,' in *Mazaar, Bazaar: Design and Visual Culture in Pakistan*, ed. Saima Zaidi (Karachi: Oxford University Press, 2009), 12–13 (Fig. 4).
54. Jürgen Wasim Frembgen, 'Islamic Stickers from Pakistan and India. Eye-catching, Protective and Carrying a Message,' *Journal Fünf Kontinente* 3 (2018/19a): 152–65.
55. Cf. Jamal J. Elias, *Aisha's Cushion: Religious Art, Perception, and Practice in Islam* (Cambridge: Harvard University Press, 2012), 42 and 64.
56. Frembgen, *The Friends of God-Sufi Saints in Islam*, 132–4.
57. Boivin, *Artefacts of Devotion*, 124.
58. Frembgen, *The Friends of God-Sufi Saints in Islam*, 132.
59. Frembgen, '*Rehmat ka Sayah*,' 12.
60. Bruce Kapferer, *A Celebration of Demons: Exorcism and the Aesthetics of Healing in Sri Lanka* (Bloomington: University Indiana Press, 1983), 191.
61. Gell, *Art and Agency*, 120.
62. Jürgen Wasim Frembgen, *Kleidung und Ausrüstung islamischer Gottsucher. Ein Beitrag zur materiellen Kultur des Derwischwesens* (Wiesbaden: Harrassowitz, 1999), 241.
63. Cf. Ibid., 103–19.
64. Frembgen, *The Friends of God-Sufi Saints in Islam*, 67 (Fig. 24); and Frembgen, 'Icons of Love and Devotion,' 228 (Fig. 1), 231 (Fig. 3), 232 (Fig. 4), and 233 (Fig. 5).
65. Ibid., 65 (Fig. 23); Frembgen, 'Icons of Love and Devotion,' 238 (Fig. 9).
66. Observation on February 16, 2013.
67. Boivin, *Artefacts of Devotion*, 52.

68. Ibid., 94–5.
69. Cf. Baldick, *Imaginary Muslims*, 21, 23, 30, 91, and 98.
70. In 2007, craftsman Abid Husain from Lahore started producing such rather cheap aluminium colliers to be sold to devotees.
71. Stuart Cary Welch, *India: Art and Culture, 1300-1900* (New York: Metropolitan Museum of Art, 1985), 324–5 (Cat. No. 220: Calligraphic hawk standard made of gilded copper; Deccan, late seventeenth century).
72. Cf. Jürgen Wasim Frembgen, 'The Symbolism of the Boat in Sufi and Shi'a Imagery of Pakistan and Iran,' *Journal of the History of Sufism* 6 (2015): 85–100.
73. Observation on February 16, 2013.
74. Jürgen Wasim Frembgen, 'Calligraphy in the World of Sufi Shrines in Pakistan,' in *The Aura of Alif: The Art of Writing in Islam*, ed. Jürgen Wasim Frembgen (Munich: Prestel, 2010a), 225–35.
75. On the 'focused gaze' of devotees for instance on calligraphies and other sacred texts evoking emotion, see Bärbel Beinhauer-Köhler, *Gelenkte Blicke. Visuelle Kulturen im Islam* (Zürich: Theologischer Verlag Zürich, 2011), 36 and 42.
76. Cf. Elias, *Aisha's Cushion*, 24, 271, and 282.
77. Centlivres and Centlivres-Demont, 'Une présence absente,' 147–9.
78. Frembgen, 'Calligraphy in the World of Sufi Shrines in Pakistan,' 226 (Fig. 141) and 229.
79. Frembgen, 'Icons of Love and Devotion,' 239–40.
80. Jamal J. Elias, 'Truck Calligraphy in Pakistan,' in *The Aura of Alif: The Art of Writing in Islam*, ed. Jürgen Wasim Frembgen (Munich: Prestel, 2010), 212 and 214.
81. Arjun Appadurai, 'Introduction: commodities and the politics of value,' in *The Social Life of Things: Commodities in Cultural Perspective*, ed. Arjun Appadurai (Cambridge: Cambridge University Press, 1986), 3–63.
82. Mihaly Csikszentmihalyi, 'Why we need things,' in *History from Things: Essays on Material Culture*, eds. Steven Lubar and W. David Kingery (Washington: Smithsonian Institution Press, 1993), 26.
83. Kalhoro, for instance, observed at the Guru Mangal Gir Ashram near Thano Bula Khan in Sindh: 'There is an alcove in a temple at the Ashram which is called "Lal Sain Ji Khudi" where there is placed a poster of Lal Shahbaz Qalandar' ('Ashram of Ascetics,' 4).
84. Cf. Frembgen, '*Rehmat ka Sayah*,' 12.
85. Susan Buck-Morss, 'Aesthetics and Anaesthetics: Walter Benjamin's Artwork Essays Reconsidered,' *October* 62 (1992): 3–41.
86. Gregory Starrett, 'The Political Economy of Religious Commodities in Cairo,' *American Anthropologist* 97/1 (1995): 61; Pinney, 'Piercing the Skin of the Idol,' 161; and Elias, *Aisha's Cushion*, 174.
87. Cf. Pedram Khosronejad, 'Introduction,' in *The Art and Material Culture of Iranian Shi'ism Iconography and Religious Devotion in Shi'i Islam*, ed. Pedram Khosronejad (London: I. B. Tauris, 2012), 10.

II FROM POPULAR DEVOTION TO MASS EVENT
Placards and Banners of Punjabi Pilgrims

Introduction

The festival of the Qalandar's death anniversary turns into a carnival-like mass event combining the fervour of devotion and ecstatic performances of trance dance with more mundane fun and amusements. Among the hundreds of thousands of Punjabi devotees especially dedicated to the saint, information about the *'urs* is spread by word of mouth, placards (*ishtehār*), and banners (*baenar*).

Colourful placards and banners invite people mainly to join in the pilgrimage (*ziyārat*) and participate in the *'urs* in Sehwan but also in other preliminary commemorative ritual events (*shām-e Qalandar, jashn-e Qalandar*) organized at different places across Punjab. They are media of religious advertisement providing a deeper understanding of the institutionalization of this saint's cult, particularly about the organization of pilgrimage, local networks of devotees, and expressions of Qalandar piety. As already mentioned in an article dealing with placards of saints' festivals in Punjab, these rather 'traditional' print media of mass communication represent a hitherto neglected source for the study of popular shrine-oriented Islam in Pakistan.[1] The present chapter supplements this more general overview and follows the same structural outline in describing and analyzing such prints. Whereas my earlier documentation on Punjabi saints' festivals is based on a larger data base of 119 placards, I could collect or photograph thus far a total of 43 polychrome placards and banners focusing only on the veneration of Lal Shahbaz Qalandar between 1999 and 2012.[2] As a result of the enormous popularity of his cult nationwide, the most celebrated Sufi saint of Pakistan is advertised by far the largest number of different print media. The same holds true for the variety of devotional posters depicting him and his shrine.[3]

Placards and Banners

Placards measure on average between 50x75 cm and are, with one exception, all in vertical format. They are printed on paper in Lahore and distributed from there. This demonstrates the special attachment of Punjabi devotees and the wealth and economic power of their sponsors. In comparison with other placards from Punjab Qalandar pilgrimage placards from Lahore are mostly larger in size, show a greater number of pictures and are printed in better quality with several colours. Many of them are framed with thin metal borders at both short ends and have an attached loop for hanging. These are not as usually pasted to walls in the urban public space but hung in shops, restaurants, and tea-houses, and are therefore more durable.

Contrary to placards, large banners are nowadays made of synthetic material and mostly digitally printed on vinyl. They are manufactured in a variety of sizes measuring up to several metres in width, all in horizontal format. Before the introduction of this technology, banners were made of cotton cloth and calligraphers used to write on them by hand. Banners are proudly carried and displayed by associations of Qalandar devotees (*sangat*,[4] *grūp*) on their pilgrimage to Sehwan and prominently installed at their camp as billboards marking the presence of the respective group (Fig. 52). Large banners are often also put up as signboards at junctions directing devotees to their respective camp.

Images

Without repeating characteristics of composition and calligraphy which Qalandar placards have in common with other '*urs* placards in Pakistan I want to focus on the fact that many of them are literally loaded with images. The same holds true even more for large banners. The main motifs, placed in the upper part of the placard, are depictions of the saint's shrine and his richly decorated tomb found on each of the 43 prints documented here. With one exception only photographs have been used. They show the facade of the shrine (18 times), the tomb (15 times), the tomb in

combination with the shrine (seven times), and the mausoleum of
Hazrat Imam Husain RA in Karbala as a substitute (three times). The
figural depiction of Lal Shahbaz Qalandar, shown for instance on
a placard dating from 1999 in his typical postures of praying and
dancing, was borrowed from a Sufi poster; recently more placards
and banners show him together with his beloved disciple Bodlah
Bahar.[5] Given that the saint's iconic image is ubiquitously found
in contemporary devotional mass media, the comparatively still
small number of the saints' images seems first surprising, but one
needs to take into account that the space of the placard is first
of all meant for written information and personal portraits of the
devotees. Usually, the depiction of the shrine and tomb just fills
the upper space indicating an emblematic character and framing
the specific portraits and texts (Fig. 53).

The photographic portraits of devotees and sponsors, found
on 24 prints, are either placed in the lower part of the placard
or banner or arranged as a frame around the main sacred motif
which is either a picture or a calligraphic reference to the ritual
event. Prints containing such portraits are generally composed
more symmetrically than those only containing text. The number of
images can be reduced to one or two but more often they grow into
a veritable picture gallery.[6] These portraits are set into rectangular
or oval frames.

To present a few examples, I first want to mention a placard which
shows, in addition to the Qalandar's tomb, just a single photograph
of a living saint, Hazrat Baba Jamil Ahmad Naqib Alvi Qalandar
from Lahore (Fig. 54).[7] Measuring 11x16 cm, his photo is larger
than any other portrait of a devotee found on Punjabi saints' placards.
Apparently, his saintly status did not permit his picture to be lumped
together with those of common devotees. Whereas the latter are
almost always depicted in the frontal bust position of passport
photographs, a saint can also be presented with a specific devotional
gesture as in this case where the bearded Baba, shrouded in a veil,
carrying prayer beads around his neck, holds a rosary in both hands
stretched out in the position of offering *du'ā*. Together with another
Qalandar Baba carrying the *nasab* Alvi, his name is mentioned first
in the list of organizers of the pilgrimage to Sehwan Sharif.

The next placard is extremely rare featuring two photographs of female fakirs in addition to a the Sehwan shrine before its renovation. It announces a *shām-e Qalandar* (nocturnal commemorative ritual) in the Walled City of Lahore celebrated in honour of the great Qalandar saint in name of two ladies (the grandmother and mother of Mai Kausar, the head of a female Qalandari circle portrayed in detail in Chapter IV of this volume). Both, the elder Mai Chiragh Bibi and her daughter, Mai Hajan Bibi Qalandari, are depicted with hair uncovered. In comparison to other placards, this print is rather unpretentious in composition and layout without ornamented shapes for textual information and without prominent calligraphy. Thus, it can be assumed that it was printed in a small press probably in the Walled City of Lahore.

In the third example, the photograph of the Qalandar's tomb and the elaborate calligram *'urs mubarak* (blessed *'urs*) in the centre is surrounded by a picture gallery consisting of 50 passport portraits (Fig. 55). Most of the latter are arranged in three long rows in the lower part of the placard. The only exception from these bust portraits is a photograph of a devotee named Poli Sain, who wears necklaces, is shrouded in a red *chādar*, and is circled with money in a traditional gesture. Generally speaking, the insertion of portraits (even those of infants) into a placard is done on special order; otherwise the printer just provides a template-design with a photograph of the shrine, the calligraphed name of the saint, and blank shapes to be filled with the text supplied by the customer. Interestingly, the organizers who commissioned the placard in question in 1999, in which the most prominent members of their association of devotees, the '*Jhūle Lāl sangat*',[8] are depicted in portraits, opted for an almost un-iconic placard two years later. This placard, with only two portraits now, has the names of the *sangat*'s members written in button-like oval shapes.

A group of devotees hailing from Burewala in south Punjab displayed their banner right above the entrance to their rented compound in Sehwan's Makrani Mohallah. The central depictions of Lal Shahbaz Qalandar with Bodlah Bahar as well as the golden-domed shrine in the upper part of the banner are flanked by views of other saints' shrines, three on each side. These shrines were visited by the Burewala *sangat* on their pilgrimage to Sehwan. The lower part of the picture contains visual references to 20 prominent members of the group, 17 of them are portraits and three give personal names in calligraphy. A picture of the pilgrims' bus occupies the centre of this row of portraits.

Texts

Sacred Words and Pious Formulas

Similar to other *'urs kē ishteharāt* from Punjab, most Qalandar pilgrimage placards have calligraphic or pictorial references to God and the Prophet Muhammad PBUH as usual placed in the uppermost part side by side with the *bāsmalah* and further invocations of the holy family (*panjtān pāk*) of the Prophet PBUH. Nevertheless, the most sacred part of the print is more prominently adorned by verses eulogizing Lal Shahbaz Qalandar, for instance, by the well-known Persian couplet beginning with *haīdariam qalandaram mastam* as well as the following verses and formulas in Urdu:

> *Damā dam mast Qalandar – 'Alī dā pehla nambar –*
> *Sākhī Shahbāz Qalandar.*
> Through your breath, oh Qalandar intoxicated (by the divine) – Ali is the number one – oh bounteous Shahbaz Qalandar.

> *Chaukhat hai Qalandar kī gharīboñ kā sahārā, miljātā hai har gham us-se jab bhī pukārā.*
> The threshold to the Qalandar is a help for the poor; every sorrow will come to an end if we call upon him.

> *Har dil meñ har ankh meñ hai armān Qalandar kā Jhūle Lāl, qismat wālā bantā hai mehmān Qalandar kā Jhūle Lāl.*
> In every heart (and) every eye there is the longing for Qalandar Jhule Lal; if you are fortunate, you will be made the guest of Qalandar Jhule Lal.

> *Nigāh-e Qalandar meñ woh tāsīr dekhī, badaltī logoñ kī taqdīr dekhī.*
> In the eyes of the Qalandar I found such qualities, (and) I saw the fortune of the people.

Other placards show Punjabi verses; the first became famous when crooned by Noor Jahan:

Shahbāz kare parwāz jāne rāz dilāñ dē, jiundere tē lāl Qalandar ān-milāñge.
The royal falcon flies, he knows the secrets of the hearts; if we are still alive, we will meet at (the shrine of) Lal Qalandar.

Ka'abe 'alī dā tē jhukde sikandar, tarīqat dā pehlā namāzī Qalandar.
The king bows before the highest Kaaba, the Qalandar is the first pious on the mystic path.

Jhūle Lāl dē khushiañ tē gham tal.
Jhule Lal, give me happiness and remove difficulties!

In addition, there are invocations to Data Ganj Bakhsh, the patron saint of Lahore, to Shah Bilawal Nurani, the saint from a remote place in Balochistan near the mythical Lahut Lamakan, to the Qalandar's beloved disciple Bodlah Bahar, whose shrine is also in Sehwan as well as frequent formulas eulogizing Hazrat Ali RA and the twelve Shia Imams. As the Twelver Shias, especially from Punjab, claim Lal Shahbaz had been Shia, Hazrat Ali RA is often mentioned together with him, for instance, in the formula *Jāne Yā 'Alī Jhūle Lāl*, the famous Arabic invocation quoting Ali's— the first Shia Imam's—sabre *dhū'l-fiqār* and in Persian verses emphasizing the Prophet's nomination of Hazrat Ali RA as his rightful successor.[9] The connection between the first Imam of Shias and the Qalandar is also highlighted in the following Urdu verse through a reference to Hazrat Ali's burial place in Najaf:

Be sabab chumte nahīñ Sehwan kī zamīn ko, is mattī se khushbū-ye Najaf ātī hai.
It is not without reasons to kiss the soil of Sehwan, (as) from this earth the fragrance of Najaf emanates.

Placards with such verses and invocations are a public affirmation not only of Sufi devotionalism, but particularly of Shia identity.

Titulature of Lal Shahbaz Qalandar

In addition to sacred words and pious formulas, the upper or more often central part of the placard contains the name of the Qalandar and his honorific titles. Thus, stringing grand titles together, he is officially named *Hazrat Sayyid La'l Shahbāz Qalandar*, often accompanied by the sobriquets *sākhī sarwar sarkār* (bounteous leader and master), *lajpāl* (the lord who gives us life), and *kibrīyā* (the great). On one placard he is also praised as *makhdūm-e auliyā'* (master of the Friends of God) and on another as *sar-e musarāt* (head of happiness, referring to his benedictions). Occasionally, his vernacular *laqab* Lal Shahbaz and the *nisbah* Qalandar is followed by his personal name Usman and the *nisbah* Marwandi referring to his place of birth in northwest Iran. He is praised as *'Alī La'l* (highest Lal),[10] *mast* (the intoxicated one),[11] and in idiomatic Punjabi as *jattī-sattī* (powerful).[12] Furthermore, he is reverently addressed as *pīr-o-murshid* (Sufi master and spiritual guide) and *walī-ye-Sindh* (saint/ruler of Sindh). On two prints the saint is only addressed by his nickname Jhule Lal; on another this name appears in repetition on the red border.

Basic Information

Alongside the mention of the *'urs* (in the form of a prominent calligraphic sign in the centre of the placard or banner), the number of this annual event is given (for instance 748 in the year 2001), the dates in the Islamic lunar and in the Gregorian calendar as well as the location, that is to say Sehwan. If it is, however, a *shām-e Qalandar*—preceding the *'urs*, also the date and place of this devotional ritual is mentioned. Necessarily genuine pilgrimage placards and banners contain information about the pilgrims' date of departure—the caravan (*qāfilah*)—and the place where they are to assemble. Often the procession starts from the house of the main organizer and moves to the railway station in town from where the journey starts from Punjab to Sindh in the south. On the other hand, there are banners just mentioning the mobile number of the respective organizer; such prints, which often show images in abundance, are generally put up at the pilgrims' camp in Sehwan where they fulfil the role of a statement of being there. Thus, they are not specifically meant as an invitation to join the pilgrimage but mark devotees' presence.

Organization—The Network of Devotees

The textual information in the lower part of placards and banners not only provides insights into the organizational framework of the respective *sangat* but also into the social fabric of these regional networks centred upon devotional practices. Such local associations of Qalandar devotees are known by specific names, for instance, *Jhūle La'l sangat grūp No. 21* (Lahore), *sangat yā 'Alī jīwan tērē la'l* (Lahore),[13] *Jhūle Lāl sangat* (Faisalabad), *'alī La'l sangat* (Faisalabad), *sangat dīwāne mastāne* (Rahim Yar Khan). Sometimes, associations call themselves simply *Qalandarī grūp* or *Qalandarī sangat* and then add their respective city, for example, Burewala, Arifwala, or Khanewal. In other cases, a *sangat* is named after the main organizers. *'Urs* placards inviting devotees to join in the pilgrimage to Lal Shahbaz Qalandar are also printed by the *sangat*s of other great saints, such as in the case of the *sangat Hazrat Dātā Ganj Bakhsh* (Lahore).

Lists of names are generally arranged in hierarchical order whereby the prominent organizers and devotees are often brought out by their portraits. They reflect an exclusively male corporate membership. Names and titles are revealing in the sense that they tell about the individual's origin, religious denomination, or official position (through *nisbah*), ethnic affiliation (through *nasab*), professional, and occupational background as well as individual idiosyncrasies (through *laqab*).

Associations organizing the *qāfilah Qalandarī* (literally 'caravan of Qalandar pilgrims') to Sehwan and their stay in this town are apparently less institutionalized than those organizing the actual *'urs* of a saint. A comparison of Lahori and Punjabi *'urs* placards shows the former only inform about a handful of organizational functions whereas the latter reflect the bureaucratized management of shrines. The placards and banners at best give the headings *zēr-e sarparastī* (under the direction), *zēr-e nigrānī* (under the auspices), *zēr-e qiyādat* (under the leadership), or *zēr-e sadārat* (under the presidency) denoting those leading the caravan of pilgrims. Sometimes, the organization committee is just subsumed under the headings *intezāmīah* (under the care of), *muntazamīn* (listing the superintendents and managers), or *minjānib* (in the name of). Guests can be addressed as *mehmān garāmī* (appreciated guests) or *mehmān khusūsī* (special guests). Occasionally, the *langar*-in-charge (persons organizing the 'communal meal' during the stay in Sehwan) and *dhammāliē* (dancers) are named. Often no office holders at all are mentioned, the *sangat* just represents itself as a collective.

The chief organizers are usually leading Sufis and Khalifahs of saints, but also senior bureaucrats who humbly call themselves *haidarī-malang* although, of course, they do not lead the lives of religious mendicants. Many of them are Sayyids and as such they are listed on top of the other devotees. Among the dignitaries and special guests, we find politicians, landlords, high officials (such as commissioners and people from army and police), and businessmen. Remarkably, politicians do not refer to their political affiliation which seems to indicate a taboo of representation in this religious context. The devotees of a *sangat* sometimes humbly call themselves 'servants of the Qalandar' or 'servants of the Friends of God'—much like the impressive fakirs staying permanently in Sehwan (Figs. 56–58).

A peculiarity of Lahori pilgrimage placards and banners is that they also mention nicknames, so typical and colourful especially for old Lahore. However, for the study of the social composition of devotees' associations and their networks, the *nasab*, the *nisbah* indicating the place of origin, and the *laqab* indicating the occupation are more revealing. For instance, the placard of the *Jhūle La'l sangat grūp No. 21* in Lahore, which honours Lal Shahbaz Qalandar in the name of the late Chaudhry Imtiaz Husain, lists altogether 98 personal names. *Nasab* like Jat, Bhatt, Gujar, Satti, and Arain show that the *sangat* is a collective entity cutting across the boundaries of *qaum* (ethnic group), *zāt* (caste), and *birādarī* ('brotherhood' of extended kin within a caste).

Secondly, the frequently mentioned *nisbah*, Samundri-wale, points to the origin of these individuals from the *qasbah* Samundri in the vicinity of Faisalabad in central Punjab. This highlights the well-known social pattern in Lahore, that many of its inhabitants, in fact, migrated to the city from the countryside. *Nisbah*s mentioning place names on our prints indicate that devotees predominantly live in and around the Walled City as well as in other traditional quarters. Nevertheless, there are also Qalandar networks where some of the main followers of a living Qalandar saint from Lahore come from other towns in Punjab, such as Gujrat, Jhelum, Chakwal, Narowal, or Sahiwal. Thirdly, occupational *laqab* document that members of *sangat grūp No. 21* work as fish-sellers, butchers, and barbers or in restaurants, for instance, as cooks. Names on other placards and banners prove a similar variety of professions, from bank officers, police inspectors, and car dealers to cloth dyers, bread bakers, chicken vendors, and makers and sellers of tea, *lassī*,[14] *pān*,[15] potatoes, and lentils. In the case of the *sangat Hazrat Dātā Ganj Bakhsh*, who organizes a lavish *jashn-e shān-e Qalandar* in Lahore before the actual pilgrimage to Sehwan, a large subgroup, in fact, consists of butchers, many of who are most probably no more working in this profession.

The reference to distinctions apparent in names and titles does not contradict the nominally egalitarian character of *sangat* members and can even be seen as an emphasis that people from all walks of life are welcomed in their specific community. Bound together as members of the same *sangat* during the devotional rituals of pilgrimage, *'urs* and *shām-e Qalandar* create a sense of brotherliness and equality.

The bottom of the placard sometimes contains the names of wealthy devotees, often together with their company's name, who sponsor printing and distribution as well as the ritual proceedings. They can be the owners of a forwarding agency, of a company for metalwork and packages machinery, building contractors and agents for cranes, of a company selling ice-blocs, but also of a textile store or *pān* shop. One placard explicitly mentions that the donation (*'atīah*) for printing the placard had been received by a man from the Walled City who works as a *baig-wālā*, that is to say somebody selling travelling bags. The names can be introduced by pious invocations such as *adā'ī ul-khaīr* (please pray for me!).

Programme

Unlike *'urs* posters which give detailed information on the rituals and ceremonies taking place at the saints' festivals, pilgrimage placards and banners advertise and publicize the event as such. They usually provide basic data about the date of the festival, the departure of the *qāfilah Qalandarī* from Lahore's City Railway Station or from another town in Punjab and the place of residence (*qiyām*) in Sehwan, sometimes also about the *langar*, that is to say the 'free' kitchen which honours the principle of charity and is run as a perpetual sacrifice. The *langar* is mentioned in a small section entitled *progrām* at the bottom of the placard. *Shām-e Qalandar* placards, on the contrary, focus more on different ritual events, such as the actual Qalandar night, *mēhndī*, and *dastar-bandī* ceremonies as well as the departure of the *qāfilah* to Sehwan. Another programme starts with *Qur'ān khwānī*, *chādar-o-dhamāl* performed after evening prayers, followed on the next day by *mēhfil-e samā'* (mystical audition) mentioning the names of the *qawwālī* singers and *pehlī dhamāl qadīmī*. The *La'l Shahbāz Qalandar mēhfil-e samā'* is ended by *rasme sēhrā*, the ceremony of the binding of garlands.

Conclusion

Placards and banners announcing and advertising the pilgrimage to Lal Shahbaz Qalandar on the occasion of the saint's *'urs* are above all printed in Lahore and distributed elsewhere. Examining their visual and textual information through the network lens helped analyze the institutionalization of the Sufi saint's cult especially popular among Punjabi devotees since the 1960s/1970s and borders on fandom. I argue Qalandar pilgrimage placards and banners are media of mass communication offering insights into contemporary Sufi devotional practices as well as the hierarchical organizational framework and the social composition of pilgrims' associations.[16] *Sangat*s constitute inclusive moral communities which cut across the boundaries of *qaum*, *zāt*, and *birādarī*. Within the confined context of devotion to a Sufi saint their members share a collective identity as followers of Lal Shahbaz Qalandar. Finally, it should be emphasized that the material, presented here very briefly, calls for a closer study of such Sufi networks across Pakistan.

Notes

1. Jürgen Wasim Frembgen, 'Words and Images in the Muslim Public Space: Placards announcing Sufi Saints' Festivals in the Pakistani Punjab,' *Baessler-Archiv* 65 (2018/19b), 51–66. In addition to placards and banners, there are treatises serving as guides to visit the tombs of Sufi saints alongside Muslim calendars in which the festivals of Muslim saints are listed. For an exemplar of such a manual from the eighteenth century, see Carl W. Ernst, 'An Indo-Persian Guide to Sufi Shrine Pilgrimage,' in *Manifestations of Sainthood in Islam*, eds. Grace M. Smith and Carl W. Ernst (Istanbul: The Isis Press, 1993), 43–67.

2. The following placards and banners are part of the collection of the Museum Fünf Kontinente in Munich: Inv. Nos. 99-321 518, 99-321 519, 99-321 520, 99-321 521, 02-324 016, 02-324 016, 04-326 224, 10-334 325, 10-334 348, 10-334 352. Photographs of other placards and banners were taken by the author in Lahore and Sehwan.

3. Frembgen, 'Icons of Love and Devotion.'

4. The term *sangat* (originally a Sanskrit word)—meaning 'union', 'association', or 'society'—is also used for branches of a Sufi order. In other contexts, this term is commonly used for circles of Shia mourners (*mātamī sangat*) and circles of poets.

5. Frembgen, *The Friends of God-Sufi Saints in Islam*, 67 and 69.

6. Ibid.

7. The *nasab* Alvi shows that the person in question is a descendant of Hazrat Ali RA, the fourth caliph and first Shia Imam, but from other wives than the daughter of the Prophet.

8. An equivalent term is *anjuman ghulāmān Sākhī Lāl Shāhbāz Qalandar*.

9. Concerning Shia symbols in the cult of Lal Shahbaz Qalandar, see Michel Boivin, 'Representations and Symbols in Muharram and Other Rituals: Fragments of Shiite Worlds from Bombay to Karachi,' in *The Other Shiites. From the Mediterranean to Central Asia*, eds. Alessandro Monsutti, Silvia Naef, and Farian Sabahi (Bern: Peter Lang, 2007), 166–8.

10. This invocation echoes the *'Alī Allāh* formula written on banners and displayed during the *'urs* above the main entrance of the *darbār* of the Qalandar (cf. Ibid., 167).

11. This alludes to the Qalandar characteristic of being 'perpetually spiritually intoxicated' (*Damā dam mast Qalandar*), a state particularly attributed to Lal Shahbaz Qalandar.

12. This Punjabi echo word refers, in fact, to a rural Jat woman (*jattī*) who is admired as strong, robust, and hard working.

13. The name of this *sangat*, which means in translation, 'May the offspring of Ali live long', is actually the title of a famous devotional song venerating both Hazrat Ali RA and Lal Shahbaz Qalandar.

14. Beverage made in Punjab of yoghurt mixed with water, milk, salt, and spices.

15. Fragrant mixture of areca nut with various ingredients wrapped into a betel leaf.

16. What Carl W. Ernst remarked about the use of printed books in traditional Sufi genres (such as hagiographies, discourses, essays, manuals on prayer, and meditation) also holds true for the placards and banners: '[…] through the wider distribution made possible by print, such publications have both served local Sufi networks and at the same time functioned as proclamations that have at least potentially formed part of the public legitimization of Sufism. Through these modern public media, Sufism is no longer just an esoteric community constructed largely through direct contact, ritual interaction, and oral instruction' ['Ideological and Technological Transformations of Contemporary Sufism,' in *Muslim Networks from Hajj to Hip Hop*, eds. Miriam Crooke and Bruce B. Lawrence (Chapel Hill: The University of North Carolina Press, 2005,) 198–9].

III ENTRANCED WITH LOVE FOR THE QALANDAR
Sufi Networks of Punjabi Pilgrims

Introduction

The cult of Lal Shahbaz Qalandar has clear trans-regional, trans-ethnic, and even trans-religious character. Beyond the saint's shrine in Sehwan, the 'catchment area' in terms of recruitment of his devotees not only includes the rest of Sindh but parts of neighbouring Balochistan, Khyber Pakhtunkhwa, and Rajasthan in India and in particular the 'land of five rivers'—Punjab—the most populated province of Pakistan. As examined in Chapter I, the booming music and film industry of Lahore, the capital of Pakistani Punjab, spurred a marked rise in Qalandar piety and pilgrimage since the 1970s. Its affinity with music contributed decisively to the 'success' of the initially regional Qalandar cult reaching out to a far greater audience, especially province-wide from where crowds of pilgrims started frequenting Sehwan by the late 1970s. It is locally estimated that Punjabi devotees comprise about 70 per cent of all pilgrims. Not all followers of Lal Shahbaz Qalandar, however, are Muslim; many Hindus, some Christians and Sikhs also pay homage in Sehwan too.

This chapter investigates social aspects, devotional practices, and customs of Punjabi pilgrim groups in the cult of Lal Shahbaz Qalandar. First, I examine their affiliation with the healing and miracle-working Sufi saint and networks of holy men belonging to the mystic Qalandar tradition together with the social structure and organization of these groups. Their members call themselves 'lovers of the Qalandar', an expression echoing Ibn Barrajan's (d. 1141) and Ibn Arabi's (d. 1240) term *muhibbūn* (lovers of God), or even call themselves *Qalandarī dīwānaiñ*—those entranced with love for the Qalandar. The focus, thereby, is on the 'corporate body' of such devotional communities and pilgrim groups respectively known as *sangat*s and *qāfilah*s. They are based on the cohesion of

55

like-minded people who are united by their love for the 'Friends of God'. Second, I investigate the annual pilgrimage cycle of these Sufi networks, their anticipatory public and semi-public rituals as well as their piety practices while visiting Sehwan. Thereby, the focus is on collective devotion. Finally, dimensions of friendship, solidarity, and brotherhood are analyzed.

Studies on South Asian Sufi cults have barely addressed questions of the organizational framework of devotees who regularly visit the shrine of their beloved saint and undertake annual pilgrimages hitherto. In the course of my ethnographic fieldwork I tried to understand how the cult reproduces itself in time and space, how it is mapped in space, and is managed in form of viable organizations. Devotional communities studied here are part of a loosely organized, 'informal' Sufism which has a rather mundane and everyday character. Contrary to austere reform-Sufism and in opposition to the spiral of religious-political radicalization in Pakistan, the socio-religious dimension of popular Sufi Islam highlighted in this chapter centres on intense, tangible rituals and human bonds. It shows how 'vernacular' Sufi religiosity is closely entwined with society, especially among the underprivileged.

Qalandarī sangats, qāfilahs, and *masnads*

Affiliation with Lal Shahbaz Qalandar

In the wake of the growing popularity of the Qalandar through songs, hymns, and trance dances presented in musical performances and films, wealthy businessmen and enthusiasts started to celebrate their devotion in circles of personal friends and members of their *birādarī*. The destitute, who traditionally went on pilgrimage to Sufi shrines, the so-called *darbār-wālē* or *mañgne-wālē*, flocked around such patrons. The latter were often members of major Sufi orders and, in addition, became now founders of predominantly male associations of Qalandar devotees and leaders of pilgrim groups. A number of these patrons and devotees had earlier affiliations with the Qalandar inherited from their forefathers; and some founded their own *sangat* to fulfil a vow when Lal Shahbaz Qalandar blessed them with the birth of a son. The majority, however, were, so-to-speak, swept away by passionate love for the saint and his enormous popularity bordering on fandom. Thus, Lahore, the centre of Pakistan's music and film industry, became the hub of the Qalandar cult. As the saying among Qalandar devotees goes, 'in Lahore in every second small street there is a Jhule Lal *sangat*'.

The Punjabi and Hindi word *sangat*, commonly used in Lahore and in central and southern Punjab, means 'being in the company of friends'; *sang* is said to be equivalent to Urdu *sāth*—'help', 'support'. In the context of the Qalandar cult, *sangat* means an association of devotees related to a specific *birādarī* that dominates the group. As explained by *sangat* leaders, 'their members sit in the company of Lal Shahbaz Qalandar and participate in ritual activities devoted to him.' However, in Potohar, the northwest region of Punjab, the term *sangat* is not common at all; instead, such Sufi networks call themselves *qāfilah*s, groups of pilgrims moving as a caravan. There are very small caravans, for instance, those headed by dervishes or 'big' *malang*s who are accompanied by just five to 20 fakirs and devotees as well as larger groups. Devotees, who are, for example, traditionally affiliated to Shah Abdul Latif Kazmi (Bari Imam) (d. 1705/06), a major Sufi saint of the Qalandar tradition whose shrine is situated in Nurpur near Islamabad, form large caravans of hundreds of pilgrims that annually proceed to Sehwan, 'because Bari Imam wishes to honour the great Qalandar,' a taxi-driver who had undertaken the pilgrimage for many years told me. Likewise, the large *sangat* of the great Sufi master Hujwiri (d. 1071), Lahore's patron saint popularly known as Data Ganj Bakhsh, which is said to have more than 1,300 male members, annually conducts the pilgrimage to the tomb of the Qalandar.

A third, albeit less common term to denote a Sufi network in the Punjab is *masnad*, an Urdu word derived from Arabic meaning 'throne'. Thus, the dignitary sitting on the throne is a king or reigning prince; in the present context it refers to the head of a devotional community. In his report of a pilgrimage to Sehwan, the devotee Qais Ajmi explains the term *masnad* as a 'basic unit of Qalandari creed where initiates sit together once a week or a month and pray. Attendants put questions and the Murshid teaches them'.[1]

The author, Qais Ajmi, was a member of a *masnad* consisting of over 60 men aged between 17 and 64 who accompanied their spiritual guide Sayyid Tanwir Sibtain Naqvi. Most hailed from the village of Mehlowala in northeast Punjab (north of Narowal), others came from Gujranwala, Wazirabad, Rawalpindi, Sangla Hill, and Sheikhupura.

These *sangat*s, *qāfilah*s, and *masnad*s form localized groupings centred on the veneration of Lal Shahbaz Qalandar. Their gatherings in cities, Lahore and elsewhere, help recruit new members. They do express a distinctive 'we-feeling'.

Networks of Qalandar Holy Men

Apart from the *sangat*s, *qāfilah*s, and *masnad*s directly affiliated with Lal Shahbaz Qalandar there are devotional communities related also to other Sufi saints and holy men belonging to the Qalandar tradition. Be they major Qalandar saints such as a Bari Imam and Baba Lal Shah (d. 1967) from the village of Sorassi near Murree or minor saints such as Mama Ji Sarkar (d. 1991) and Lala Ji Sarkar (d. 2012)—both buried in Nurpur as well as Sayyid Shabbir Husain Shah who lived in Lahore—or even saints-to-be: they all emphasize their spiritual bonding to the great Qalandar. While discussing the proliferation of Sufi shrines in Punjab, David Gilmartin notes that '[…] in many cases a large and well-known shrine became the centre of a network of much smaller shrines which were monuments to the disciples and descendants of the more well-known saint.'[2] This process is also at work in the context of the Qalandar cult. Thus, written and oral hagiography, devotional poster-portraits, and photographs as well as inscriptions displayed at Sufi shrines are manifestations of networks among holy men, which substitute for formal genealogies common among established orthodox Sufi orders. Such regional spiritual networks extend into many parts of Punjab and adjacent regions of Kashmir and Khyber Pakhtunkhwa. 'Big' dervishes (*malang*s, *faqīr*s), to whom spiritual authority is attributed by their followers, do keep their own networks of sedentary or peripatetic holy men and helpers. During the annual *'urs* festivals celebrating the mystic nuptial of the saint with God as well as *jashn-e Qalandar* festivals commemorating the saint's affiliation with the 'Red Sufi', they exchange invitations for ritual events and discuss details of the annual *qāfilah* to Sehwan.

Such networks of saints and dervishes as well as the traditional *pīrī-murīdī* system, connecting Sufi saints and their disciples, are deeply rooted in rural and urban areas. They create the warp and weft of devotional communities venerating the Qalandar. In the following two subchapters I examine the social structure and organization of both *sangat*s, typical for *birādarī*s of central and south Punjab, especially Lahore, as well as large and small *qāfilah*s found across the province, but especially in Potohar.

Social Structure

From my conversations with leaders and members of Qalandari *sangat*s I learned that although many were founded and dominated by a particular Punjabi *birādarī*, they also invited people from other 'brotherhoods' and ethnic groups (*qaum*) too. For instance, Pashtun (Pakhtun, Pathan). Spokesmen emphasized the flexibility and openness to accept devotees hailing from various ethnic, social, and religious groups. Personal friendship is the decisive factor when crosscutting ethnic, kin, village, or religious loyalty. In a metropolis like Lahore, locality constitutes another important factor for membership: similar to *qāfilah*s, *sangat*s are associations often closely related to a suburb or to a specific quarter or neighbourhood of the Walled City too, sometimes as closed and hidden as a *kathrāh*,[3] a self-contained settlement inhabited by a single caste-like group (*zāt*). In smaller towns of Punjab, *sangat*s often boast a mixed composition. Small networks in Lahore count about 20 to 30 members while the largest ones go into hundreds. The *Jhūle La'l sangat grūp No. 21*, for instance, has over 200 members; headed by Chaudhry Bilal, a wealthy forwarding agent. The *sangat* is dominated by his own Jat *birādarī* but also includes Gujar, Bhatt, Rajput, and men from other castes. As far as affiliation to ethnic groups, caste and *birādarī*s is concerned, placards and banners printed and distributed by Qalandari *sangat*s are an important source of information. My studies about the names and titles mentioned on Punjabi pilgrimage placards show that members belong to various social groups and professions: from bank officers, car dealers, and cloth merchants to cloth dyers, bread bakers, tea vendors, butchers, and barbers (see Chapter II). Most members are ordinary people belonging to the lower classes whereas their leaders and patrons, especially in the case of larger devotional communities, are rather well off, often belonging to the class of the new rich. If the latter are active in political parties or movements, they understandably also use *qāfilah*s and *sangat*s as a vote bank. Religious charisma and authority in leadership seems to be of lesser importance. However, minor living saints are sometimes given a prominent honorary position in the 'weak' hierarchy of a Sufi network.

A typical Lahori Qalandari *sangat* is, for instance, the *Pahlwān barfwālā sangat* founded in the mid-1970s by Nazir Pahlwan Barfwale (d. 1989). When he remained childless for years, Nazir Pahlwan prayed to Lal Shahbaz Qalandar to intercede with God on his behalf for the birth of a child. If he would be blessed with a son, he vowed to dedicate his whole life to the Qalandar and to establish a *sangat* for his veneration. So it happened. Their first *dērah* or *addā* (meeting place) was the Crown Hotel at the General Bus Stand close to the Qalandari Barf Store run by the Malik family. When the Crown Hotel became too small a meeting place, they shifted to their own small poultry market opposite Sheranwala Gate of the Walled City. For two years this medium-sized male association with about 50 to 60 members has been better known by the names of his two sons as *Mālik Asad – Chan Qalandarī sangat* (cf. Fig. 49). About a quarter of its members belong to the Malik *birādarī*, originally oil pressers (Teli); the others are Gujar, Bhatt, Jat, and Shaikh. When two of them, Bhola and Mian, developed discordances with the Malik brothers, they separated from the *sangat* and founded the rather small *Bhōlē sangat* with their own *dērah*. The Malik brothers, for their part, keep a network of contacts to other associations of devotees in Peshawar, Nurpur near Islamabad, Rawalpindi, and Okara, inviting leaders of the groups to their *shām-e Qalandar* in Lahore and reciprocally being invited to other saints' festivals.

In comparison to this *birādarī*-dominated *sangat* from Lahore, the famous *Shah Chan Chirāgh qāfilah* from Rawalpindi, for instance, consists of about 70 men belonging to different castes, such as Jat, Kamboh, Shaikh, Gujar, Malik, Bhatt among others. Its members come from various parts of the city but are all devotees of the city's patron saint, Shah Chan Chiragh, whose shrine is situated in Purana Qila. The founding leader of this caravan of Qalandar pilgrims was Sain Nazir Lahuti (d. 1998); today a carpenter and cushion-maker from the quarter of Amarpura is one of the leaders.

The largest *sangat* in Lahore is the one from Mochi Gate led by Agha Reza, a cloth merchant in Shahalam (Walled City), and the largest *qāfilah* from the city is associated with the famous Sabzi Mandi (vegetable market) *qāfilah* with thousands of men headed by wealthy Arain traders who are Sufis of the Qadiriyyah. They first started the pilgrimage in the mid-1970s. With the additional support of a Qadiri Sufi Shaikh and Mufti from Sukkur, they built the Lal Haveli (red castle) in Sehwan's Khosa Mohallah in 2002 as a hostel for Punjabi pilgrims. Small *qāfilah*s, on the other hand, might only consist of a small circle of friends with their families, including women and children. Obviously, in such smaller groups the fluctuation of members is lesser than in larger associations. Although, as mentioned above, *sangat*s and *qāfilah*s are predominantly male associations or 'brotherhoods' in the strict sense of the term (also jokingly called *nar-wālē* in the vernacular), there are remarkable exceptions from the rule such as the *Chirāgh Bībī qāfilah* from Lahore headed by women (see Chapter IV).

Generally, *sangat*s and *qāfilah*s consist of both, Sunnis and Shias. At times, Christians too join. Exceptions are Qalandari networks which evolved from *mātamī sangat*s whose members practice ritual mourning on occasion of various religious festivals in particular in Muharram. An example is the *sangat* led by Sayyid Mohsin Ali Shah (Walled City). These Shia dominated devotional communities also have Sunni members at times.

Organization

Studying the textual information on the placards of Punjabi *sangat*s, in which the annual pilgrimage to Sehwan is announced, revealed a rather modest degree of organization within their association. Thus, the *qāfilah Qalandarī* is either headed by a committee or more often by a single leader who maintains local patronage structures legitimized in *birādarī* idioms. Sometimes the person in charge of the *langar* and the trance dancers accompanying the caravan are mentioned on pilgrimage placards too (see Chapter II).

I also gathered empirical data from conversations with leaders of several smaller *sangat*s and *qāfilah*s who did not print special placards. My old friend Liaqat Ali Bhatti from Rawalpindi, for instance, whom I know since 1988, is the leader of a Qalandar caravan now comprising of 30 to 35 men from different caste-like groups, such as Bhatt, Malik, and Jat. In 1990, when he took his first caravan to Sehwan, the group consisted of just six friends. From then onwards it grew into an association in which he and his vice-chairman delegate different tasks to six or seven other members. As a rule, he himself makes the travel arrangements by train and bus whereby every member pays for his own ticket. If one is poor, however, he is invited for free. This generosity is reported across all Sufi networks known to me. Moreover, Liaqat purchases the *chādar*s spread on saints' tombs and oil lamps burnt there. Two members arrange food, including tea, for travel and stay in Sehwan. One of Liaqat's friends, who is wealthier than other *qāfilah* members, is responsible for the *langar*. Others help him distribute the food. One person takes care of the blankets and another makes sure the oil lamps are lit every evening. In Sehwan, they stay in a room belonging to the Makhdumi *kāfī*, a Sufi lodge and sanctuary belonging to one of the companions of the Qalandar. Liaqat, in fact, inherited this privilege to stay for free in the room from a deceased friend who had undertaken the pilgrimage since the late 1960s. One member of the *qāfilah* acts as a *chaukīdār* (watchman) keeping the key to their room.

Expenses for the pilgrimage as well as lodging in Sehwan are shared by members of the respective network. Thus, every traveller in a *qāfilah* contributes between PKR 1,500 to 2,000; this money is administered by the leader. At times, there is an alternative system of collecting the money. Thus, in the *Mālik Asad – Chan Qalandarī sangat*, mentioned above, the *chanda* (from *chand*— moon) is a monetary contribution collected every month and held by the leader.

Pilgrimage to Sehwan

Rituals in Anticipation

In the days before Qalandari *sangat*s and *qāfilah*s embark for Sehwan, the larger and more affluent of these associations celebrate commemorative rites such as *shām-e Qalandar*, *mēhndī*, or *sedāī Qalandar*. In anticipation of the death anniversary of the Qalandar these rituals are performed especially in Lahore and to a certain extent also across other cities of Punjab.

In some cases, *sangat*s already celebrate Qalandar nights (*shām-e Qalandar*) in Rajab some weeks before the 'urs of Lal Shahbaz Qalandar from Shaban 19 to 22 (Figs. 59–61). Particularly auspicious for the ritual are Rajab 13 which is the birthday of Hazrat Ali RA, Rajab 27 when the tomb of the Qalandar in Sehwan is ritually washed, Shaban 3, the birthday of Hazrat Imam Husain RA, Shaban 4, the birthday of Hazrat Ghazi Abbas Alamdar, Shaban 7, the birthday of Hazrat Qasim ibn al-Hasan, and Shaban 15, the birthday of Muhammad al-Mahdi (who Shias believe to be) Imam Mahdi and also the claimed birthday of Lal Shahbaz Qalandar. Most Qalandar nights are celebrated some days before the pilgrims actually start their journey by train or bus but, because of necessary arrangements for travel, not on the very last night. The extended ritual time between early Rajab and the final Qalandar 'urs in Shaban, which punctuates the ritual calendar, is used by organizers to collect money to purchase splendid tomb covers (*chādar*, *ghilāf*) later taken to Sehwan and spread on the saint's grave. As a rule, these devotional textiles are already proudly displayed at the *shām-e Qalandar* on the stage where the musical gathering takes place. The textiles are reverentially kissed by devotees. Generally, a Qalandar night starts with praise for the Prophet Muhammad PBUH and Hazrat Ali RA, followed by a *mēhfil-e mosīqī* (musical concert with Qalandar songs), *dhamāl* (trance dance), and *langar*. Often the whole commemorative rite is professionally filmed on video and in part individually documented using mobile phones. Expenses for this ritual are covered by the leader and the most affluent members of the *sangat*.

The *shām-e Qalandar* is a tradition said to have been invented in the late 1960s and early 1970s by the Lahori music composer Nazir Ali and his *murshid* (spiritual guide) Sain Lal Das. The latter had been a dedicated follower of the Qalandar since his youth. He originally hailed from a Hindu Kashmiri family and had been professionally active in the then nascent film industry of Lahore in the 1930s. He finally became the *chirāgh-wālā* (ritual 'lamp-lighter')[4] of a Hindu *kāfī* (private Sufi lodge) in Sehwan and in this capacity blessed the young Nazir when the latter implored the Qalandar to give him the talent to become a successful composer. Subsequently, Nazir composed popular devotional songs in the genre of *Qalandarī dhamālaiñ* for different Punjabi films produced in Lollywood (see Chapter I). He became the alleged lover of Noor Jahan for seven years beginning 1969. During this period, the first Qalandar nights were organized at Lahore's Shahnoor Studios, presided by both Nazir and Noor Jahan's *murshid* Sain Lal Das. Afterwards, many actors, singers, dancers, and other people of the film business in Lahore became devotees of the Qalandar and *murīd*s (disciples) of Lal Das. Since the early or mid-1970s till date, a *shām-e Qalandar* is organized on the 21st of each month at Shahnoor Studios with devotional songs and *dhamāl*.[5] In tandem with the creation of Qalandari *sangat*s, thus, also the performance of Qalandar nights celebrating the evocative poetry honouring Lal Shahbaz Qalandar became gradually popular for associations which could afford the expenses, though a number of *sangat*s started as late as in the 1990s to organize their first event of this kind.

An example for a typical *shām-e Qalandar* is the event organized by Khurram Abbas on Mohni Road opposite Taxali Gate in Lahore. Khurram Abbas is a tall, middle-aged man who worked as a WAPDA (Water and Power Development Authority) lineman for long and recently became the bodyguard of a local politician. Having been much impressed in the late 1980s by the decorative splendour of a Shia gathering in Arifwala, the town of his parents-in-law, he not only encouraged performance of the ritual mourning by the Shia *sangat* he led for years with greater pomp but alongside also the establishment alongside a *Qalandarī sangat*. In the mid-1990s,. this network consisting of about 60 men, women, and children of the Mirasi caste started to celebrate their first Qalandar night on Shaban 12. Khurram emphasizes he gives directives for running the annual event but everybody in his *kathrāh* would know what to contribute for the *langar*. He also collects money to pay musicians and to cover the expenses for their transport. The event starts in the evening with the *mēhndī* ceremony deep inside the *kathrāh* at a small courtyard and an adjacent imambargah which contains replicas of Hazrat Imam Husain RA, Hazrat Ghazi Abbas Alamdar, and Hazrat Qasim's shrines. Only women, children, and some boys of the neighbourhood are allowed to participate in the ritual (Fig. 60); men and outsiders are generally excluded. The women celebrate the *mēhndī* of Lal Shahbaz Qalandar, a marriage ceremony largely in the female domain. If a wish has been fulfilled by the grace of the Qalandar they donate ritual gifts (*nazr*) such as baskets laden with henna, trays bearing candles, and food for the *langar*. For women, the *mēhndī* accompanied with *dhamāl* in the secluded inner space of the *kathrāh* constitutes a substitute for pilgrimage to Sehwan, only performed by their menfolk. Similar women-only *mēhndī*s take place in other parts of the Walled City and its vicinity. After the *mēhndī*, Khurram performs a devotional dance on the street. He carries a domed miniature clay mausoleum on his head which contains four burning oil lamps (Fig. 61). This *chirāghī-dhamāl* refers to a famous devotional saying in a version of the Punjabi song *Lāl mērī pat rakhīo* (see Chapter I) which goes:

Chār chirāgh tērē bālan hamisha, panjwān maiñ bālan ā'ī bālā jīwe lā'lan
Four oil lamps always burn for you, I have come to light the fifth for the Praised One. Long live La'l (cf. Fig. 5)

For the whole night, Mohni Road is blocked for traffic, red pennants are hung across the street and stage and a sound system with amplifiers is set up. From my observation on August 2, 2009, I estimate approximately 200 to 300 people from the surrounding areas visited this semi-public devotional event— mostly men, but also families and couples. The musical concert or *fanktshen* (function, event) started with praise for the Prophet Muhammad PBUH and Hazrat Ali RA by an elder. Then the singers took their turns. Khurram proudly mentions that famous artists, such as Naseebo Lal, Hasan Sadiq, and Sain Khawar have performed at earlier *shām-e Qalandar*s. Other singers, who regularly perform on such occasions in Lahore include Afshan, Samina, Rani Qalandari, Boby Ali Khan, and various *qawwālī* groups. Musical programmes are usually framed by the drum beat of *dhōl* players (Fig. 62). It is religiously meritorious (*sawāb*) to offer *langar* for the visitors: large pots of *biryānī* (rice-based dish with meat and spices) and *pālak* (spinach) are traditionally prepared by *sangat* members in Lahore who share the 'blessed' food.

There are larger and smaller *shām-e Qalandar*s in Lahore. The Qalandar night annually celebrated at Moon Market in Lahore's Allama Iqbal Town, for instance, was attended by at least 800 to 1,000 men on August 1, 2009. (Fig. 63). There was a steady flow of visitors, so the size of the audience could have easily multiplied. A separate *shamiānah* (tent) was set up for the comparatively small number of women (ca. 30–40). This is probably the largest *shām-e Qalandar* in Lahore, sponsored by some wealthy businessmen. One of them is the eldest son of music composer Nazir Ali who lives in the United Kingdom. His younger brothers, Gogi and Sajid, were the main performers on the occasion. For events of this size, organizers need special permission from local authorities and must also hire a security service. When I tried to interview main organizer, Kalim Panwala, on my next visit in early November, 2009, his shop was unfortunately closed. On December 7 that year two bombings killed over 50 people, wounded over 150, and gutted many shops at Moon Market. I have not returned there since then. The deteriorating security situation in many parts of Pakistan has not only affected Sufi saints' festivals and music concerts but also preliminary rituals of Qalandar devotees. In July, 2010, I observed the number of visitors, for instance, at Khurram Abbas' *shām-e Qalandar* on Mohni Road had considerably dropped and other organizers shifted devotional musical events to the courtyards and rooftops of private houses. On July 24, 2010, I accompanied singers Gogi and Sajid to a comparatively modest-sized Qalandar night of the *Sohnā Lāl sangat* in Lahore's suburb Kot Khwajah Saeed (Fig. 64). The head of this *sangat*, a merchant from Azam Cloth Market (said to be Asia's largest textile market) had invited around 80 to 100 people primarily from his extended family, men, women, and children on the spacious second floor terrace of his house. The presentation of devotional music followed by *dhamāl* started at 11pm and lasted till four in the morning.

Finally, several staunch Shia groups celebrate a hybrid ritual called *sedāī Qalandar* (call of the Qalandar) which appears to be an amalgamation of the prominent commemoration of Hazrat Imam Husain RA with the devotion to Lal Shahbaz Qalandar. Celebrated always on Shaban 12, the ritual starts with prayers, invocations, and *nauhah* (lament) recitation in the imambargah followed by flagellation in a courtyard. The imambargah features large banners showing the mausoleum of the Qalandar in connection with the occasion.[6]

Visiting Sufi Shrines on the Way to Sehwan

In the first half of the twentieth century pilgrims usually travelled by foot or bullock-cart to the shrine. Some also arrived by boat on the River Indus while others travelled by vehicles. However, since the 1960s and 1970s, roads and railways have considerably improved and from then onwards most Punjabi pilgrims have travelled to Sehwan using either by road or by train. Buses and cars are often lavishly bedecked with iconic images and devotional items. Traditionally, devotees use to pay their respects to other Sufi saints as well before reaching the threshold of the Qalandar. Thus, every Qalandari *sangat* and *qāfilah* follows its own route on the way to Sehwan. Such visitations of major Sufi shrines reflect the affiliations of local pilgrimage groups not only to other Qalandar holy men, as mentioned above when discussing their networks, but also to other major saints mainly from Punjab who belong to noted Sufi orders. The slow movement of approaching the Qalandar creates an experiential climax for the pilgrims when they finally reach the court of their spiritual ruler in Sehwan, by far the largest shrine during the whole journey (apart from Lahore's patron saint Ali Hujwiri, popularly called Data Ganj Bakhsh). This enhances the communitas feeling of the devotees who travel together.

A few examples should suffice to present an idea about traditional routes of Punjabi *sangat*s and *qāfilah*s travelling by bus. Thus, the journey of the *MD Bābā qāfilah*, named after Sayyid Ahmad Ali Shah Baba Multanwale (MD being a modern corruption of 'Ahmadi') from Nurpur near Islamabad, takes 25 days: first the 30 to 35 men pay their respects (*salām karnā*) to Bari Imam in Nurpur and seek his blessings and his permission for the pilgrimage. Then they proceed east to Khari Sharif in Mirpur, the abode of the Sufi poet and saint Mian Muhammad Bakhsh (d. 1904). From there they move south to Gujrat, where they visit the shrines of Shah Daula (d. 1674/75) and Sain Kanwanwali (d. 1934), and finally Lahore. With the blessings of Data Ganj Bakhsh and other saints of Lahore, they travel southwest first to Sultan Bahu (d. 1691) in Jhang, then to the graves of Hir-Ranjha near Jhang and afterwards to Multan, the city of many renowned Sufi saints. From there they go for *ziyārat* (ritual visitation) to Sakhi Sarwar (12th/13th c.) near Dera Ghazi Khan before travelling further south to Sehwan in Sindh. Like many other *sangat*s and *qāfilah*s, after the *'urs* of the Qalandar, the devotees of MD Baba also travel together with their saint to Lahut Lamakan in Lasbela, a mythical place in the mountains of Balochistan related to Hazrat Ali RA. They return from Lahut Lamakan by road via Karachi where they pay their respects to Abdullah Shah Ghazi (d. 768), the patron saint of Pakistan's largest city, and sometimes also to Mangho Pir, the saint of the crocodiles whose shrine is situated in the northern outskirts of the city. In comparison to this rather long journey, other pilgrim groups considerably shorten their trip. For instance, the *Jhūle La'l sangat* from Dera Ghazi Khan, founded in the mid-1980s, only visits three Sufi shrines on the way to Sehwan, all in south Punjab and on return two or three more holy sites such as the shrine of Baba Farid in Pakpattan (d. 1265).

Before Sehwan or after the 'urs of the Qalandar, many a pilgrim group from Punjab also makes sure to get blessings from Shah Abdul Latif (d. 1753), the famous mystic and poet from Sindh who is buried in Bhit Shah on the left bank of the River Indus. When I spoke to several leaders of devotional communities, I learned that the number of shrines to be visited obviously also depends on respective financial possibilities. Sangats from Lahore are, of course, usually visiting Sufi shrines first in their own city and then in central and south Punjab. Sangats from Multan start their journey by visiting first the local shrine of Shams Sabzwari (commonly, but mistakenly, called Shams Tabrez) and then on Bhakkar island near Sukkur, the mausoleum of Sadruddin Arif Shah (d. 1286), where many pilgrims stay for three days. According to legend, Lal Shahbaz Qalandar metamorphosed into a falcon and flew to the saint's abode once to rescue him and on another to serve him water for ritual ablution. The Qalandar is also said to have performed a 40-day-long period of fasting and praying at Sadruddin Arif's place. A number of pilgrim groups combines two modes of transport: thus, the Jhule La'l grūp of my friend Liaqat Ali Bhatti from Rawalpindi first travels by train to Rohri in upper Sindh and then takes a bus to Sehwan whereby the qāfilah at times stops to visit Sufi shrines.

However, many devotional communities from Punjab travel either by train directly to Sehwan or first to Hyderabad where they visit at least the qadamgāh of Hazrat Ali RA before taking a bus to reach the final destination of their pilgrimage. Thus, also the members of the masnad of Sayyid Tanwir Sibtain Naqvi from Mehlowala first took a train from Rawalpindi to Hyderabad, where they visited qadamgāh and then proceeded to Sehwan by bus stopping only at the grave of one Hajji Baba whose duty it had been to receive pilgrims at the shrine of Lal Shahbaz Qalandar by blowing his dervish horn.[7] A large number of Lahori sangats used to book their tickets with Shaikh Tariq affectionately called 'Baba-e train'. Weeks before the 'urs this Qalandar devotee and shoe factory owner sets up a table in front of a shop in Lahore's infamous 'Hira

Mandi' (one-time red light) quarter of the Walled City which serves
as an open-air office. Equipped with a special licence since 1986 he
has been allowed to sell tickets for many special trains for pilgrims.
As Shaikh Tariq told me in a conversation on August 4, 2009 as a
maximum he was once allotted 21 special trains (each train having
22 bogeys) in the late 1980s under the government of Benazir
Bhutto. He claimed he was able to send around 50,000 pilgrims
annually to Sehwan. Later, he was only granted three trains a year
and just one in 2009.

When I travelled together with the *Bābā Nazīr 'Alī sangat*
(Fig. 65) nearly a 100 people met us on the platform at Lahore
City Railway Station where music composer Nazir Ali's sons Gogi
and Sajid unrolled a carpet and first sung *Qalandarī dhamālaiñ* in
the memory of their late father (cf. Fig. 30). At every major halt
on the way to Sehwan they performed again. In Sehwan, they are
even allowed to sing inside the mausoleum of the Qalandar where
they 'offer their devotional music as a prayer' in their own words.
This again shows the intense sacred emotion which represents the
core of Qalandar piety.

Camp Life and Conduct in Sehwan

To make the pilgrimage more comfortable a number of *sangat*s,
*qāfilah*s, and *masnad*s deposit luggage such as tents and cooking
utensils from one year to the other with trusted locals in Sehwan and
in Shah Nurani near Lahut Lamakan. Leaders of larger devotional
communities often travel a week or two before the *'urs* in Sehwan
to make proper arrangements for the arrival of their group. With
the help of a few men, they prepare the campsite and organize the
supply of drinking water and food for the *langar*.

Most pilgrim groups, however, transport *shamiānah*s, tarpaulins,
flat woven carpets (*qalīn*), mats, bedding, cooking pots, goats
(or even young buffaloes) for the *langar*, often also a clay oven
and even chairs, shrine replicas, devotional banners, and flags by
bus or truck. In Sehwan they either camp on the outskirts of the
town, for instance, in Lal Bagh (Fig. 66), around Purana Qila or
in one of the graveyards, or they rent local houses and courtyards.

On arrival, they first pitch tents and mark their campsite through tent walls. Large banners indicate the presence of the *sangat* or *qāfilah* in question. Members of the group collect firewood and one of them digs a pit for the clay oven used for baking flatbread. Other food is cooked on charcoal fires. Some networks, such as the *Būrīwālā Qalandarī sangat*, a men-only group of about 200 people from south Punjab, customarily resides in two large *shamiānah* tents at a graveyard between Mela ground and Makrani Mohallah. Next to them is the tent of a *sangat* from Arifwala which consists of about 150 men.

In the report of his pilgrimage, Qais Ajmi mentions a code-of-conduct which every member of his *masnad* had to sign before embarking on the journey.[8] Thus, he writes: 'Each pilgrim should consider himself at lower status as compared to the rest' and 'every member of the group should behave himself as the ambassador of *tarīqah* of Lal Shahbaz Qalandar'. And furthermore: 'In the limits of Sehwan, according to the tradition of our *masnad* no one will wear shoes.' As far as the position of their leader is concerned, he emphasizes: 'To safeguard our *murshid* they [the members of his group] should all form a circle around him.'

Unlike this particular group of Sufis who visited the holy city of Sehwan in the company of their spiritual guide, members of other groups, according to my own observation, mostly pass the day sleeping, chatting, smoking hashish and drinking *bhang* (intoxicating drink made of hemp), playing cards, preparing food, hanging around in the bazaar, and by participating in various rituals of devotion.

Corporate Rituals of Devotion

Sufi Islam centres on love and aims at connection. Therefore, for every pilgrim seeking to connect with the Qalandar, the saint's *darbār* or monumental sanctuary in Sehwan is the ultimate core of devotion.[9] His tomb is the focal point of devotional practices because it is the source of *barakat* which flows from his final abode in abundance and radiates throughout the sacred town, especially at his *'urs*. Here pilgrims encounter the numinous, the divine power of the Qalandar, who acts as an intercessor to God and as charismatic healer and miracle-worker. Seeking the saint's blessings, they offer prayers, touch, and reverently kiss the tomb covers (*chādar*, *ghilāf*) literally 'loaded' with *barakat*.[10] These devotional practices and customs have a syncretistic religious background typical for the lowlands of Pakistan.

As a rule, every *sangat* and *qāfilah* rallies around its spiritual leader (Fig. 67) and leads its own procession to the *darbār*. Their members move slowly and gracefully, at times also dancing ecstatically (Figs. 68–69), but with a heightened sense of emotion. Accompanied by drummers and dancers they walk barefoot from their camp to the shrine carrying *chādar*s. Sometimes it is just one big rectangular *chādar* but often devotees carry several pieces knotted to each other at the short ends, creating a long colourful chain of textiles. In the inner sanctuary they solemnly place these *chādar*s on the tomb, one by one on top of each other, scattering red rose buds on them. The green or red cloths are usually cheaply produced in factories in the Far East and stamped with calligraphic verses from the Quran.[11] Yet other cloths are lavishly embroidered and at times show remarkable pictorial emblems of Qalandar piety such as the motif of the saint's shrine, tomb, boat, and heart-shaped stone. Thus, for instance, the *Alī Lāl sangat* from Faisalabad every year orders a professional to design a new precious *chādar*. This cloth is first proudly displayed at their camp site and carried in a procession to the shrine.

Similar to tomb cloths, a number of *qāfilah*s from the Potohar region in northwest Punjab carry shrine replicas (*dālī*) all the way to the *darbār*. In this way other saints of the Qalandariyyah, such as Bari Imam from Nurpur or Shah Chan Chiragh from Rawalpindi, pay their respects to the great Qalandar. These shrine replicas are displayed for some time in the sanctuary and later either disposed in a river (much like a Shia *ta'ziyah*) or carried back.

The most important ritual to be performed at the shrine is the devotional trance dance called *dhamāl* analyzed in detail in Chapter VI. Devotee Qais Ajmi emphasized in his report: 'Dhamal is the outstanding article of our path, as harmony of physical body and soul is possible through this.'

Shia devotees venerate the Qalandar as a descendant of Hazrat Imam Husain RA. Therefore, the Shia organized in a *mātamī sangat* who perform public flagellations in Muharram also do so in Sehwan to honour the Qalandar. They perform several times during their stay, often at the huge Shia standards ('*alam*) in front of the main shrine but also in the courtyard and even inside the inner sanctuary. Every Shia *sangat* has developed its own customary sequence and style of mourning performances. Thus, Sayyid Wasim Gardezi, the leader of a large *sangat* from Katrah Wali Shah in the Walled City of Lahore, informed me they would do *mātam* every evening on the three main days of the '*urs*: on the first day at the *darbār* of the Qalandar, on the second at the shrine of Bodlah Bahar, and on the third day again at the *darbār*.

On July 29, 2010 I witnessed a ritual of devotion celebrated by a small *sangat* from Lahore-Paknagar on the rooftop of a guesthouse in Sehwan. It started with the recitation of verses eulogizing the *panjtan pāk* (family of the Prophet Muhammad PBUH) followed by Shia prayers and *hadīth*. These were uttered by all participants facing a vertically displayed, finely embroidered red *chādar* which appeared as a sort of altar with five oil lamps and five bowls each with a candle in front of it. Afterwards, free food was served with *biryānī* and sweet rice (*zardah*).

Friendship, Solidarity, and Brotherhood

Devotees underline the permeability and flexibility of their *sangat*s and *qāfilah*s in terms of accepting new members; they emphasize 'anybody is free to join'. Their common point of reference is the veneration of Lal Shahbaz Qalandar which creates a 'trans-subjective mode of thinking' among pilgrims, to use an idea formulated by Jürgen Habermas in his work on communicative ethics,[12] but more specifically proves affective bonds based on custom and religion so typical for Punjabi society.[13] As far as the recruitment of Sufi networks is concerned, personal friendship plays a pivotal role. *Sangat*s and *qāfilah*s develop of clusters of friends, relatives, affines that transcend the *birādarī* of the respective leader. They also include men from other social, ethnic, and religious groups, thus cutting across caste and religious distinctions, for instance, between Sunnis and the Shias that otherwise regulate social encounters. In short, the devotional community forms a local social nexus where members share deep personal friendships. *Sangtī*s, members of a *sangat*, constitute a circle of men like brothers. This is often passed down from generation to generation. It is governed by criteria of allegiance, *birādarī* loyalty and faithfulness.[14]

Punjabi society is at times in the vernacular characterized as 'hard-eating' and among men, in addition, also hard-drinking (tea, *bhang*, alcohol), and hard-smoking. These popular characteristics are very much alive in the gatherings of *sangtī*s who share food and often meet daily to drink, smoke hashish, play cards, and chat. In conversations with *sangtī*s, some of them admitted that at times during *shām-e Qalandar*s conflicts could surface which even ended in gunfire. There are also *sangat*s whose leaders and members are involved in the underworld and generally in criminal activity.

Within the brotherhood of a *sangat* or *qāfilah*, solidarity is a highly estimated value. The smaller the network or community, the more organic social solidarity is practiced. Every *sangtī* is expected to contribute at least something to the expenses during pilgrimage. Of course, those who donate more generously are respected in proportion to their contributions. Leaders and influential members try to help other *sangtī*s find employment and assist in case of illness or difficulty. If the police nab one for taking drugs, they try to secure his release. There is a distinct sense of solidarity among all members of a group. For example, rickshaw driver Anwar who belongs to a small *sangat* located near Allama Iqbal Town in Lahore said, 'We hold hands and help each other in every respect in every situation in life. I would cut off my arm [whereby Anwar emphatically gestured this] than let go of the hand of my friend. If one of our *sangtī*s passes away, we also carry his bier—it is a matter of love.' This corporate solidarity based on similitude transcends mechanical kin-based solidarity.[15] It is enacted on a horizontal social level where members equally participate in commemorative rites, celebrate together and collectively merge in the spiritual and musical ecstasy typical of the Sehwan *'urs*.

Conclusion

Devotional communities of Punjabi pilgrims who venerate Lal Shahbaz Qalandar constitute loosely organized, rather informal networks of mostly men based on friendship, *birādarī* affiliation, and locality. They can be characterized as emotional communities of largely urban, underprivileged, like-minded devotees who celebrate the *'urs* of the Qalandar with fervour. Travelling together to Sehwan, visiting other Sufi shrines on the way, walking together in a ritual procession to the shrine of the Qalandar, and performing devotional rituals mark a period of intimacy which deemphasizes social distinctions, submerges kinship, and celebrates egalitarianism.[16] As far as the social structure of *sangat*s and *qāfilah*s is concerned, these rather informal Sufi networks cut across the boundaries of *qaum*, *zāt*, and *birādarī* though the latter remains a decisive factor in establishing a larger corporation. In the true spirit of Sufism, they tend to break away from stable social categories. The love of the Qalandar thus literally stands 'unbounded'. *Sangtī*s join together in ardent love for their saint.[17] Their collective identity is characterized by a powerful sense of sharing, belonging, comradeship, and spiritual bonding. Devotional communities venerating Lal Shahbaz Qalandar thus show how popular Sufi Islam is contextualized in its social environment and strengthens the sustaining value of society.

Notes

1. Qais Ajmi, *Three Days' Journey into the Wonderland of Sehwan* (Lahore: 2001; unpaginated typed manuscript, 78 pages).
2. David Gilmartin, 'Religious Leadership and the Pakistan Movement in the Punjab,' *Modern Asian Studies* 13/3 (1979): 447.
3. Sometimes also called *kathrī*; the Urdu term for such a densely-packed quarter would be *bastī*.

4. Cf. Jürgen Wasim Frembgen, 'Devotional Service at Sufi Shrines: A Punjabi *Charāgwālā* and his Votive Offering of Light,' *Journal of the History of Sufism* 4 (2003–4): 255–62.

5. With the exception of the months of Ramazan and Safar when only *dhikr* (ritual commemoration of God) is performed (information by Irshad Husain, boom-operator and soundman at Shahnoor Studios).

6. For instance, observed on August 4, 2009 at imambargah Sayyid Wazir Ali Shah (Bazar Hakima, Walled City/Lahore).

7. Ajmi, *Three Days' Journey into the Wonderland of Sehwan.* Here I would like to acknowledge the support of my friend Atiya Khan in Karachi who made it possible for me to study this rare manuscript.

8. Ibid.

9. Michel Boivin, *Artefacts of Devotion*, 29–30.

10. Jürgen Wasim Frembgen, 'Assemblage und Devotion: Macht und Aura von Objekten in muslimischen Heiligenschreinen im Punjab,' in *Die Dinge als Zeichen: Kulturelles Wissen und materielle Kultur*, ed. T. L. Kienlin (Bonn: Verlag Dr. Rudolf Habelt, 2005), 171–3.

11. Frembgen, 'Calligraphy in the World of Sufi Shrines in Pakistan,' 229 and 232.

12. Jürgen Habermas, *The Inclusion of the Other: Studies in Political Theory* (Cambridge: MIT Press, 1998).

13. David Gilmartin, 'Biradari and Bureaucracy: The Politics of Muslim Kinship Solidarity in 20th Century Punjab,' *International Journal of Punjab Studies* 1/1 (1994): 6.

14. Gilmartin notes for example: 'In spite of the underlying ideology of solidarity based on descent, *biradari* leaders are defined not primarily by genealogical position, but by the bonds of reciprocal obligation they have established with other *biradari* members, largely as a result of the ability (through wealth, landholdings, personal energy, official connections, political savvy, skill as mediators, etc.) to provide service to their *biradari* cohorts' (Ibid., 4).

15. Richard Kurin and Carol Morrow, 'Patterns of Solidarity in a Punjabi Muslim Village,' *Contributions to Indian Sociology* 19/2 (1985): 248.

16. Cf. Ibid., 236.

17. Cf. Alix Philippon, *Soufisme et politique au Pakistan* (Paris and Aix-en-Provence: Éditions Karthala & Sciences Po Aix, 2011), 115 and 123.

IV A FEMALE CIRCLE OF PILGRIMS FROM LAHORE
The Life Story of Mai Kausar

Introduction

The following personal observations and reminiscences are meant to contextualize the life story of Mai Kausar Lahuti Qalandari presented over this chapter. They should thus merely serve as a prologue.

On February 11, 2013, I left the home of a *sarangī* player in a neighbourhood not far from Pani-wala Talab in the Walled City of Lahore. Instead of returning the same way, I followed the narrow lane in the other direction. I was aware I was in a locality inhabited by the Mirasi (hereditary musicians). Since decades I had loved classical music of the subcontinent. After walking slowly for a while, I noticed a building standing out as it had been painted red in the iconic *qalandarī la'l*. Decorated, additionally it was with large Sufi posters. It was immediately apparent that the house must be related to Lal Shahbaz Qalandar. The main door was wide open. The strong pull of an ethnographer's sense of curiosity made me cautiously enter. I glanced at the Sufi posters, placards, and devotional items on the walls and offered my greetings with a humble gesture to the persons present, mostly women and girls, but also one man. I introduced myself first to the lady sitting on a string cot leaning on a cushion ostensibly presiding over the group. The lady, then in her early fifties, turned out to be Mai Kausar (also called Kausar Bibi or Mai Sahiba), the head of a *qalandarī* lineage by the name of *Chirāgh Bībī qāfilah*. The man in question, Ghulam Shahbaz Labba, was a singer. The encounter with Mai Kausar and her relatives, neighbours, and friends proved to be a moment of serendipity as I found myself in the midst of a devotional community venerating the Qalandar. In fact, they emphasized that they would proudly call themselves 'lovers of the Qalandar'.

In the ensuing conversation Mai Kausar talked about her female ancestors. Her maternal grandmother, Chiragh Bibi Qalandari, attached her family to the 'Red Sufi' over a 100 years ago. Her mother, Mai Hajan Bibi Qalandari (respectively *Amāñ Hājan Mangla Qalandarī*), kept the tradition alive till her death about 15 years ago (Fig. 70). She now leads this predominantly female community, a group which consists of about 200 to 300 women, men, and children primarily from Lahore but also families from Sahiwal, Gujranwala, Faisalabad, and Multan. In Sehwan they stay with the saintly Sayyid Murad Ali Shah, a Lakkiyari Sayyid. Mai Kausar's ancestors first moved from Kabul to Kashmir centuries ago. They then settled in Jalandhar in Punjab. From there they moved to Lahore in the twentieth century.

During my next visit to her *baithak* on December 20, 2013 Mai Kausar gifted me an illustrated booklet printed by Lahore-based Simorgh–Women's Resource & Publication Centre in 2010 which featured her story in Urdu. I also met her younger brother, Hajji Toni, who works in the Water and Power District Authority as a lineman. He strongly emphasized that their circle of 'lovers of the Qalandar' was unlike a *sangat* where 'men just smoke, eat, and loiter' but a devotional community that was a family-based *silsilah*, a spiritual chain of devotees 'linked' by kinship. To mark this difference, I use 'lineage' in the present context at times. In her narrated autobiography which follows, Mai Kausar also uses the term *faqīrī silsilah* (Sufi lineage).

On September 19, 2014 I visited Mai Kausar again in the company of my youngest son. We waited a little outside as young women were cleaning the *baithak*. A *dhikr* (ritualized invocation of God's names) had been organized the day before after *juma*ʿ (Friday) prayers. Mai Kausar ordered a string cot and a fan be brought out and served us tea. This time we talked about her travels, her pilgrimage from Sehwan to Lahut Lamakan[1] where Hazrat Ali RA and Fatima RA are said to have supposed to have dwelled in ancient times, the neighbouring shrine of Bilawal

Shah Nurani,[2] which she visited two times with her mother, her pilgrimage to the shrine of Imam Reza in Mashhad in her thirties, and an almost year-long stay in England where she lived with her relatives in Birmingham.

Further social visits followed in February, 2015 (together with my wife) and in April, 2017 where I also observed that Mai Kausar regularly blesses children and learned that she accepts *murīd*s through the common Sufi ritual known as *ba'yat* (allegiance).

The Life Story of Mai Kausar Lahuti Qalandari

Preliminary Remarks

In 2010, Shazia Shaheen compiled the *sawānih-e hayāt* or biography of Mai Kausar Lahuti Qalandari in Urdu on behalf of Simorgh. The 'research' (essentially the process of recording and compiling the narrative of Mai Kausar) for this publication was done by Shaheen with Nazia Hasan, Sabiha Latif, and Shazia Azam. The 47-page booklet includes 10 black and white pictures. The text is structured in paragraphs but without titled chapters. Only at the beginning is a main heading in bold. It contains the riveting life story of Mai Kausar's family as narrated by herself in first person. Unfortunately, the compilers did not remedy many inconsistencies in the text. On my request, my friend Aly Bossin, professor of French at Lahore's Aitchison College and a gifted photographer, visited Mai Kausar on March 2, 2019 to plug some important knowledge gaps. The information collected by him in conversation with Mai Sahiba and her brother Hajji Sohail is inserted in her *sawānih-e hayāt*.

In 2015, I commissioned my friend Asif Jehangir, a British mathematics instructor and translator of Sufi texts, to translate this text from Urdu into English. My own comments on the Urdu text and additional explanations are inserted in square brackets and presented in endnotes.

The Story of the 'Ashiqān-e Qalandar ('Lovers of the Qalandar') from 1910 to 2010: Amritsar to Lahore

My maternal grandmother, Chiragh Bibi, lived in the Indian district of Jalandhar in Punjab (Fig. 71). She was born into a Quraishi family there in 1871; they originally belonged to Kashmir and spoke Punjabi. Chiragh Bibi was a beauty and her siblings were so too. They were six sisters and one brother. The brother was the youngest whereas she was the eldest. Her brother, Fazal Muhammad, was my 'grandfather' [she addressed him such].[3] One day, while Chiragh Bibi and Fazal Muhammad were playing on the roof of their house they both suddenly fell off the roof or some supernatural being (*jinn*, *bhūt*, or demon) flew over them and caused them to fall. The truth of why and how they fell has never been established. When their parents heard them falling they found them bleeding profusely. They had the children seen to. A few days after both recuperated (although no one had them treated spiritually because even they didn't know what had actually happened to them). The family forgot about the incident with the passage of time.

In earlier times, most people were illiterate and, in our house too, nobody emphasized [on] education very much. In 1885, my maternal grandmother's family got her married at the age of 14. On account of her beauty, the Chaudhrys of Hoshiyarpur asked for her hand in marriage. We were Quraishi by caste whereas they were elephant-*wālā*s and employed by Sikh maharajas. Due to Mai Chiragh Bibi's exceptional beauty alone, she was married at a young age, but she lost her eyesight [which could be interpreted as the body renouncing the world] on the night of her wedding. Her in-laws (understandably) were left extremely distressed. The family of my maternal grandfather told their son (the husband of Chiragh Bibi) that she would recover but she didn't. In fact, her health deteriorated. Chiragh Bibi began to experience fits as a result of which she gradually lost her mental balance. She did not recover for 15 years. In addition to being visually impaired, she had not eaten any grain which left her emaciated. However, no one sought any spiritual remedy for her because no one understood what the reality behind her condition was.

On the other hand, the brother of my maternal grandmother [below simply called with the kinship term 'Nani'] Fazal Muhammad, got married too. He had only been married for three months when he had mental health issues and began experiencing fits. Both brother and sister were leading a helpless life. Relatives began indulging in gossip, such as 'in this family everyone is mad and they all become worse after getting married'. Because of the 'propaganda', the remaining sisters got married outside the family.

One day my Nani was sitting outside her house in a state of holy folly [majnūnāne kaīfiyat] when a passing fakir saw her. Sain Karimullah belonged to the cobbler [Mochi] caste. He enquired what the matter was with her, to which my Nani's mother-in-law told him that her daughter-in-law became blind on her wedding night. She told the fakir that they had tried to cure her many times in vain. The fakir asked if she also had fits and the mother-in-law answered in the affirmative. The fakir said she could get better if his instructions were followed. My Nani's mother-in-law agreed.

That fakir, a man of God and knowledge, decided to settle there and pledged to leave only after having cured my Nani. He said 'to cure her you have to do exactly as I say'. On the instructions of the fakir, my Nani was ritually bathed as the dead and then perfumed with musk and camphor. She was then covered in a shroud and placed on a charpoy in an empty room. The fakir then entered the room and asked my Nani if she could recite any Islamic prayers such as the kālimah [creed] or the āyat ul-kursī (Verse of the Throne). Nani replied she had memorized the first three words of the kālimah by heart. The fakir asked Nani to keep repeating these as a litany. He closed the door, made a circle on the ground, and sat outside [of the circle]. Nani kept on repeating the litany till she fell asleep. In a dream she saw a large open courtyard in which a holy man wearing only a waistcloth and carrying a baton was repeating the name of Hazrat Ali RA continuously. Many people were standing near the man who was going to each in turn. When the man went to Nani he held her hand and said, 'We looked upon you with grace but your family did not do well by getting you married. Nevertheless, on Rabi-ul-Awwal 21, your sight will stand restored as the King of King's special favour is upon you.' When my Nani awakened and came out of the room she was in a state of spiritual ecstasy [*wajd*] and appeared as if she had regained her youth in full.

As soon as my Nani came out of the room she told the fakir about her dream. The fakir affectionately placed his hand on her head and told her his work was finished and that she had earned the favour of his spiritual preceptor too. Saying this he left that place and never looked back at her. The words of the holy person, whom my Nani had seen in the dream, proved true for her eyesight returned and she also stopped having fits on Rabi-ul-Awwal 21.

My grandfather[4] Fazal Muhammad had jumped into a well at the shrine of Imam Nasiruddin in Delhi (where clay pots are given as offerings)[5] in a state of *dīwāngī* [divine intoxication]. Close friends and relatives asked him to come out but he remained there for 12 years. Everything—food, drink, and clothing—was handed down to him using a rope. If he ever did come out of his own will, he would (soon) return.

One day fakir Sain Faiz Muhammad came to the shrine and when he heard about my grandfather and saw the state he was in, he had a spiritual meeting with Imam Nasiruddin inside the shrine. The saint requested Sain Faiz to treat my grandfather spiritually. Therefore, Sain Faiz told him that Allah's grace was upon him and he'd be cured following the intercession of the great Qalandar. My grandfather was also healed. His ecstatic states and spirituality, however, disappeared never to manifest again unlike my Nani. Perhaps some holy man had spiritually bound him.

My Nani was from the Quraish tribe and her family often travelled to eke a living.[6] Mubarak Ali, a relative, also went to Sindh to find work and on reaching Rohri heard a great deal about Sarkar Sakhi Shahbaz Qalandar and the thousands who gather at his shrine (Fig. 72) which could prove auspicious for him. On returning, he related the information to Chiragh Bibi and her relatives adding that if they went there their income would increase. Chiragh Bibi travelled towards Sindh with her relatives after.

When their caravan reached the Rohri Railway Station, her gaze fell on one Sain Ashiq Ali. He too was a man of God. When Nani saw Sain Ashiq Ali she reached *hāl* [a spiritual state of ecstasy granted by God] whereupon she manifested signs of great spirituality. Sain Ashiq Ali saw this and instructed her family to take Nani to the shrine of the great Qalandar. As Nani was also looking in the direction of the Qalandar's shrine during *wajd* [ecstasy], her caravan reached the shrine of Sain Bodlah Bahar in Sehwan first.

The area around Sehwan was surrounded by jungle in those days. Their caravan had embarked on a long journey reposing faith in the Almighty and had suffered many hardships on the way. When they reached the shrine at Sehwan, they met Sain Lal Das as he was sweeping the floor.[7] As soon as he saw Nani he said take her to the *gaddī-nashīn* [custodian] of Sain Wali Muhammad, Sayyid Sain Gul Muhammad Shah's mansion [Sufi lodge or *kāfī*, known as Aulad-e Amir, belonging to the Lakkiyari family],[8] where her real place is. On arrival, she was greatly honoured and lodged there.

At that time the *havēlī* and shrine shared a wall and a guest house. That night they all stayed there. The same night, Sain Gul Muhammad Shah was given glad tidings in a dream on the great Qalandar having cast his special favour upon Chiragh Bibi and her placing garlands on his blessed hand for the rest of her life. When he arrived at the guest house after his morning bath, he related his dream to everyone's delight.

Sayyid Sain Gul Muhammad Shah showed Nani great respect and treated her elders with exemplary hospitality. The caravan returned to Amritsar after halting some more days. After returning, Nani's health improved and she started looking after the household. People began requesting her to fulfil vows they had taken and wishes they had made. Gradually word got out that she was the object of the great Qalandar's special favour.

In 1910, my Nani was the first to take a garland to the shrine of the great Qalandar at Sehwan. This was neither a votary offering nor greed but faith she had and a gift of the love rooted in Gul Muhammad Shah's dream. When my Nani returned following the first offering, she had four sons and two daughters. The eldest son was named Muhammad Iqbal Saifi, the second Badruddin, the third Abdul Rashid, and the fourth Fakhruddin.

Two sons worked as tailors and were among the most famous of the time with many stars/celebrities wearing their creations in

films. The other two were noted artists. Their daughters were called
Bashira and Nazira. Bashira died shortly after getting married and
Nazira, also known as Amañ (mother) Mangla Qalandari, got
married to my grandfather's son, Gulzar Ahmad, who lived in the
house opposite our current residence.

My Nani's life took another turn after she began to take garlands
to Sehwan. Due to the presence of elders there she began to
experience spiritual clairvoyance and people's wishes started to
be granted. In her era the custom of having large gatherings on
Fridays began. In such gatherings most participants were women
and the custom is still prevalent. In such gatherings, women recited
hymns in praise of the great Qalandar, played the *dhōlak* [small
two-sided drum] and Nani would receive spiritual visits from great
saints. Women would share their problems and Nani would give
them answers based on advice she received from saints. God gave
her such honour and she, acting on His commands and in the name
of the great Qalandar, continued bestowing blessings.

Nani's in-laws also accepted the state of affairs and with the help
of her husband she moved forward. Her mother-in-law was initially
a bit harsh which is why she also ejected her son and daughter-
in-law from her house. My grandfather supported my Nani a lot
and never left her. He would make ends meet by selling roasted
chickpea and helped her in carrying out necessary ceremonies. My
Nani did not have any sisters-in-law and they all lived together.
After my maternal grandfather [died], her sisters looked after
her. For the Friday gathering, somebody would make the dough,
someone else would cook, and another would perform other duties.
This way they took care of the Friday gathering together. This also
provided an excuse for all to eat and take food home. People's
livelihood is secured in this way to this day.

After the creation of Pakistan Nani and her family immigrated
here and kept the same routine. In this neighbourhood most
belong to my family. The neighbourhood is called *Sēthoñ-wālī-
galī* [Merchant Alley]. It had the same name before the creation of
Pakistan as rich Hindu and Sikh families used to live here. When
we arrived, many houses were padlocked and only a few were
open. Those people who had lived here must have barely managed

to escape the violence, murder, and looting which erupted on both sides when the creation of Pakistan was announced, with their lives intact, empty-handed, leaving their possessions behind. My father's sister told us that our caravan took seven days to reach Lahore City Railway Station from Amritsar with Sikhs attacking the train at every halt. Young girls were taken away and pregnant women had their bellies cut open with scythes. We came empty-handed and had to start our lives afresh. Since we didn't know anyone here all marriages were also arranged among close relatives.

My Nani continued holding her Friday gathering and soon a large number of people began approaching her with their problems. Gradually, she gained expertise too. She became known in Lahore and women would bring their daughters so she could pray for their marital prospects. All attendees at the Friday gathering would first offer congregational Friday prayers. The gathering would commence after.

The water left after my Nani and grandfather had bathed was blessed—it cured children with rickets. If poured over dying plants or trees they would become verdant again. Likewise, if a childless woman sprinkled it on her belly, the Almighty would bless her with a child.

Sayyid Baba Zahur Ali Shah from Amritsar was linked to (the shrine of) Jhandiala Sharif [of the poet Waris Shah (d. 1798)]. He was a great saint and the custodianship of his shrine spanned centuries. His shrine is known as *Kānoñ-wālī Sarkār* [the Master of Ears]. He later settled in Okara. Due to a common spiritual chain he had a connection with my Nani and was aware that she had a connection with the great Qalandar. He always worked with Nani and mentored her as well.

My Nani was sick when Baba Zahur Ali Shah died and was unable to pay her respects on the occasion. On the day Chiragh Bibi died, however, his son, Sayyid Sain Manzur Ali Shah, was present. The saintly elders had told him by spiritual means to go to Lahore because Chiragh Bibi was about to leave the temporal world. It was his first time in our house and he wasn't very familiar with our family. He didn't know who would be able to fully appreciate the *silsilah* [spiritual chain of transmission respectively 'Sufi lineage'] after the passing of Chiragh Bibi, which is why, when, in accordance with family traditions, he selected an official successor on the fortieth day after her death following the advice of the family elders, his choice proved wrong. It was not his fault as he did not know, but because of this decision Allah Almighty showed them all a miracle. In fact, the person who was made the successor of Chiragh Bibi was unable to bear this responsibility or the heat of the esoteric knowledge which accompanied it. Hence, this spiritual chain was passed on to my mother, Nazira Bibi (Fig. 73).

My mother did not wrest the *silsilah* from anyone nor did she beg for it. It was bestowed on her by Allah. She kept the spiritual chain going with the blessings of her *murshid* and the grace of God. In 2010, it will be 100 years since the beginning of this ritual of the *'ashiqān-e Qalandar* ['Lovers of the Qalandar']. Perhaps my Nani didn't pass the spiritual chain on to her sons due to their wives being outsiders who didn't understand it the same way my mother did. My maternal aunts believed in the spiritual chain but not with the same devotion as my mother. My Nani spoke to her about everything on her mind and since she was the only daughter, she was the closest to her mother. My Nani involved her in every matter and she in turn understood her every indication, state, and spiritual mood. After the death of my Nani, when my mother went to the annual *'urs* of the great Qalandar in Sehwan, it was asked who would now fulfil the ritual of *sēhrā-bandī* [tying the garland] in Chiragh Bibi's place. My mother answered she would till her last breath. The *dastār-bandī* [tying of the ceremonial turban] initiation ceremony of my mother took place on the occasion 35 years ago before all the members of our family, and in exchange for this ceremony, my mother rolled up her sleeves and carried out the responsibility for this chain ever since with great joy.

In other people's homes there are often conflicts over property, but in our family the conflicts have always been about the succession to the custodianship [literally *gaddī-nashīn*, the 'spiritual throne']. We spent our childhood in great poverty. The amount of poverty in our house was equal to all the mercy of God in the world but, even so, God is gracious.

My father was the son of my mother's uncle and in the same spiritual chain [here meaning 'devotional community'] as my mother. Father believed in the spiritual power of the *silsilah* and always helped mother in moving it forward. He was poor and his children young. He was, however, hardworking, educated, prayed regularly (including *tahajjud*), and had committed the Quran to memory (*hāfiz*).

His good looks could be likened to the full moon. In comparison, my mother was pitch dark like the night but people still recall their love even today as exemplary. He would labour and save money to give to my mother saying 'use it for '*urs*'. My father has helped my mother very much. In my entire life I have never heard my father use the word 'wrong' for my mother. If my mother had not had my father's support, she would not have reached this status. He worked hard to feed his children and help his wife and walked in step with her his entire life.

My mother had three daughters and two sons. Two other sons perished in an accident. Only once did father overstep—he asked mother if she always had to go to Sehwan every year with her mother. That very night the roof of the house collapsed and my brothers and grandfather were 'martyred'. My father's back was left broken and mother went mad with grief. At that time my brothers were aged eight and six, I was just six months old. When three funerals departed the house simultaneously, my father believed his sons had become victims of an accident as he had dishonoured the great Qalandar. Father never denied the spiritual chain thereafter.

My mother spent her entire life organizing the Friday gathering and only gave us *langar* distributed there to eat. She was never intimidated of poverty. Poverty never scared her, nor did it ever cause her to step back; indeed, she gradually kept this *silsilah* going according to her capacity. Until she was on her last breaths, my mother continued this chain with the grace of Allah.

My mother Mai Hajan Mangla Qalandari [Mai Hajan Bibi Qalandari] died at the age of 55 when her star was at its brightest. I was initiated in the spiritual chain after the separation of my mother and God showed me great mercy. In this manner, the *silsilah* continues from woman to woman. The men in our family have not been able to inherit this spirituality due to fate. In this chain, the gender is never a consideration, one's intention is. Mother treated all her children the same and I didn't ever want to take over. I thought I'd never be able to fill her shoes but, after setting foot, I bid farewell to the mundane and faced many hardships. Our family believes in the *silsilah*, all help and pay their respects to me. Every child of the family accompanies me to Sehwan (Figs. 74–75). What is important, however, is what resides in the heart. I consider this spiritual lineage my passion and feel responsible. There are people who would like to start full-fledged organized institution but aren't ready to take responsibility. I thank the Almighty for equipping me to single-handedly take care of this responsibility cheerfully.

I was the liberated sort, fearful of marriage. Many men from the family wished to marry me but I always refused. During mother's lifetime, I was very fashionable. I had also studied in London[9] and worked some very good jobs but I relinquished everything for the spiritual order.

I was very beautiful and took great care of my appearance. I wanted to fly like a free bird but the connection with the great Qalandar was written (Fig. 76). I forsook everything and became his *jōgan* [female yogi]. I was my mother's favourite and spoilt since she had already lost two of my brothers and Hajji Toni and Hajji Sohail were born later.

Relatives often taunted me saying all sorts of people frequent her house. For this reason, my sisters found it difficult to quickly get married. I thought getting married would pose no challenge since I was educated and good-looking and kept rejecting (suitors). I preferred remaining single. This is why I first tried to get my younger siblings married. Due to remaining in the *silsilah* for long, mother had become a little cranky and not attentive towards her children. I felt it was my responsibility to get them married.

There was a time when we were not short of money. Father and my brothers worked in Saudi Arabia. They had also undertaken the pilgrimage to Makkah. Mother remained in Lahore and looked after the *silsilah*. After mother left the world, I often felt she had merged into me. The night she died was the night her spiritual prowess transferred to me. I didn't know she'd leave come morning. I was

great friends with her. Even our breath was in sync. I loved and
served her. We were in love with each other. Mother died two
months after Hajji Toni's marriage on February 25.

She had not taken ill before. She suffered a fatal heart attack.
When mother passed, I had nothing: no money, empty from the
inside, and my spiritual mentor, Sayyid Manzur Ali Shah, had
also left the world. He had provided great guidance to mother and
literally led her by the finger. Sayyid Manzur Ali Shah was *sayyid*
[descendant of the Holy Prophet PBUH and the *panjtān pāk* ['the
Five Pure Ones'] from the family of Ghaus Pak [noted Qadiri
saint Abdul Qadir Jilani (d. 1166)]. He always considered mother
among his closest associates and helped her. Mother treaded on the
spiritual path with the manifest and hidden help of both him and the
great Qalandar. Every person needs a mentor needless to say. After
mother passed, Baba Rafiq Sain of Sialkot guided me.

Mother had not left me with much except for explaining a few
things to me which I only understood afterwards. When she was
talking to me on the final night of her life, I panicked thinking
'why she was trying to scare me'. She made me cognisant of some
spiritual mysteries, how to remember them and how to perform
select tasks. Mother never fell asleep that night. I was massaging
her body as she told me about spiritual lessons, litanies, and secrets
of the path. As she was telling me these things, I panicked thinking
why is she telling me all this tonight? She taught me how to pray
the litany which Nani and she had performed and gave me some
of her mother's keepsakes. We were still talking when, in the latter
part of the night, her condition worsened and I took her to the
hospital alone since she had forbidden anyone else to accompany
me. The life went out of her limbs only a few yards from our house.
I tried to support her, but she was unable to get up, and Sohail
arrived at that time too. We both put her in a rickshaw and took
her to the Mayo Hospital.

When we reached Bansan Wala Bazaar she exclaimed, 'Oh
Kausar!' I asked her to be quiet saying we would reach hospital
soon. Her body was cold and perspiration ran down her brow. Her
soul had left her body when I had asked her to be quiet. I, on the
other hand, thought she'd gone quiet as I asked. When we arrived

at the hospital, the two of us tried to carry her from the rickshaw but were initially unable to.

After a lot of effort, we finally managed to remove her, after half the night had passed, and sprinkled water on her face, but she never opened her eyes. We placed her on a stretcher and brought her to the ICU. She was wearing a red dress and rings on her fingers. Sohail was standing at her head and I at her feet. 'Mother is never quiet! Why is she so quiet today?' I asked him. I looked at her face and felt she had passed. That very moment it felt as if a force had wrested my heart. Sohail took mother inside the ICU and I went home and knocked very loudly on the door. Toni, Banu, Naila, and another woman from the neighbourhood were there. I told them mother had left us but they refused to believe me saying I had gone mad. They rushed to the hospital leaving me alone. Before they reached, Sohail heard about mother's death and had left the hospital in grief. A grief-stricken Sohail rammed into an electricity pylon. When relatives reached the hospital, they saw that blood oozing from his head. He needed six stiches. They brought him home after. He was unable to speak for three months except one word: mother—but mother had died and he couldn't even recall her burial. At that time, we were all in a state of great grief, as if a mountain of sorrow had fallen on us. Gradually, I consoled everyone and became the head of the house. In this manner, I adopted the role of mother after her passing. Mother used to chew a lot of *pān* but I never had the courage to eat betel in front of her. After she passed, I too began eating *pān* and now my brothers do not have the courage to eat *pān* in front of me!

I have taken after my mother. My speech, presence, and face have all become like hers. I was not always like that but over 12 years, I aged (Fig. 77). My hunger, thirst, and sleep—all evaporated. It was as if my mother had taken away every constraint from me when she died. After she passed, I felt as if a *chādar* [heavy shawl used to cover the head with] had been taken from me. She was my protective shadow. I understood the real meaning of being helpless after she passed and I had to shoulder formidable responsibilities. Now, I have become accustomed and toughened. No one can dare to take my place now. After I entered into the *silsilah*, people harassed me a lot. Some even tried to wrest it from me. When people look at me with a bad intention or touch me (inappropriately) I immediately understand their nefarious intent and say: 'Good people, go. You will not receive any benefit from me for I am of another world.'

Sometimes I have to be even sterner. I carry myself as a man amidst men. Now, if a bearded person comes to me, I can handle him (on his level) and if a rascal or a criminal comes to me, I can handle him too. Nonetheless, I like the company of men as among them I can learn to make myself stronger and I also get to learn about the affairs of the world.

I walk around Sehwan in an awe-inspiring manner as if I were a lion and not a woman. I may be physically small but my voice is powerful. It emanates from me as if a *jinn* had possessed me! If I didn't put on such an act, people would tear me to pieces. Allah has given me so much honour that no one can stand in 'my spot' in the shrine without my permission. Once I was sitting amidst the entire gathering in Sehwan with siblings, relatives, and other Sayyids. Henna and *dhāga*s [blessed threads to be tied on the wrist] were lying near and the shrine of Pir Lajpal [literally 'the lord who gives us life', meaning here Lal Shahbaz Qalandar] was in front. People would walk forward taking either henna or the threads. The night was nearing conclusion and the mood was festive. A very tall *malang* with shoes tucked under his armpit came to me and bowed. I placed my hand on his head but, instead of rising up from his prostration, he pulled my foot. At this, I kicked him. My brothers and other people then beat him to a pulp, tied him with rope, and reported him to police. I didn't know if someone had sent him after me or if he had mental health issues. I am relating this to show that walking on this path is not easy; one faces difficulties and disgrace too. Before stepping onto this path, one must kill all of one's desires, passions and control one's heart.

I am not old yet but I don't wear bright colours out of consideration for what people would think as I have sisters-in-law. If someone asks, I tell them to buy pastel or Sufi-colours.[10] If however, someone still brings me bright colours I wear them on routine rather than special days. I don't wear half-sleeves.

I too am human. I live in a closed room; I too feel the heat but I have relinquished everything and adopted a simple life. I always worry what 'outsiders' would think if they were to see me. I have performed many lesser pilgrimages ['umrah], obtained an education, visited shrines of saints and, due to my strength of character, been able to move forward.

When I visit the shrine of my mother, I stand erect in the bus over the whole journey. I torture myself to express the pain that ensued mother's separation. Even if people tell me to sit I refuse. I feel serene. For 12 years I have placed a chādar over the grave of mother and crown on the grave of father's. I wish to serve my parents with reverence. They never told me to do so but I do as my heart says.

On one occasion a flag-pole installed on mother's grave broke and I went to buy a 14-foot pole. Because the pole was long and would not fit into a rickshaw, I considered hiring a van. When I enquired the price, I was told it was Rs 400. I thought to myself how a poor woman could justify lavishing the sum on a pole. I then bought some material from a shop selling cut pieces of cloth, rolled it and began carrying it on foot. Whilst I was walking, I was also crying and asking my mother to reward me for this as I am living as a man in this world and don't observe pardah when it comes to matters of the 'urs, whether you take me there on a horse-drawn carriage or via the Hira Mandi Chowk for I don't consider myself a woman any longer afraid that someone will see me or will become attracted to me.

When the spiritual state of jalāl ['majesty', rapture] overpowers me I feel I am alone. I can see no one else when the saints surround me. When people see me in this state they do not say, 'Kausar is standing there.' Rather they see Mai Mangla Qalandari standing. Thousands of people mistakenly think Amañ is standing there when in reality it is me. When I say something people say, 'Mai has said.' I may be Kausar but my mother has 'united' with me. Sometimes, when I look at photographs, I too fail to distinguish between mother and myself.

I have received a lot of honour because of my parents' prayers and the grace of Allah. I beseech Allah saying, 'Oh Allah, protect my honour, for you alone know what is in one's heart!' If a woman goes (out with someone) after marriage, she is the (bearer of the) honour of her husband, and if she does before marriage, she is the honour of her parents, and that is also my view. This, perhaps, is one reason why I was unable to find someone I liked. I have kept my honour intact. I have, in fact, not married due to my mother and siblings as aforementioned.

I have no money in the bank, for I have no father or husband from whom I could receive money. I earn from the sweat of my brow or my followers present *nazar* [gifts] which I depend on. I am aware that all relations are based on money in this world. Everyone is a worshipper of material things! Whoever you give money to becomes your companion.

I play with hundreds of thousands [*lākhs*] of rupees (i.e. I am talking about *lākh*s). Every year I spend around five to six *lākh* rupees on the festival [of Lal Shahbaz Qalandar]. Another reason no one competes with me is that I play [this game] like a man: you cannot play without money, be it chess or horse-racing, one has to spend money to make money. My disciples give me presents so that I fulfil their wishes and try my best to meet their demands in the name of Allah. God helps me maintain my honour. Allah fulfils wishes of people and keeps my respect intact too. Perhaps Allah has written my destiny such for only He has the right to grant greatness to people as He is the Creator and the Sovereign of all. The great Qalandar is just an intermediary by whose name Allah listens.

I am happy in this state for I have full control over my life. I am neither afraid of anyone nor does anyone keep watch over me. I can come and go as I please wherever and whenever I want.

Ever since my sister-in-law died, I have borne full responsibility for her children. This is why I now try to avoid travelling extensively. Twelve years prior, I went as I fancied. Thatta, Iran, Bannu, Peshawar; I travelled wherever spiritual indication led me. I have not been to Murree to this day as the prospect frightens me, Lahut [meaning the sacred place of Lahut Lamakan, see the introduction to this chapter] I've been thrice. This is all destiny since Lahut is more dangerous than Murree! Murree is nothing compared to Lahut.

Lahut is an eight-hour journey from Karachi, a little far from Chaghi; before it come the shrines of Mohabbat Faqir and Nurani Nur [Bilawal Shah Nurani]. Lahut is 14-day from Sehwan on foot. Once I made the journey with mother, 14 days after we returned home, she passed away. I returned to Lahut after her demise. I took a train from Lahore to Karachi. After resting for a night, I proceeded to Lahut by bus. To reach there you have to pass a perilous jungle infested with snakes, bats, and *bhūt* [demons]. A large watch of many fakirs, however, resides there too. The place is extremely strange indeed and an 'ordinary' person cannot pass through that jungle—it requires great courage and strength.

The third time, I went to Lahut with my 'son' Faraz Husain (he is actually my sister's son who I raised). Once I thought about going to Lahut from Sehwan on foot but both my brothers and sister-in-law stopped me saying they did not wish to lose me. My brother and sister-in-law look after me well. Even if a thorn pricks me, they become worried. No one has ever disrespected me. I have treated my sisters-in-law as if they were my daughters-in-law. When I've become a mother-in-law, I've acted like a mother-in-law should.

I've raised them with love and they love me too. They are my blood, they are my soul, and I cannot bear to see them in pain. Similarly, all these people cannot bear to see me hurt either. If my blood pressure goes high, my brothers and sisters become worried that our sister is not feeling well. If I come across as rather stern with them, it is not to prove myself better or to hide my faults, but I consider it my duty to teach them the difference between right and wrong. I am the elder in our house. I do not throw my weight around, I owe them this. I have given them every luxury; I buy all the rations for the house which includes everything from detergent to wash dishes to washing powder for clothes. I try to provide everything for the house according to my mind, whether it is a box of matches or *ghī* [clarified butter] which is why my daughters-in-law don't fight among themselves either. Until now our household is run on a common basis in which everyone's food and drink is shared, wherein even my brothers give me their income to do with as I please and never ask me what I did with it. I take care of the expenses of their wives and children too, including everything from their food to their clothes.

A short while after mother's death, the time for the *mēlā* [religious fair] neared. The *mēlā* takes place every year on Shaban 9 and 10 at Sayyid Mitha Bazaar, Kuchah Sethan.[11] That year, I struggled to organize the *mēlā* as I had nothing. By the time the next came around I tried to make myself firm-footed and stable. Twelve years have now passed and I have achieved mastery over such (organizational) matters. Those who have God's special favour achieve mastery over these things … If I say that I am very pure and truthful, nevertheless I am still human and not an angel and humans make mistakes. Since birth, I have tried never to wrong another person. I have performed Umrah, and try to perform all my obligatory actions, such as the obligatory prayers, fasting (in the month of Ramadan), and reading the Quran, and now I truly have no desire left for any worldly thing.

A short time after my mother's death, I learnt the litanies for *kashf* [spiritual unveiling] in order to communicate with her. It is possible to speak to the dead with the help of *kashf*. For others, my mother may be dead, but for me she is alive. We laid mother to rest in Miani Sahib Graveyard[12] where father is buried too. In order to communicate with mother, I made her rise and spoke to her for two or three hours around noon. I said: 'Mother rise and speak to me.' I met her but not face-to-face. One of her legs was in the grave towards her head and the other leg was towards her feet and she was as high as the sky; I do not know what she was? I could only hear her voice.

I visited mother's grave like a lover frequents the grave of his beloved. I couldn't live without her. I stopped eating what my mother liked. She liked *karēlah* [bitter gourd] and runner bean a lot. I don't even look at them now. Not everyone can act like this, only a true lover. I don't know if anyone will ever do this for me, for I don't even have any children. No one destroys themselves the way I have destroyed myself in the love of my mother.

Perhaps she knew that I would follow her footsteps. This is why she tried to keep me close from the very beginning. A companion of mother's called Rubina said, 'I have never forgotten that day when we bathed and washed her, and dressed her in a red dress, put henna on her hands, put bangles made of garlands of flowers on her, perfumed her with *'itr* [essence of the rose], and sat her down in the gathering saying, "this is now your future and you have to perform the rites of the great Qalandar in place of your mother".' I was 35-years-old then and didn't realize that I will have to soon bear such a heavy responsibility. I was in a state of sorrow. My body was as if asleep and I couldn't see anything. I stood in a state of shock and I was being made up. I couldn't even cry, but Rubina was weeping whilst trying to provide me with emotional support. That time, those moments, that day is forever fixed in my life, I can never forget that day—it was the day that loaded me with responsibilities, it was the day which made me much older than my years and that day was the day which ended my freedom and my desires. That time has now passed and it is has made me so old in just 12 years. I was not like this, I was someone else, but the trust which my mother thrust upon me as she passed away has made me become its trustee.

Rubina is my best friend. She earlier served mother. She would always tell her, 'help Kausar after me.' Once during the annual *'urs* [of Lal Shahbaz Qalandar], mother had the ceremony of having her headdress tied by Rubina, to the chagrin of many as she chose her instead of her own children. In reality, this was mother's way of telling Rubina to help me as much as she had helped her. Whatever her wishes, Rubina takes them to Sehwan, whether it is to ask for her family or to ask for *rizq* [increase in provisions] it is always granted.

By the time of the fourth *'urs* after mother's death I was completely prepared. Now I am convinced that it was my Lord who brought me to this level of preparation. In this work you cannot do anything which is not totally honest. When a person is in the state of spiritual ecstasy anyone may do with you as they please. These are the people who do not (even) refrain from pranks. Here anyone is capable of mischief and you should also bear in mind the fact that this area is very dangerous, it is not like Chichawatni, Pattoki, or Changa Manga. Here no one can be sure about anybody; it is in the interior of the city. To lead the life of a fakir is not easy here.

You come across all sorts of people—the honest and the crooked. I live near Hira Mandi, situated close to Lohari Bhati Gate and Gumti [bazaar]. These areas are historical, not places no one knows nothing about. This is such a historic area that thousands were made saints here and a multitude more became 'saint-like dogs'. This is such an area that, if nothing else, people chase you with a *jharū* [cleaning broomstick]. Here they set dogs on you which bark, '*ue ue*' ['woof woof'] as they chase you. We are sat in such a dangerous area here that every moment we repent to God and say, 'Lord, you alone can save our honour.' The whole world knows that this is such a neighbourhood, but my work has never been affected by this.

Once I was at Data Darbar [Ali Hujwiri, the patron saint of Lahore]. A young woman came and sat among the *malang*s [dervishes]. She was wearing the *niqāb*. She had big eyes and her long nails were painted. She was telling *malang*s false stories about herself saying she regularly goes to Sehwan, she had performed the *sēhrāh-bandī* ceremony and till she had stood up, the *tāj-poshī* [crowning ceremony] of the saint hadn't gone ahead [once]. I sat there wondering 'who could have the audacity to narrate such tales with such trustworthiness and aplomb'. I asked her where the great Qalandar resided and she replied Sehwan. I said to her, next time you go, take me along for I too long to visit the shrine of the great Qalandar. She agreed to take me and continued that she was well known in the court of the shrine. I spoke to her for two hours. She told so many lies that I became angry and verbally abused her, and when she realized that I knew everything and my place at the shrine she ran away as fast as she could.

Often many bad things take place at Sufi shrines. Once, behind Karbala Game Shah[13] near Data Darbar, in Bilalganj area, a person had hung a wooden sign reading, 'The Shrine of the Chishti-Nizami Sufi order'. He was caught with two prostitutes there. Such ugly things happen at shrines too and Sehwan too is no exception.

From the very beginning Sayyid women of Sehwan had explained that all sorts of dubious characters frequented shrines and I, as Nazira's daughter, was welcomed to stay with them.

When I used to visit Sehwan with my mother she'd communicate using her eyes and I would understand. She was extremely principled and had a strict personality. Once Rubina and I put on make-up before going to the shrine. Mother saw and only had to glare once for us to understand she didn't approve. We immediately went back, washed our faces and after that I never went to the shrine made-up. Once during the *'urs* of Sayyid Manzur Ali Shah, mother slapped my sister because she had come to the gathering wearing make-up.

Nature has given women the ability to know when somebody is lusting after them. In much the same way, I am also able to recognize such people but I never reveal it to anybody. I have always tried to maintain a stellar character to ensure that people respect me.

The organization of our annual *mēhfil* [gathering, here meaning the *mēlā* or *shām-e Qalandar*] is in my hands and only a conscious person can be in charge of the entire organization, a madman cannot. I am always worrying about the arrangements, for example, whether the ice has arrived or not, whether the shawls have arrived, whether the floor mats have arrived, have the candles been ordered? By the time night falls till the beginning of the henna ceremony, my clothes and state are both filthy and I don't even have the time to go wash and change.

The next day, when the call to prayer sounds come pre-dawn, I get busy organizing the cooking of the food because we have to have 12 large *dēg*s [cauldrons] cooked. After the food is cooked, I distribute it fairly among everyone. Come late afternoon, crowds begin pouring in to listen to the *qawwālī* and by evening the whole alley is full of pilgrims. I feel as if I am possessed by a great female leader who makes me do all this. This is why I do all the work without anyone's help. When the time for the *mēhfil* comes, I suddenly become lively. No person can make me do so much work. In my joy and madness, I work like a machine and at the same time berate others saying, 'If you don't want to work, don't! And if you do work you're not doing me any favours as I will do it all by myself. I don't need anyone else's help!'

In reality I don't find it difficult to get any job done. Everyone respects and looks after me well. There are three reasons why my siblings, relatives, and others respect me. The first reason is my personal character. I have a firm conduct and never gave anyone an excuse to point a finger. Second, no one in our family ever looked after their parents as I did. I did not look after them to show off nor to get anything from them, rather I did it just to fulfil the rights of a daughter. Third, people respect me as I joined this *silsilah*. My Lord [*mālik*] has, due to the blessings of this path, accorded me respect among my siblings, *birādarī* ['brotherhood' of extended kin in a caste], neighbours, relatives, and people of the entire region. Their wishes are fulfilled because of the (accorded) respect.

Every year prior to the *mēhfil*, I get my entire house painted and the area from my house to the bazaar cleaned. I get the floor mats washed too as 200 people come here to continuously recite the Holy Quran from seven in the morning. I take the name of Allah and His Messenger PBUH before having the drums beaten. The Holy Quran is continuously recited 700 to 800 times at the event and the spiritual reward gifted to The Sovereign of Both Worlds, the Five Pure Ones, all great saints of Islam, and the Qalandar himself. The recitation begins at 7 am and ends at around 1.30 pm. Only men from madrassas from the interior of the city participate. I used to feed them all earlier. Now I present Rs 500 per madrassa which they share among themselves. I don't have the food right after the recitation as it is early in the day, all the women are tired, and it becomes difficult to wash the crockery and cooking utensils. I also don't invite women to recite the Holy Quran as it is difficult for them to come so early.

There is no 'set time' for *hāzrī* [visitation of saints' spirits] on me. It doesn't just happen like that, you have to prepare, and the most important preparation is being in a state of ablution. It is all about *nīyat* [intention]. When you stand on a prayer mat, you will have to make the intention first, only then will your prayers be accepted. Even if you want to perform a *mujrā* [dance performance with singing; exclusive preserve of courtesans during the Mughal era; today synonymous with raunch], the courtesans get themselves ready (by bedecking themselves) before they start. Once you've made the intention, half the task is already done. I sit with the intention for visitation. I hope that they [the spirits of the saints] will come. The person upon whom the visitation will take place has to draw a circle around themselves and sit inside it. On Friday, when *langar* has been cooked I distribute the food. Every year this gathering takes place on a Friday over which approximately two *mann* [*maund*, about 37kgs] of food is handed out. Every object belonging to the great Qalandar is ritually washed. I may have inhaled incense, eaten liver curry, and gorged on *chapatti* [flatbread], but I begin trembling during the middle of the *langar* and it feels as if something is trying to possess me. On the day of the annual *qawwālī*, only men are permitted in the gathering. Before the *qawwālī*, I take care of all the arrangements myself. I do not rush to take a *ghusl* [ritual bath] and it seems as if someone has placed a lock on my mouth and I am unable to utter a single word.

Even the prospect of *ghusl* leaves me terrified. My sisters stand outside the bathroom with my clothes while my state begins to change the very moment I start pouring water (on myself). I do not comprehend anything, I am not aware of anything, it feels as if my entire body is tearing apart. When I come out of the bathroom, my mouth is closed. Someone places bangles on me, another places a garland (around my neck), and perfumes me. I feel there is no one else present but myself. I do not even know who the *qawwāl* [musician] is, who my enemy is, who my friend is. At that time I have no desire, nothing. Neither *pān* [betel] nor food. Everyone yearns for my hand or scarf to touch me. I also have a lot of money in my pockets and I simultaneously worry about someone taking away the cash from my pockets as we all depart for Sehwan the next day and all the costs are my responsibility.

When I step out of the room, people claim my face is not my own no more and that they see mother instead. The crowd outside swells. After this the *qawwālī* performance commences and my legs begin to shake; it feels as if the life is going out of them. At that moment, the great saints are pulling me towards them saying, 'Mother come, mother come!' People say I emanate such light from my face that it seems I have make-up on.

Because women are not permitted to attend the *qawwālī*, I am mostly surrounded by men in the gathering. There are also <u>khwājāsarā</u>s ['third gender' people often also called Hijras, Khusras, or Khadras]. On the occasion I use about Rs 2,000–3,000 worth of (woollen) threads [dhāga] which I buy a month earlier from the bazaar. Tying knots and cutting pieces leaves me with blisters on my fingers and tongue. Similarly, during the 'urs in Sehwan, I get blisters but as soon as the festival concludes my blisters too vanish. The more [litanies] I recite, the more my mouth burns. It feels as if it's on fire. If I chew betel I develop more wounds in my mouth.

The intention with which people take the pieces of thread [to be wound around the wrist or neck], is fulfilled. While presenting the pieces I make a supplication, 'Oh Shah Husain! May the wish come true!' These threads go as far as Sehwan, the United States (of America), Canada, and Japan. The visitors, when their wish has been fulfilled, come the following year to the 'urs and bring clothes and henna as gifts. In our own house we have over a mann-and-a-half of henna and what others bring is in addition to this. I distribute the henna in the gathering which leaves my hands coloured. I pray over the threads and whoever requires a piece of it, I point towards Toni and tell them to obtain one from him. People usually take the henna as an offering for weddings, homes, sons, brothers, and children. Some even stubbornly make me sit next to them and insist their wish be fulfilled. I tell them Allah will definitely fulfil their desire and I ask them to give something in charity or give them some incantation to recite, but they insist that I alone can 'get' the Almighy to do this since they don't want to do anything themselves. I plead with them to leave but they pester me further by snatching my pān and sometimes a bottle [of water]. They sometimes jokingly say they will kill me wearing a serious expression and I say, 'Okay, go now, I will try!' I do not agree immediately but the other person [meaning the spirit of the saint] does not agree right away. Then I sit up all night beseeching, 'King of Kings [the Qalandar] please do this for me' (Fig. 78). Then at once a voice instructs me to tell so-and-so to drink water from a mosque, from a river or go to River Ravi.

On that day I neither meet our Maula Ali RA nor Ghaus Pak [Abdul Qadir Jilani]. I have been on this path now for 12 years. I recite the name of the great Qalandar so much that I wish he would meet me just once in person, but until now no one has met me. I

wonder when I will meet the Qalandar. Who are those fortunate
people who meet these great people in this manner?

I do not believe that any woman can experience a visitation
by Maula Ali RA. If someone says so I ask for proof. It is a lie. It
is all a drama. Neither can Ghaus Pak visit someone nor Maula
Ali RA, or Baba Farid. Yes, this can happen that a great elder's
blessed gaze falls on you, a fakir's, a friend of God's, a dervish's, or
Ghaus Pak's. A person's shoulders cannot bear the heavy [spiritual]
weight of such an experience. However, a spirit (*hawāltī*)[13] can
enter a person in an unknown manner. These superhuman 'things'
[phenomenon] include *jinn*, *bhūt*, *balā*, *maī* ['mothers', 'spiritually
intoxicated women']. Such forces can come upon a human but if
one claims Maula Ali RA, Data Sahib [Ali Hujwiri], or Ganj Shakar
[Baba Farid] did then this is certainly not the case. They have a
very high station. We cannot bear the weight.

Cloth, joss sticks, sweets, and clothes collected during the
'urs are carried to the shrine of the great Qalandar. In his *'urs*,
alongside the *sēhrā* [floral headdress, garland], 11 dupattas and
dresses, and Rs 100 per dress used to be taken. Now, we present
Rs 1,000 with every suit. I also give gifts to the custodians of his
shrine [*kāfī* Aulad-e Amir]. The current custodian is Sain Murad
Ali Shah. He is the one who carries the garland and we also give
everything collected to be placed on the shrine to him (Fig. 79).
The sister of the custodian helps him perform the ritual ablution.
When Sain Murad Ali Shah Sahib enters the shrine, he is flanked
by government functionaries and commoners alike. His sons tie the
garland, the henna comes from a Hindu—the same family bringing
it since the time of Chiragh Bibi.

On Shaban 22, *fuqarā* [ritual of fakirs] takes place. During
this, the boat of the great Qalandar is taken out in which 125,000
fakirs take part; Chiragh Bibi also used to participate. After her
Mai Mangla [Mai Kausar's mother] did and now Hajji Toni and
I do. The leader of this order is Sayyid Sain Hajjan Shah and he
organizes the ritual.

I never give amulets to relieve people's difficulties. Allah is the
one who bestows honour and people take threads believing in the
great Qalandar as an intermediary. Allah creates an intermediary.

Women mostly ask for money, suitable marital matches for sons, and especially to have a (baby) boy. Whatever the problem, it is the great Qalandar who does everything. I don't do anything. I only supplicate: 'Oh Great Qalandar, you must keep my honour intact!' If somebody comes with their problem I don't say anything at once but give them hope by telling them that God-willing the Almighty will fulfil your wish. Both men and women come to me but women constitute the majority as women face more difficulties. We have had some relationship among our families [with the Qalandar] too ever since the days of Amritsar.

Neither my ancestors were motivated by greed, nor my mother or I. I only undertake as much I can accomplish. Avarice doesn't solve anything. Allah does everything. If doing something is beyond my reach, I prevent people from it and if I am able, I say: 'Yes, I can do this.' The great Qalandar has kept my honour intact more so than even my parents. My life has been fairly difficult. I have achieved success through the household of the *panjtān pāk* [literally the Five Pure Ones] and Allah rewarded me because I looked after my parents.

There is no difference between men and women. Both have the same soul, strengths, and intellect. Their flesh, eyes, and nose are the same, only the bodies are different. A woman is not delicate—rather, if she is really determined, she can be stronger than a thousand men. Then she is unstoppable. If, in this society, no one can stop a woman from doing something evil, then how can she be stopped from doing something good? Those who consider women weak are in reality weak themselves from the inside and they use various means to try and prove their 'manliness'. Only those who lose themselves on this spiritual path can really understand the difficulties of this path. I have annihilated myself, sacrificed every happiness and rest, which is why today I am able to speak with such an elevated tone. Nowadays people make advertisements in the name of famous saints and set up shop on every corner. Everyone has their own business and they play with the emotions of people, especially of women, minting money, fooling people in the name of white or black magic. I try never to fraud anyone using the name of Allah. It becomes more difficult for a single woman on this path because people think you are helpless and they try to loot you as if you were war booty. But, if a woman is of strong character and of determined intention in her heart, then nobody can loot her.

All *silsilah*s [Sufi orders, spiritual paths] are the same but methods differ. Our path is neither completely that of the Sufis or *sharī'a*. The *sharī'a* is the absolute truth which we travel alongside.

In Sufism there is love, passion [*'ishq*], the Beloved, and the truthful Lover. Our path is such that we believe in Sufism but not venture (beyond) the *sharī'a* either. If we reflect we realize that religion (Islam) and *sharī'a* are essentially expressions of love. The martyrdom of the family of the Prophet PBUH too exemplifies passionate love. Passionate love has no definition, no form, and even such people are incognisant of what kind of search, state, fire it is, and from where one finds succour. Such are the ways of the heart, ways to reach the soul and kill it. Those who manage to do so are alive—separate from worldly desires, ostensibly not completely in control of their senses but Allah (for them) opens their inner eye. When the *'urs* of the Qalandar nears, I become restless, I desire to fly to Sehwan. I cannot stop myself; a sort of madness takes over. I do not perform the *dhamāl* even when I get there but become spiritually intoxicated [*mast*], my soul overpowering me. I often go to give my respects there and other shrines besides Sehwan too. Whenever I feel restless or suffocated, I leave the house and find solace at a shrine.

I wish this *silsilah* [spiritual lineage] continues. Only time will tell who will become the guardian after me. Only someone with *himmat* [aspiration] will be able to do justice. I have no children who could carry the lineage forward but I pray to my Lord to give me honour and strength to continue the *silsilah* forward till I am alive to feel worthy of having succeeded mother.

Conclusion

The self-representation of Mai Kausar's devotional community, reflected in her life story, is riveting courtesy not only the miraculous details of her life and relatives, personal reflections, attachment to the Qalandar, but also as a portrayal of female religiosity showcasing how, among other things, religious tradition is orally transmitted among women.[15] It vividly shows how women transfer charisma and become ritual agents. In ethno-sociological terms, the Qalandari *silsilah* of Mai Kausar represents a matrilineal descent group; in mystic terminology, it is a line of spiritual descent which we may term 'Sufi lineage'.[16] The latter is a remarkable exception in the realm of Sufi masters because women are traditionally excluded from lines of transmission. In the present case, spiritual authority lies in the hands of Mai Kausar, her mother Amañ Hajan Mangla Qalandari and especially Mai Kausar's charismatic maternal grandmother Chiragh Bibi Qalandari, who founded the *silsilah*. In addition to members of their clan and caste, the matrilineal 'chain' also welcomes other individuals, raising follower count. This way the *silsilah* constitutes a larger, more effective religious group able to stand its ground during the annual *'urs* in Sehwan vis-à-vis other devotional communities.

Notes

1. *Lahūt* means the divine nature in opposition to the human nature (*nasūt*); *lā-makān* means 'beyond space', 'inexistent', 'nowhere'.
2. Jürgen Wasim Frembgen, *Das Rätsel des Pfeils. Begegnungen mit Sufi-Meistern* (Frauenfeld: Waldgut, 2017b), 76–81.
3. As communicated to Aly Bossin by Mai Kausar on March 2, 2019.
4. Mai Kausar here explicitly mentions her *dādā* (paternal grandfather) although the person in question, Fazal Muhammad, is the brother of her maternal grandmother. Here it has to be taken into account that in vernacular use of Punjabi kinship terminology maternal grandparents are often addressed and referred to using the same terms as paternal grandparents. This has also happened in the case of Mai Chiragh's brother.
5. This could be a misunderstanding on the part of Mai Kausar who may have mistaken Shaikh Nasiruddin Chiragh-e Dehli (d. 1356) for Sheikh Abu Bakr Tusi Haidari (thirteenth century), a saint of the Qalandar tradition, who is popular by the name of Matke Pir, that is to say the saint to whom clay pots are donated which are then deposited in trees around the shrine.
6. As the caste of musicians is considered by other Punjabis to be on the lowest rung in the local system of social stratification their members often claim descent from the noble Arab Quraishi family. The fact that Mai Kausar mentions here that 'her family often needed to travel to other towns to make a

living' tries to conceal but nevertheless indicates that her family also travelled to Sehwan (as mentioned in the following) in all likelihood to perform. Later, on page 7 of the original Urdu text, it is said that two sons of Chiragh Bibi became 'artists'.

7. The Hindu Lal Das was the respected 'lamp-lighter' (*chirāgh-wālā*) at that time (cf. Michel Boivin, *Artefacts of Devotion*, 40.

8. The identity of Sain Wali Muhammad was clarified by Aly Bossin in conversation with Mai Kausar on March 2, 2019. For more information on this Sufi lodge, see ibid., 60–1.

9. By claiming 'to have studied in London', Mai Kausar obviously wanted to make things seem better. Actually, during her stay in England she visited different cities, also London, and finally had to enrol in an English language course in Birmingham but, as she confessed to me, she did not learn anything and showed up just to mark her attendance.

10. Interestingly, Sufi colours were the topic of a conversation I had with Mai Kausar on December 20, 2013. She pointed out five colours, namely 'Qalandar red', green, black, *jōgī rang* (orange), and blue.

11. This *mēlā* is, in fact, a kind of *shām-e Qalandar* described in detail in Chapter III.

12. This is the main old graveyard in the centre of Lahore not far from the quarter of Mozang.

13. Imambargah of note in Lahore. All major '*Ashura* processions terminate at the site.

14. The expression *hawāltī makhlūqāt* means 'spirits' or 'superhuman beings'.

15. On female fakirs in Sehwan, also see Omar Kasmani, 'Women [un-]like women. The Question of Spiritual Authority among Female Fakirs of Sehwan Sharīf,' in *Devotional Islam in Contemporary South Asia. Shrines, Journeys and Wanderers*, eds. Michel Boivin and Remy Delage (London and New York: Routledge, 2016), 47–62.

16. Alexander Knysh translates *silsilah* as 'spiritual genealogy' and 'lineage' [*Sufism: A New History of Islamic Mysticism* (Princeton: Princeton University Press, 2017), 386].

V BETWIXT AND BETWEEN
Figures of Ambiguity in the Sufi Cult of Lal Shahbaz Qalandar

Introduction

It is an essential trait of popular and informal Sufi traditions in Sindh and Punjab, deeply embedded in indigenous cultures, to allow otherness and shades of ambiguity. The cult of Lal Shahbaz Qalandar is in particular known for its tolerance of ambiguity. This is especially true for the ritual context of pilgrimage to the saint's shrine in Sehwan and above all his annual *'urs*, which opens a space of tolerance for transgressive performances in presence of the Qalandar. Liminal figures of 'popular religion', such as peripatetic dervishes, enraptured men and women, the 'third gender', take on important roles as actors throughout the cult and perform in public alongside musicians, trance dancers, and Shia flagellants.[1] The event is celebrative and spectacular marked by a high emotional intensity of Dionysian character in which the divine is experienced day and night with all senses.

Following theories of Arnold van Gennep and Victor Turner, the ritual of pilgrimage includes the phase of liminality with its experiences of 'communitas' and temporary abolition of hierarchies among devotees. This is why the *'urs* of the great Qalandar saint, including its preparatory *shām-e Qalandar* rites (examined in Chapter III) in Lahore and other cities in Punjab, represent a unique arena for 'figures of ambiguity' to step out from the margins of society and indulge in transgressive performances. It allows 'holy fools' to show their antics and eccentricities in the ambiguous, liminal period of the *'urs*, to appear in peculiar outfits. For instance, a dancing dervish in Sehwan whose jute-made sleeveless smock was embroidered with shiny fabric and stitched all over with a variety of colourful beads, buttons, tassels, and 'objets trouvés', and who, in addition, was wearing a large number of necklaces. Another pilgrim had his black hair back-combed in the shape of a towering crown. Thus, the playful comical and carnivalesque, with its characteristic inversions, are an integral part of this performance-oriented event. Ambiguity is also articulated on another level in Sehwan and at other Sufi shrines: the domain of mystic music (as well as in the genre of classical vocal music), when, for instance, a male singer like the legendary late Nusrat Fateh Ali Khan (d. 1997) praised God in a female voice; and vice versa, when female singers such as Abida Parveen, Jyoti Nooran, or Masuma Anwar sing *sufiyāna kalām* in a deep, male vocal timbre. In fact, the model for such temporary forms of gender transformation had been the famous mystic poet Amir Khusrau (d. 1325) who sung for his Sufi master, the saint Nizamuddin Auliya (d. 1325) from Delhi, in a woman's voice like a bride longing for her bridegroom.[2] This mode of 'vocal masquerade', which points beyond male and female, seems to indicate an ideal of complementary perfection achieved through the merging of opposites.[3]

Through focusing in the following on the threshold status of three ritual agents, this chapter interrogates aspects of otherness, gender, and inversion. Also addressed is the debate on 'orthodoxy' and 'heterodoxy' as the eccentric deeds of these individuals seriously challenge behavioural norms of formalized scriptural Islam as promulgated by theologians. I met these three 'figures of ambiguity'—which I call by the invented pseudonyms Sain Ali, Sayyid Jamal, and Parwana to protect their anonymity—on different occasions in Sehwan and the two first-named in addition in Lahore between 2003 and 2009 in the course of field research on the cult of Lal Shahbaz Qalandar.

Sain Ali, the 'Bangle-wearing *malang*'

Rejecting conventions and formalism of mainstream society, dervishes and fakirs affiliated to 'free' *bī-shar‘* Sufi orders or associated to certain enraptured saints such as Lal Shahbaz Qalandar, Shah Husain, or Bari Imam, often transgress boundaries

Fig. 1 Panoramic view over Sehwan Sharif with the river Indus, taken from the remnants of the ancient fort associated by legend with Alexander the Great (May 2012)

Fig.2 Panoramic view over Sehwan Sharif with the golden-domed mausoleum of Lal Shahbaz Qalandar in the centre, the green-domed shrine of Bodlah Bal.ar in foreground on the right and the white-domed Pathan dervish-lodge far on the left side (May 2012)

Fig. 3 Shrine of Lal Shahbaz Qalandar during the 'urs (July 2010)

Fig. 4 Dancing dhamāl close to the main shrine in
Sehwan Sharif (July 2010)

Fig. 5 'Four lamps are ever burning for you. I have
come to burn the fifth for the exalted one.
Long live Lal.'

Fig. 6 Singers Gogi and Sajjid, the sons of Baba Nazir Ali, with members of their *sangat* at Lahore Railway Station shortly before starting the pilgrimage to Sehwan Sharif (August 2009)

Fig. 7 *Shām-e Qalandar* with Madam Afshan (August 2009, Bagh Munshi Lata, Lahore)

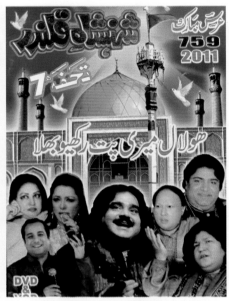

Fig. 8 DVD with the famous Qalandar hymn *hō lāl mērī pat rakhīo bhalā* featuring renowned artists such as (from the right): Abida Parveen, Sher Miandad Khan, Nusrat Fateh Ali Khan, Arif Lohar, Shahida Mini, Rahat Fateh Ali Khan and Madam Noor Jahan

Fig. 9 Sindhi pilgrims on the river Indus arriving in Sehwan Sharif (August 2009)

Fig. 10 Devotional dance in
Sehwan Sharif (July 2010)

Fig. 11 Pilgrims leaving Lahore Railway Station; an 'urs placard is pasted
on the train (August 2009)

Fig. 12 Depiction of Lal Shahbaz Qalandar on a contemporary Sufi poster

Fig. 13 The flying Qalandar; detail of a Pakistani Sufi poster

Fig. 14 The Qalandar praying and miraculously flying in the air; contemporary Sufi poster

Fig. 15 Sufi poster with Lal Shahbaz Qalandar in three different postures

Fig. 16 Eid-greeting card with the depiction of the dancing Qalandar

Fig. 17 The dancing Qalandar; folk painting, Sukkur-Qasimabad (November 2017)

Fig. 18 Begging bowl with the depiction of the dancing Qalandar, belonging to the dervish Ghulam Akbar; Karachi (November 2016)

Fig. 19 Lal Shahbaz Qalandar with his beloved disciple Bodlah Bahar; contemporary Sufi poster

Fig. 20 Hand-painted image of the Qalandar in contemplation mounted on a bus carrying pilgrims to Sehwan Sharif (December 2011)

Fig. 21 The dancing Qalandar painted on the back of an oil-tanker; Shirin Jinnah Colony, Karachi (November 2014)

Fig. 22 Painted truck with the image of the dancing Qalandar; Baldia,
Karachi (November 2013)

Fig. 23 Mural painting of the Qalandar in contemplation and dancing; shrine of
Baba Taj Sain, Lahore (April 2006; destroyed in the meantime)

Fig. 24 Plastic pendant with a sticker showing Lal
Shahbaz Qalandar in prayer

Fig. 25 The dancing Qalandar; model for a sticker in
a sample book, Lahore (November 2009)

Fig. 26 Sticker artist Mohammad Kashif working on an image of the Qalandar; Lahore (November 2009)

Fig. 27 Sticker of the dancing Qalandar on the wind-screen of a motor-rickshaw, on the left a photograph of Sayyid Shabbir Husain, a saint belonging to the Qalandariyyah, Lahore
(November 2009)

Fig. 28 A Pathan dervish on the streets of Sehwan Sharif, displaying an image of the Qalandar with Bodlah Bahar (July 2011)

Fig. 29 'Urs placard with a depiction of the shrine in Sehwan Sharif, Lahore (July 2010)

Fig. 30 Large banner with a view of the shrine of Lal Shahbaz Qalandar; *sangat* of Baba Nazir Ali, Lahore Railway Station (August 2010)

Fig. 31 Folk painting showing the mausoleum
of the Qalandar; local shrine in Sehwan
Sharif's Makrani Mohallah (July 2010; painted
over in the meantime)

Fig. 32 Hand-painted image of the shrine of Lal Shahbaz Qalandar on the 'crown'
of a truck; Sehwan Sharif (July 2011)

Fig. 33 Replica of the mausoleum of the Qalandar carried by pilgrims to be loaded
on the train to Sehwan; Lahore (August 2009)

Fig. 34 'Urs placard inviting devotees to join the pilgrimage
to Sehwan Sharif (Lahore, 1999)

Fig. 35 Folk painting with the image of the falcon symbolizing the Qalandar; local shrine in Sehwan Sharif's Makrani Mohallah (October 2009)

Fig. 36 Calligram with the Qalandar's name in the shape of a falcon; Sehwan Sharif (July 2010)

Fig. 37 Silver pendant in the shape of a falcon; personal
accessory of the drummer Pappu Sain
(November 2017)

Fig. 38 Mural painting with the boat of the Qalandar; meeting place of a
Qalandari *sangat* near Lahore Railway Station
(October 2013; destroyed in the meantime)

Fig. 39 Richly embroidered and inscribed piece of cloth
with the image of a sailing boat; Sehwan Sharif (July 2011)

Fig. 40 Wooden replica of the boat of Lal Shahbaz Qalandar displayed during a
shām-e Qalandar on Mohni Road, Lahore (July 2010)

Fig. 41 Calligraphic wall decoration with the inscription *Jhūlē Lāl Qalandar mast* in the dervish lodge of Bodlah Bahar; Sehwan Sharif (May 2010; destroyed in the meantime)

Fig. 42 Embroidered calligraphic invocation of the Qalandar; shrine of Sayyid Naban Darya Bukhari, Sehwan Sharif (October 2009)

Fig. 43 The Qalandar's nickname Jhule Lal written on a board; Lea Market, Karachi
(December 2011)

Fig. 44 The Qalandar's nickname Jhule Lal written on a sewing machine; Sabzwari
Mohallah, Sehwan Sharif (November 2014)

Fig. 45 Calligraphic sticker with the Qalandar's nickname Jhule Lal pasted on a bus; Lahore (November 2008)

Fig. 46 The Qalandar's nickname written on the back of a motor-rickshaw, notice the word Qalandar written on the little flag; Lahore (September 2014)

Fig. 47 Motor-rickshaw with inscriptions praising Lal Shahbaz Qalandar;
Karachi (July 2011)

Fig. 48 The Qalandar's nickname Jhule Lal written in the flowery style of truck painting on
the back of a motor-rickshaw; Lahore (February 2012)

Fig. 49 Malik Chan Qalandari, the leader of a *sangat*, with his motorbike, notice the name
Jhule Lal written in red; Lahore (November 2009)

Fig. 50 The Qalandar's nickname Jhule Lal written on a motorbike;
Lahore (February 2012)

Fig. 51 Jhule Lal prominently written on the bonnet of a
devotee's car; Sehwan Sharif (July 2010)

Fig. 52 Banner belonging to a *sangat* from Arifwala in the Punjab;
Sehwan Sharif (July 2011)

Fig. 53 Placard announcing the *'urs* of
Lal Shahbaz Qalandar

Fig. 54 Pilgrimage placard with the portrait of Baba
Jamil Ahmad Naqib Alvi Qalandar from Lahore

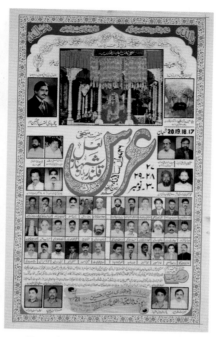

Fig. 55 'Urs placard by a community of
devotees from Lahore

Fig. 56 Lal Pari Mastani (d. 2013) who stayed at
the shrine of Lal Shahbaz Qalandar
(November 2008)

Fig. 57 Fakir Mohammad Husain in Sehwan Sharif
(November 2008)

Fig. 58 The elaborate wooden snakes carried by
Mohammad Husain (December 2011)

Fig. 59 Placard announcing a *shām-e Qalandar* held
2002 in Lahore

Fig. 60 Celebrating *shām-e Qalandar* inside an old quarter at Mohni Road,
Lahore (August 2009)

Fig. 61 Khurram Abbas carrying a little earthenware replica of a shrine with oil lamps during a *shām-e Qalandar*, Lahore (August 2009)

Fig. 62 The renowned *dhōl*-players Pappu Sain and Jhura Sain performing at a shrine in the wilderness of the Salt Range, Punjab (October 2003)

Fig. 63 *Shām-e Qalandar* at Moon Market in Lahore with the performers Gogi and Sajjid, the sons of Baba Nazir Ali (August 2009)

Fig. 64 *Shām-e Qalandar* of the *Sohna Lal sangat* held on a rooftop in Lahore (July 2010)

Fig. 65 Pendant and membership card of the *sangat* of Baba Nazir Ali from Lahore (August 2009)

Fig. 66 Pilgrims camping at Lal Bagh, Sehwan Sharif (July 2010)

Fig. 67 Members of a devotional community paying homage to their Pir; Sehwan Sharif (August 2009)

Fig. 68 Dervishes dancing in the streets of Sehwan Sharif (photograph by Aly Philippe Bossin, August 2009)

Fig. 69 Dancing dervish (photograph by Aly Philippe Bossin, August 2009)

Fig. 70 Poster announcing a ritual of the *silsilah* of
Mai Kausar; Lahore

Fig. 71 Picture with Mai Chiragh Bibi (right), Mai Hajan (left), and the young
Mai Kausar (centre)

Fig. 72 Folk painting of the mausoleum of Lal Shahbaz Qalandar; put up at the shrine of Haidar Shah Bukhari, Soldier Bazaar, Karachi (November 2013)

Fig. 73 Painting of Mai Kausar's mother, Mai Hajan Mangla Qalandari; Lahore (February 2015)

Fig. 74 Dervish blessing a devotee with sacred
lamp oil; Sehwan Sharif (August 2009)

Fig. 75 Members of a sangat during the *'urs* in
Sehwan Sharif (August 2009)

Fig. 76 Jhule Lal, the nickname of the Qalandar,
written on a wedding chariot; Soldier Bazaar,
Karachi (November 2013)

Fig. 77 Mai Kausar (photograph by Aly
Philippe Bossin, March 2019)

Fig. 78 Hand-painted image of the dancing Qalandar on the back of a motor-rickshaw;
Sukkur (November 2017)

Fig. 79 Women sorting out rose buds to be placed on saints' tombs; courtyard of Bodlah Bahar, Sehwan Sharif (October 2013)

Fig. 80 Finger rings of a dervish; Lahore (October 2013)

Fig. 81 Enthusiastic female devotee in the courtyard of the Qalandar's shrine; Sehwan Sharif (October 2009)

Fig. 82 Trance dance in the courtyard of the shrine; Sehwan Sharif
(photograph by Aly Philippe Bossin, October 2012)

Fig. 83 Dhamāl of the fakirs of Bodlah Bahar; shrine of Lal Shahbaz Qalandar (photograph by Aly Philippe Bossin, March 2009)

Fig. 84 Dhamāl of the fakirs; shrine of Bodlah Bahar,
Sehwan Sharif (photograph by Aly Philippe Bossin,
March 2009)

Fig. 85 The dhamālī Abdul Qayyum (on the left);
Sehwan Sharif (October 2009)

Fig. 86 An accomplished habitual trance dancer;
Sehwan Sharif (October 2009)

Fig. 87 Devotees doing dhamāl in the courtyard of the shrine of Bodlah Bahar;
Sehwan Sharif (May 2012)

Fig. 88 Sayyid Asif Ali Zaidi doing dhamāl in the courtyard of the Qalandar
(photograph by Salman Zaidi, August 2010)

Fig. 89 Ecstatic dhamāl during the *'urs* of Lal Shahbaz
Qalandar; Sehwan Sharif (July 2010)

Fig. 90 Dr Ashfaq Khan (second from right) with Baba Arif Sain
(centre) and the author (March 2011)

of expected norms. Some ascetics are chained on example of the fourth Shia Imam—Zain ul-Abidin—others smear bodies with ash, wear the 'dress of nakedness', or put on the gay-coloured patched frock of ritual clowns, attracting scorn and derision in line with the ideal of the Malamati 'who try to conceal their spiritual achievements'.[4] Some of the 'unruly Friends of God' have matted hair with long, braided locks. Others shave body hair: from hair on the head to beard and eyebrows. Many wear fancy jewellery such as rings (Fig. 80), bracelets, and anklets, necklaces, earrings, etc. The latter attributes indicate a particular *malang*-type, marked 'effeminate' in terms of costume and hairdo, adopting a feminine role and playing the role of the female lover to a Sufi saint or God.[5] This corresponds to transcending of gender divisions by male 'homines religiosi' on their way to sainthood described by Scott Kugle as 'men become saints by tapping "feminine" qualities that are normally hidden or repressed in men'.[6] In an essay on gender ambiguities he further explains:

… gender crossing signifies that a man takes up the social markers of woman: to wear women's clothing: to adopt women's speech, song, and gesture; to take on a woman's role in erotic interactions or even in sexual interactions. In a complementary but distinct way, male Sufis may shed many of the signs of social status, including the patriarchal status of masculinity, as a sign of surrender without performing these signs of surrender in the outer form of feminine gender. They might do this by wearing outlandishly coloured clothes, wearing no clothes, shaving their beard and moustache, leaving family and ascribed status, or inviting condemnation and blame.[7]

One of this free-thinking often peripatetic holy men is Sain Ali who I first met in October, 2004 in a makeshift tent opposite Data Darbar in Lahore and subsequently during the *'urs* of the Qalandar in Sehwan. Then in his 40s, sporting sunglasses, a dark-brown Chitrali cap, and a long, brown and flowing garment with a yellowish shawl, his grey hair shoulder-length and his full beard well-trimmed. In addition to rings on his right hand, a necklace of rose petals, a necklace with a pendant featuring an iconic image of the Qalandar, and a string of beads on his right upper arm, he was wearing a large number of glass bangles on both wrists. Because of the latter accessories he came to be known by his dervish *laqab wangāñ-wālā* which in Punjabi means someone wearing bangles. He said he was left mesmerized by Punjabi folk singer Arif Lohar's song *Wangāñ* which talks about selling bangles at Lahore's Data Darbar. The bangle-wearing *malang*'s own speciality was the theatrical and highly-emotional performance of singing *qalandarī* songs as well as folk songs, focused on love till he was so charged he wept long, passionately and loudly—behaviour associated with women and also Shia ritual mourning in Muharram.

*Malang*s such as Sain Ali hold an ambiguous position in a double sense: on the social level they are men living in the male-dominated 'public' sphere; yet as celibate ascetics they exist outside the 'normal' social world: diametrically opposed to the world of families and women. Nevertheless, as mentioned above, male dervishes often adorn themselves with typically female accessories and social markers such as glass bangles in the case of the Sain or they dress like married women otherwise. Thus, on the spiritual level they are male seekers of God who cross-dress as 'true brides' (*sāda suhāgan*) of Allah.[8] Within the South Asian concept of 'bride mysticism' male dervishes try to 'approximate' the female gender in order to fulfil the inverted role as a 'bride of God' yearning to unite with her beloved.

The most famous examples of Sufis who transgressed gender boundaries and danced in abandonment donning women's clothes and bangles are Musa Sada Suhag (d. 1449), who danced this way at the tomb of Nizamuddin Auliya,[9] and Bullhe Shah (1680–1757/8), who appeared like a transvestite in front of his spiritual master and exclaimed: 'If I would become a dancing girl [of the Kanjar caste], my honour would not diminish, let me appease you through dancing.'[10] Another, lesser known case in the Sufi hagiography of Pakistan is the saint Sain Saheli Sarkar (nineteenth century), whose shrine is situated near Muzaffarabad (Azad Kashmir). It is said that his whole attire was effeminate and he used to wear many flower garlands. His nickname Saheli means female friend, an equivalent of *suhāgan* (bride).

Sayyid Jamal, the 'King of the Rattling Dancing Bell'

A peculiarity of the cult of Lal Shahbaz Qalandar is to attract people otherwise positioned on the fringes of society such as *khusrē* (plural of *khusrā*), *hijrē* (plural of *hijrā*), *khadrā* (plural of *khadrō*), respectively *khwājahsarā*s ('chiefs of the seraglio in the palace') as they call themselves, that is to say cross-dressing effeminate individuals of the so-called 'third gender'; including transsexuals, hermaphrodites, eunuchs, and transvestites. Dressed as females they play important auspicious roles during rites of passage and regeneration (birth, circumcision, marriage) where they dance and ensure virility through gestures employing vulgar vocabulary thereby stimulating sexual energy of the vital life force. Dancing in abandonment himself, the Qalandar is obviously the Sufi saint loved most by *khwājahsarā*s, professional dancing girls, and prostitutes. Thus, the community of *khwājahsarā*s maintains— allegedly since the time of their patron saint Lal Shahbaz Qalandar himself—its own *faqīroñ kā dērah* or 'camp of fakirs' in Sehwan Sharif, which is known as *Khadrāñ ji marhī*. The large compound serves as a meeting place for all *khwājahsarā*s of Pakistan who visit the saint's shrine during the annual pilgrimage. As Amira, a 70- to 75-year-old resident *khwājahsarā* in the *marhī* told me in October, 2009 the elders of their community would point out that *khwājahsarā*s had even been guardians of the saint's tomb in earlier days. *Khwājahsarā*s, usually born male and only in rare cases of uncertain gender, consider themselves as fakirs or ascetics 'who have sacrificed their own sexual fulfilment and regenerative powers for others'.[11] As I frequently observed in Sindh and Punjab, *khwājahsarā*s forced to live outside a *dērah* often turn into wandering dervishes or resident fakirs at a shrine, displaying female attire and demeanour. The ambiguity of their gender and physical appearance sometimes becomes strikingly obvious, for instance, in the combination of a long grey beard with a golden women's handbag.[12]

At the Qalandar's *'urs* in October, 2003 I met a group of *khwājahsarā*s at the shrine who came from Punjab and had

assembled around the young Pir (Sufi master) Sayyid Jamal
(b. 1978), who they reverentially and affectionately called *badshāh*
(king). With henna-dyed long hair, dark moustache, a fancy
embroidered cap, bangles, and necklaces, the coquettishly smiling,
soft-spoken Jamal appeared to fit well with his *khwājahsarā*
companions who laughed about their gender-role reversals. Years
later, during the *shām-e Qalandar* celebrated on August 1, 2009
at Lahore's Moon Market in Allama Iqbal Town, I saw Sayyid
Jamal again. He was joyfully called on the stage on arrival,
garlanded and honoured into joining the recitation of a *qasīdah*
for Hazrat Imam Husain RA. People exchanged merry glances,
some boisterously celebrating his appearance. When I questioned
some bystanders, they derogatorily termed him the 'Pir of *khusrē*
and prostitutes', but added they respect him because of his Sayyid
lineage. Keeping this ambiguous remark in mind, I continued
observing this mysterious figure, reflecting on his role within
the cult of Lal Shahbaz Qalandar and later sharing my thoughts
with Pakistani friends. In our opinion, he represents the qualities
of being soft, gentle and meek, no doubt having a female soul,
thus perfectly fitting to the liminal character of the Qalandar cult,
in which boundaries are blurred and transcended. He resembled
Hermes, the winged messenger of Zeus, who in the words of Durre
Ahmed: 'was considered a mediator, peacemaker, and stood for
conciliation, tolerance, peace.'[13] In addition, Sayyid Jamal seems
to incorporate the ease, fun, and joy of life which permeates this
vibrant, colourful cult. His dress and transgender behaviour are
also strongly reminiscent of the playfulness of the ecstatic saint
Shah Husain from Lahore, who used the dimension of play as an
alternative to the asceticism of other Sufis and to the rigour of
theologians, thereby challenging ritual formality.[14] Jamal's *laqab*
Chayhañ Shah—king of the rattling dancing bell—specifically
refers to the sound of the *ghūngrū*s (rattling dancing bells) bound
around his calves. *Ghūngrū*s are also a marker for long-haired,
male trance dancers who slip into the role of female devotees
venerating God.

A cursory YouTube search reveals several slide-shows with
pictures of Sayyid Jamal. These pictures show the young, smiling

saintly person honoured by devotees at shrines or processions. He is depicted in Arab or red Qalandar dress riding a camel and also in private settings. In some cases, it is obvious that his skin has been bleached, lips reddened with a little rouge on cheeks, long hair coloured with henna, moustache well-trimmed and that he is wearing jewellery, bracelets, and rings.

Parwana, the Enraptured Conductor of Trance Dance

Mastī is a polyvalent term in South Asia mainly denoting an emotional passion of divine rapture and bewilderment between rationality and holy folly.[15] Thus, a person 'intoxicated' and 'mad' with love of God is called *mastanā* in case of a male and *mastānī* if female. They are per se transgressors and flouters of boundaries. The dancing Lal Shahbaz Qalandar himself is considered a model of embodying ecstasy, for one of his Persian poems opens with the line *haīdāriam qalandaram mastam*—'I am a Haidar (dervish), a Qalandar, I am intoxicated'. Often the imprint of rapture is a permanent one, rendering the person in question into an ecstatic mode of life, continuously in a state of liminality.

The eastern courtyard of the Qalandar's shrine in Sehwan is the main ritual arena for daily performance of devotional trance dance known as *dhamāl* (see Chapter VI). It is a sacred space for dervishes, experienced *dhamāl* dancers, and devotees who all join in as a celebrative form of interaction with their beloved saint as well as for the pilgrims who watch this spectacular performance. Unconventional mystics, men and women, regularly make their appearance in this ritual context, wearing fantastic costumes and equipped with unusual accessories demonstrating remarkable creativity, thereby attracting the eyes of the onlookers. Among these strange individuals I also happen to observe in October, 2009 and again in December, 2011 Parwana Mastani, an 'enraptured' lady and conductor of trance dance (Fig. 81).

Compared to earlier times, organizers of the daily *dhamāl* segregated the dancing men, seated male spectators and scores of

dancing, possessed women with families strictly using long ropes
that stretched through the courtyard. But, marking their special
status, the few dervishes positioned themselves as usual in front of
the male dancers segregated from them by rope. They performed
as 'artists' and 'attractors'. The straight aisle in the middle of
the courtyard allowed access from the eastern gate to the saint's
mausoleum. The flow of visitors through the aisle should ideally
be constant and smooth but because of the spectacular dancing on
both sides this was often blocked by curious onlookers. During four
consecutive days in October, 2009 I observed a *mastānī* always
positioned within the aisle but very close to the spectacular dancing
dervishes. When I later talked to Parwana at a tea stall, I came to
know she was in her early thirties and originally from Kotri, near
Hyderabad in Sindh. Every day this self-confident but somewhat
hyper and restless woman would wear a new sober dress in black,
blue, or some other colour and design always paired with a baseball
cap. Standing ambiguously in the aisle between the men's and
the women's space but closer to dervishes and often holding the
rope with one hand, she ecstatically waved with one arm or both,
conducting the dancers and directing them to the saint's tomb. At
times she went into trance herself, moving her body and wild hair to
the rhythm of the drums surrounded by male spectators in the aisle.
Then she went back to waving, thereby spurring on and conducting
dancers; her movements accompanied by ecstatic exclamations
such as *Allāh to hāl, 'Alī wāris, mast – mast* or *'Alī, 'Alī, yā 'Alī
Haīdrī*. From time to time she scared people off the aisle, trying to
keep it free from onlookers, thus fulfilling the function of a steward.
Likewise, she emptied dustbins at the shrine. Later, I observed
her gripping men by their arms, slapping them on their backs and
talking to them, transgressing moral boundaries of patriarchal
norms concerning female modesty and domesticity. While her
behaviour was straightforward and male-like, her appearance was
that of a female beauty. In December, 2011 her behaviour was
somewhat restrained and less spectacular than two years before.
Although she continued her waving movements with her hair open,
she now had her breasts covered with a glittering shawl that she at
times pulled up to her eyes.

Conclusion

The above-portrayed figures of ambiguity question and challenge the existing patriarchal-rational order, counter restrictive and purist behaviour, and cross boundaries of socially defined gender divide to get close to a sacred power. Through their inversion of customary gender roles, they display surrender and devotion.[16] Their unusual behaviour also creates subjective reflexivity among others confronted with otherness and in-betweenness. Living outside of conformity 'figures of ambiguity' frequently appear at liminal spaces such as Sufi shrines. In Foucauldian terms, the latter are 'something like counter-sites, a kind of effectively enacted utopia in which the real sites, all the other real sites that can be found within the culture, are simultaneously represented, contested, and inverted'.[17] The permanent placement of these persons in a state of liminality and their extraordinary transgressive performances at ritually framed events taking place at these shrines demonstrate the enormous potential of the Dionysian cult of Lal Shahbaz Qalandar to accommodate difference, otherness, and paradox to include the feminine and deal with complexity and plurality. In context of the cult, figures such as the bangle-wearing *malang*, the 'king of the rattling dancing bell', and the enraptured female conductor of trance dance prove the potential for revolt and experiment embedded in the very ambiguity they live and express. Transforming their gender, they almost seem to personify ambiguity. It has to be emphasized that ambiguity is generally suppressed and even eliminated in 'civilized society' and in Pakistan in particular, where the dominant absolutist mindset is impregnated by 'literalized monotheistic ideals of morality' and 'modern heroic consciousness' with its inherent exclusivist notions.[18] This is the reason why figures of ambiguity such as those portrayed here are increasingly threatened by Islamic reformism and radicalism. Nevertheless, the Qalandar cult seems to reflect an age-old local tradition of ambiguity which enshrines the idea of uncertainty about the divine.

Notes

1. Cf. Frembgen, *Journey to God*, 25, 66–101; and Frembgen, 'Charisma and the Holy Fool: Gul Mastān Bābā, the Enraptured, Saint of Udaipur,' in *Sufi Traditions and New Departures: Recent Scholarship on Continuity and Change in South Asian Sufism*, eds. Søren Christian Lassen and Hugh van Skyhawk (Islamabad: Taxila Institute of Asian Civilization, 2008b), 151–80.

2. Scott Kugle, 'Dancing with Khusro: Gender Ambiguities and Poetic Performance in a Delhi *Dargah*,' in *Rethinking Islamic Studies. From Orientalism to Cosmopolitanism*, eds. Carl W. Ernst and Richard C. Martin (Columbia: The University of South Carolina Press, 2010), 252–3.

3. See Carla Petievich, *When Men Speak as Women: Vocal Masquerade in Indo-Muslim Poetry* (Delhi: Oxford University Press, 2008).

4. Frembgen, *Journey to God*, 71–97 and 133.

5. Ibid., 99.

6. Kugle, *Sufis and Saints' Bodies. Mysticism, Corporeality, and Sacred Power* (Chapel Hill: University of North Carolina Press, 2007), 121.

7. Kugle, 'Dancing with Khusro,' 251.

8. Frembgen, *Journey to God*, 100–1; cf. Kugle, *Sufis and Saints' Bodies*, 209.

9. Ibid; Kugle, 'Dancing with Khusro,' 254–5.

10. Frembgen, *The Friends of God-Sufi Saints in Islam*,105–7. Interestingly, the verse in question about becoming a dancing girl, which I found written on a Pakistani poster-portrait of Bullhe Shah, is not part of the written and printed (probably 'purified') versions of the famous poem, *Tērē 'ishq nachāyāñ kar thaiyā thaiyā*. See, for instance, Muzaffar A. Ghaffaar, *Masterworks of Punjaabi Sufi Poetry: Bulleh Shaah. Vol. 1* (Lahore: Ferozsons, 2005), 97–8; and Aziz, *Kalaam-e-Aarifaan*, 75.

11. Georg Pfeffer, 'Manliness in the Punjab: Male Sexuality and the *khusra*,' *Sociologus* 45/1 (1995): 35.

12. The case of Ibrahim Faqir at Bhit Shah or the late Bibi Sahib (Baba Siraj) who lived in Miani graveyard in Lahore.

13. Durre S. Ahmed, *Masculinity, Rationality and Religion: A Feminist Perspective* (Lahore: ASR Publications, 1994), 97.

14. Kugle, *Sufis and Saints' Bodies*, 200 and 204.

15. On *mastī*, see Frembgen, 'Charisma and the Holy Fool,' 156–8.

16. Kugle, 'Dancing with Khusro,' 251–3.

17. Foucault 1986: 24.

18. Ahmed, *Masculinity, Rationality and Religion*, 29–31; cf. Stanley Diamond, *Kritik der Zivilisation. Anthropologie und die Wiederentdeckung des Primitiven* (Frankfurt a. M. and New York: Campus, 1976,), 109 and 158.

VI THE PERFORMING BODY
Trance Dance in the Devotional Sufi Practice at Sehwan

Introduction

Dervishes, members of *sangat*s, and *qāfilah*s as well as individual pilgrims regularly perform a trance dance known as *dhamāl* in honour of Lal Shahbaz Qalandar.[1] Considering its popularity, especially among the masses, it can be described as 'embodied religion' or as a form of 'danced religion' in the sense of I. M. Lewis.[2] In fact, the ascetic-mystical dimension in Islam known as Sufism is a very complex phenomenon with many different faces. It reflects a broad spectrum between more moderate, ethically-oriented movements or schools of thought organized in the majority of formal, well-established Sufi orders, and others—a not so small minority—with a more ascetic, world-renouncing profile, consisting of non-conformist groups of dervishes and devotees who emphasize ecstatic experiences such as dance. Listening to *samā'* (vocal spiritual music) and moving the body in rapture and abandonment nevertheless plays a role in both currents. It marks an experiential state of merging with the saint, the Prophet PBUH and God which—although debated controversially among Sufis themselves[3]—functions as an 'integrating modus operandi' particularly in Pakistan and India's Chishti Sufi order.[4]

The genre of instrumental *dhamāl*, however, is a different kind of Sufi activity mostly practiced outside institutionalized Sufi orders. It is specifically associated with dervishes and devotees of the Qalandar movement in South Asia, particularly in Sindh and Punjab. As such the rapturous dance is embedded in *mastī-o-qalandarī* which can be translated as 'Qalandarism'.[5] Thus far, dervish dance and *dhamāl* in context of spirit possession at the main Qalandar shrine in Sindh have been dealt by Michel Boivin

117

from a historical perspective, emphasizing its ancient local roots in ascetic Shivaism and other regional cults with shamanistic elements.[6] Focusing on the interpretation of drumming and dancing at the shrine of Madho Lal Husain in Lahore, Richard K. Wolf formulated an argument regarding the poetics of Sufi practice from an anthropological perspective. In his master's thesis, Rune Selsing explored the efficacy of ritual action in the *dhamāl* taking place at the shrine of Shah Kamal and other Sufi saints in Lahore.[7] He specifically examined the distinct discipline of habitual dancers to attain a state of rapture and the oral and musical transmission of the related practical knowledge in a form of ecstatic Sufism not institutionalized. The present study also urges empirical observations to investigate *dhamāl* as a concrete devotional, multi-faceted practice situated in the public space; the focus here is on its complex socio-religious context in Sehwan. I particularly differentiate between three types of *dhamāl* performers, emphasizing diversity of embodied ritual attitudes and related aesthetic styles. To highlight this plurality, I use original quotations from a variety of performers and refer to many peripheral arguments which need to be studied in greater detail in future.

My initial interest in this trance dance sparked from regularly participating in pilgrimages to Sufi shrines where I observed strikingly different embodied attitudes among performers (a problem also addressed by Wolf).[8] To understand this complexity of ritual actions and to interpret its various levels, which I grappled with during field research, I here draw primarily on Ronald L. Grimes' useful distinction between modes of ritual sensibilities.[9] That is, how can these differences be explained in context of *dhamāl*, what frames of reference are they related to? How should distinctions in performance and aesthetics be interpreted? These questions serve as a guideline and premise of the present study. First, I give a short introduction to the historical context of the dance, highlighting the genesis of *dhamāl*, its relation to the Qalandar movement and its pivotal figure Lal Shahbaz Qalandar. Secondly, ritual space and time are outlined as defining the socio-religious context of *dhamāl*. In the main part of this chapter, I describe and examine performance and aesthetics of dance in Sehwan, differentiating three groups of performers (dervishes, *dhamālī*s, and devotees) in terms of ritual structure, body techniques, gestural grammar, and gender-related kinaesthetic dance styles.[10] The next section focuses on embodied ritual attitudes culminating in a final discussion on dimensions of experience and agency.

The Historical Context of *dhamāl*

In vernacular Punjabi, Urdu, Hindi, and Gujarati *dhamāl* (literally 'noisy') means 'wild', 'boisterous', and 'over-excited'. According to common folk etymology, this term is derived from the words *dam* (breath) and *hāl* (state), *dam-hāl* literally meaning 'breath state'. Hence one of the most common devotional formulas is *damā dam mast Qalandar*—'through your breath, O Qalandar intoxicated (by the divine)'.[11] Therefore, people at shrines often muse the rhythm of breath and the heart should be synchronized with the beat of the drum in ecstasy. John T. Platts, however, claims *dhamāl* comes from *dham*, meaning the sound of jumping on or stamping the ground and explains the term as 'jumping through fire'.[12] But, according to recent scholarship, *dhamāl* is most probably derived from the Sanskrit *dharm*.[13] It needs to be remembered that the original name of Sehwan, the centre of contemporary *dhamāl* had been Siwistan, the 'place of Shiva', the Hindu god worshipped as the 'king of dance' (*nātarājā*). Thus, *dhamāl* appears to have been originally a ritual of mystical union with Shiva performed by the Pashupatas, a Shivaite school of ascetics, which has been later associated with the *qalandar* dervishes.[14]

As aforementioned, the latter belong to an antinomian movement which stands in opposition to scriptural Islam, established Sufi orders, and apparently spread from West and Central Asia during and after the Mongol invasions of the thirteenth century, in other words, at a time of war and chaos.[15] It is renunciatory in character and allows anarchist individualism which also becomes apparent in peculiar costume and insignia (cf. Chapter 5). 'Qalandarism' (*qalandarī*) in fact denotes a free-wheeling way of life open to a variety of dervishes, some formally initiated into the Qalandariyyah, others like South Asian *malang*s only loosely associated with certain Qalandar saints. Both aspire for direct divine inspiration through ardent love of God. Their hearts enraptured by the love of God, they seem to be seeking to be drowned in him not considering themselves responsible for what they do. Mendicant and peripatetic *qalandar*s are known for their provocative, socially deviant behaviour directed against prevailing moral and religious conventions, adopting *malāmat*, which means 'seeking blame': holding themselves in contempt to conceal spiritual achievements and fight hypocrisy. Extraordinary states of rapture and ecstasy characterize their religiosity.

According to the local South Asian Qalandar tradition, *dhamāl dālnā* (literally 'to put on *dhamāl*') or *dhamāl karnā* (literally 'doing *dhamāl*'), which both mean 'dancing', is attributed to Lal Shahbaz Qalandar.[16] References to the trance dance and ecstasy in general are found in Lal Shahbaz Qalandar's Sufi poetry. In his Persian *ghazal*s the saint calls himself insightfully the friend of famous martyr Mansur al-Hallaj (d. 922) sharing his emphasis on ecstasy as a means to draw oneself close to God.[17] Therefore, the last verse of one of his *ghazal*s is quoted most often: 'I know nothing except love, intoxication and ecstasy.'[18] Another starts with:

I am burning with the Beloved's love, every moment.
At one moment I am writhing on dust and in the other
I am dancing on thorns.
Come, Oh Beloved! Give me passion for music,
I dance in the open market, in the ecstasy of union,
In His love, I became infamous, but Oh pious one,
I do not mind this infamy for thy sake and I dance openly,
Although the world calls me a beggar because I dance,
I have a secret in my heart that impels me to dance.[19]

This God-given secret appears to refer to existential, esoteric knowledge which cannot be expressed in words. Lal Shahbaz Qalandar is said to have danced for the sake of love of Hazrat Ali RA without restraint to drum beat.[20] He appears to have redefined the Sindhi *samā'* by transforming an important indigenous musical ritual with shamanistic elements into a specific corporeal form of *dhikr*, using it also as a method of attracting people in the process of conversion to Islam.[21] In line with Hallaj, he considered music and dance a form of *dhikr*.[22] With regard to its local origin, *dhamāl* thus represents a link between the Sufi tradition and Indian asceticism.[23]

The Socio-religious Context of *dhamāl* in Sehwan

Ritual Spaces

The main 'locus ritualis' for a spectacular large-scale performance of *dhamāl* is the town of Sehwan Sharif, the final abode of the enraptured Qalandar, who is said to have expressed his intense love for God and his union with the divine through whirling and spinning dance movements. The saint is first of all commemorated, praised, evoked, and honoured through dance at his shrine proper which features two courts for devotional dance; the larger one, which leads from the main eastern gate to the mausoleum, is specifically intended for *dhamāl* and has a female-gendered space cordoned off from space allotted to male devotees (Fig. 82).[24] In addition to these ritual arenas of the central shrine, trance dance is also performed during the 'urs at other localities in the town such as various dervish lodges, smaller shrines, and the sacred places commemorating Lal Shahbaz Qalandar and Hazrat Ali RA. At these places, which constitute, so-to-speak, 'secondary sources of charisma',[25] and in the makeshift tents of the pilgrims, men and women bound through ties of family and kinship usually belong to the same association of devotees and share the same ritual space but they must keep to themselves and avoid body contact. Women and men (including dervishes and habitual dancers) thus maintain a general separation of genders while dancing. Among female and male devotees, girls join their mothers and other female relatives while boys dance alongside their fathers or older friends likewise. Nevertheless, in context of the dance, boundaries of gendered spaces are not always clearly demarcated and blurred and permeable at times. This also holds true for *dhamāl* performed in streets as part of processions wherein tomb-covers are ceremonially carried.

According to hagiographic traditions in Punjab, saint Baba Shah Jamal (seventeenth century) a Sufi of the Suhrawardi and Qadiriyyah orders who was apparently not affiliated to the Qalandar movement, once became furious because of the complaint of a Mughal princess.[26] As legend goes, he started to ecstatically dance to the rhythm of the drum so much so that when he reached an altered state of rapture, a multi-storeyed fortress collapsed.[27] This is why the saint is particularly associated with trance dance and venerated by local *malang*s (dervishes) who are also keen devotees of Lal Shahbaz Qalandar. Baba Shah Jamal's shrine is situated in the quarter of Ichhra in Lahore. *Dhamāl* takes place in a courtyard right below the terrace (of the shrine) where hundreds of devotees and spectators can be accommodated around a circle of 10 to 20 dancers. The *dhamāl* at this shrine, which originated as a devotional practice of dervishes dancing in a circle, is in principle an exclusively male-gendered ritual.[28] The presence of hordes of young men in the dim light of the shrine and common consummation of drugs generally prevent women from attending this nocturnal event.

Ritual Time

As far as the 'tempus ritualis' of both *dhamāl* events examined is concerned, it is important to note that ritual at the shrine of Baba Shah Jamal in Lahore is a weekly gathering held every Thursday evening after *maghrib* prayers (as is common at so many other Sufi shrines) which is not embedded in the framework of a pilgrimage. Here the performance of drummers and dancers follows a customary sequence of the ritual.

The shrine of Lal Shahbaz Qalandar, on the contrary, is the focus and destination of the largest pilgrimage in Pakistan on the occasion of the saint's annual *'urs* festival.[29] This is the liminal ritual period when the power of the respective saint is thought to flow in particular abundance. The spectrum of pilgrims covers diverse ethnic and social groups with the majority coming from the masses of the poor including scores of Hindus from Sindh who venerate Lal Shahbaz Qalandar as Raja Bhartrhari, a Shivaite ascetic of the fifth century. In terms of age, young male devotees constitute the largest group. Pilgrims stay at least three days, usually between seven to 10 days at Sehwan (sometimes even longer) including the essential period from Shaban 19 to 21 over which the most important ceremonies take place. In the context of this *ziyārat*, pilgrims feel a permanent flow of *barakat* within a celebrative event marked by an emotional intensity of Dionysian character where the divine is experienced day and night will all senses. This is what Roger Caillois has aptly called the 'intermediate rule of intoxication, exuberance and flow' in festivals where 'all conventional rules are temporarily dissolved'.[30] The liminal ritual of trance dance is embedded in the 'communitas' experiences of the pilgrims with their heightened forms of communication sharing the attachment to the Qalandar saint. It should be noted that, in addition to the visual spectacle of *dhamāl* during the *'urs*, the shrine of Lal Shahbaz Qalandar is visited by pilgrims year-round where *dhamāl* is performed daily after *maghrib* prayers (with the exception of Muharram 1–10) in the eastern court of the shrine.[31]

Performance and Aesthetics of *dhamāl*

Dhamāl can basically be described as a ritual dance which expresses a 'communal', spiritual state of trance (*hāl*; or 'presence') or ecstasy (*wajd*) in which the subject dissolves his or her 'self'.[32] In vernacular language the term *mastī* or the formula 'to be *mast*' is much more frequently used to describe this emotion of ecstatic rapture connecting the participants of the performance. Dancers in Lahore and Sehwan, who I spontaneously addressed on the roadside, described this devotional dance as 'an expression of deep love of the Qalandar', 'a close link between the heart and God', 'an opening of the gates of paradise', and 'a gift of God'. Some dervishes, with whom I discussed *dhamāl*, pointed out that this dance of abandonment leads to 'clearance of the soul', 'breaking up the self' and thus to self-annihilation 'making room for God'. The common Sufi interpretation is that in *hāl* the moment of divine presence is realized which opens the door to a spiritual space, where dancers, listeners, and musicians are united with their *murshid* (spiritual guide). This state is considered to be bestowed

by God, descending from him into a man's heart, agency attributed
to God alone.[33]

Dance movements in trance are essentially linked to rhythm
and ecstatic exclamations. Thus, *dhamāl* is also the term for the
typical rhythmic sequence mostly played on a barrel drum (*dhōl*)[34]
or—like in Sehwan—on large kettledrums (*naghārō, naqqarah,
naubat*).[35] Thus, *dhamāl* is essentially linked to drumming.[36] Master
drummers, such as the duo Pappu and Jhura Sain as well as Gunga
and Mithu Sain, who perform at shrines in Lahore and during
the *'urs* of the Qalandar also in Sehwan, use repetitive rhythmic
patterns gradually increasing in rapidity to create a trance-inducing
state. In this way, drum beats (with which specific formulas are
identified) are transformed into *dhikr*. Experienced dancers point
out they hear *dhikr* formulas (also called *bōl*) in the different
sequences of beats and also recite them silently or audibly during
their performance such as:

> *'Alī, 'Alī, 'Alī, haq*
> *Dam mast Qalandar, dam mast Qalandar*
> *Lā ilāha illā 'llāh*
> *Yā pāk, yā pāk*

> Ali, Ali, Ali, truth
> Through your breath, oh Qalandar intoxicated
> There is no god but God
> Oh pure one, oh pure one

These hymnic formulas are essential sonic elements of the dance,
uttered by dancers as well as the audience which mainly invoke
God, Hazrat Ali RA, and Lal Shahbaz Qalandar.[37] In his thesis,
Selsing focused on these *dhikr*s or *bōl*s as a central aspect of
dhamāl in more detail, emphasizing that they are bestowed by the
saint himself to purify devotees' hearts.[38] In terms of the structure
of dance, 'changes between different *zikr*s correspond to changes
in the rhythm'.[39] On March 9, 2006 I attended a *dhamāl* at the
shrine of Baba Shah Jamal in Lahore where Pappu Sain shouted
the following *dhikr*s to which the dancers and spectators responded
in chorus:

Allāh-hū, haq wujūd
Allāh-i mast, Maulā-i mast
Maulā 'Alī, mast-i Maulā
Allāh-i mast, 'Alī zabardast
mast Qalandar, Jhūle Lāl
damā dam mast Qalandar, Jhūle Lāl
Qalandar mast, zabardast

God is One, [his] truth is eternal
Enraptured God, enraptured Ali'
Master Ali, rapture of Ali
Enraptured God, Ali the powerful
Qalandar intoxicated, the ruby who rocks himself in a cradle
Through your breath, Oh Qalandar intoxicated – the Red swinging
Qalandar intoxicated, powerful

Besides this invocation of God and the saints, the initial rhythmic cycle of four beats was later doubled to eight and 16 over the course of the performance. Sometimes, the drum is accompanied by the metallic sound of fire tongs (*chimtā, dast-panāh*)[40] or a metal rattle and accentuated by the sound of the local oboe (*shahnā'ī*), dervish horn, trumpet, or conch shell. Music connoisseurs such as the late Ashfaq Khan of Lahore (cf. Fig. 90) who was widely respected in music circles emphasized that this instrumental trance music must be 'round' (*gōl*), without beginning and end, like whirling the head in ecstasy.[41]

Prerequisites for dancing to the rhythm of the *dhōl* are to move barefoot—on the earth, which God has spread like a carpet for man as Sufis use to say—as well as a certain length of hair which supports the whirling movements of the head. Often the adept also eats some ash from the sacred fire, rubs themself with sacred oil and reverently touches the drums. Following proper etiquette, the dancers first turn towards the saint's tomb, crossing their arms before the chest, gently bowing and asking respectfully for permission to perform *dhamāl*. Often they also touch the ground with their right hand, a gesture demarcating his or her dance from the complex ritual processes taking place. In Sehwan, the devotees should first, in commemoration of the 'red Sufi'

Lal Shahbaz Qalandar, tie a red thread around their right wrist before participating in *dhamāl*. The actual beginning of the ritual is marked by single, heavy beats of the drum. At the end of their performance, dancers prostrate and pray in the shrine's courtyard in direction of the saint's tomb.

Against the background of our case study in Sehwan, in the remainder of this section I will examine the performance and ritual structure of trance dance. Special emphasis is placed on the aspect of *dhamāl* as a multi-sensory performing art, a 'field of aesthetics' on the borderline between religion and drama which contains distinctive patterns of bodily techniques observable among protagonists of this 'poetics of movement'.[42] In this context, it is important to differentiate between three groups of actors characterized by overlapping categories and styles of this music-dance form:

(1) The dance of dervishes (*malang/malangnī, faqīr/faqīrānī*) that is to say of mystic and ascetic seekers of God—both, male and female—permanently or temporarily individuals-outside-the-world; classified by others as *bī-shar'* ('sans religious law') and *jalālī* (incorporating an awe-inspiring emotional state).[43]

(2) The dance of *dhamālī*s, that is to say of dedicated and experienced dancers—both, male and female—who are part of the shrine culture and sometimes earn a living by performing in public. Apart from part-time performers (*shauqīn dhamālī*s), full-time dancers over the years often turn into *malang*s or *faqīr*s and are respectfully called *sā'īñ*.

(3) The dance of devotees, that is to say of male and female laymen who are only temporarily—during pilgrimages and ritual gatherings (*ziyārat*)—in that liminal, outwordly state of an intense relation to God and the saints.

I want to emphasize that these distinctions between dervishes, *dhamālī*s, and devotees, which are aimed to focus on their performing activities, are not clear-cut, but in fact fluctuating, and should therefore not be understood as a form of classification. It should be mentioned that devotees' *dhamāl* is nowadays often influenced by the popular *filmī dhamāl* of folk singers and dancing girls which is likewise influenced by mundane Punjabi *bhangra* dance.

Dancing Dervishes

The peculiar whirling dance regularly performed in Sehwan is characteristic for the red-robed dervishes (*faqīr*s) attached to Bodlah Bahar (Figs. 83–84).[44] Their form of spinning devotion, specifically known as *lāl phērī* (lit. 'whirling of the red', 'red rotation') or *chakrī* (lit. 'gyrating') and thought to be practiced for centuries, has the character of a sacred mimesis and spiritual exercise venerating movements of the great Qalandar to attain a vision of the spiritual master.[45] Moreover, according to local oral dervish lore, the latter inherited the dance tradition from Hazrat Ali RA who after being proclaimed by the Prophet Muhammad PBUH as his rightful successor is said to have whirled three times around his own axis in a gesture of confirmation and joy. *Lāl phērī* is performed every evening in the courtyard of Bodlah Bahar's shrine to the sound of the kettledrums in which about 10 to 25 male dancers stand in three or four rows in the courtyard facing the tomb of the saint. A few simple dance steps (first the right foot is placed to the front, then the left one, wherefrom the dancers raise both arms) alternate with spinning around to the right. As a form of *dhikr* characterized by circular movements, it is reminiscent of the well-known Persian mystical motif of moths fluttering around the flame, an analogy frequently activated by word or deed as mentioned by Wolf.[46] The late Sayyid Asif Ali Zaidi (d. 2017) of Lahore, who occasionally performed *dhamāl*, claimed that it has 'a liberating effect, getting rid of all the dirt' and compared its effect to 'a soul which like a bird wants to be set free from its cage' (cf. Fig. 88).[47] After the spinning, all dancers prostrate themselves and then form two long rows, standing shoulder-to-shoulder while praying litany-like invocations to Hazrat Ali RA and other saints. The dervish ritual ends with a ceremonial greeting.

Participation in this form of ritual action at Bodlah Bahar's shrine is in principle exclusivist that only *faqīr*s initiated into the Qalandar tradition (through ritually shaving their hair, eyebrows, etc.) and wearing the proper bell-shaped red frock belong to the group of performers.[48] A few common devotees, nevertheless, also participate at times by dancing in the last row. Even female devotees are free to dance towards the side of this otherwise male-dominated space. The dervish robe in red, the symbolic colour of the Qalandar, marks the ritual identity of the performers. Their flowing, gyrating movements in abandonment are often gradually increased and raised to the level of divine attraction (*jadhb*), finally achieving the trance state of *hāl*, but always convey the impression that the dancer masterfully controls his or her *dhamāl*. Nevertheless, the visual 'Gestalt' of their structured dance appears Dionysian and wild in comparison, for instance, with the perfect harmony of the well-regulated Mevlevi ritual. On every new moon and on the 1, 21, and 29 of each lunar month as well as during the *'urs*, the dervishes of Bodlah Bahar make a procession down from their lodge to perform at the shrine of the Qalandar for one hour where they dance in front of all the other dancers cordoned off from them by a rope.

Then there are individual dervishes of the *malang*-type who do not perform collectively with a group but celebrate their own distinct style. For instance, at Sehwan I observed the spinning dance of a rather portly elderly *malangnī* known as Lal Pari Mastani (d. 2013) (cf. Fig. 56).[49] During one of the daily ritual performances (on November 7, 2008) in the eastern *dhamāl* court of the main Qalandar shrine, she rotated with full vigour, red robe swinging like a bell around her, mace-like staff and patched bag (both worn on her back) acting as a counter-weight intensifying the whirling movement. She performed with complete control of her body movements.

In addition to *lāl phērī*, Qalandar dervishes also dance in a more individual way with an emphasis on stamping the ground. When the ascetic and martial Mahlan Shahi *faqīr*s first move slowly anti-clockwise in a circle and then accelerate their stamping following the rhythm of the *dhōl* this stamping intensifies the sound of large bells worn around the waist and of the rattling ankle-bells (*ghūngrū*s). The Mahlan Shahis are a branch of the Qalandar order widespread in Punjab. I have been told that in ecstasy, dervishes may even, in rare cases, tear their garments to pieces. Such a frenzied dance was, for instance, masterfully performed by Saqi Baba on the beginning of a musical gathering organized in honour of Sayyid Mehdi Raza Shah Sabzwari, one of the guardians of the shrine of Lal Shahbaz Qalandar, during the latter's *'urs* on August 11, 2009 in Sehwan. Saqi Baba, an impressive dervish with matted hair in his fifties, was born in Gujar Khan (Punjab) and spent his initial seven-year period as a candidate to become a *malang* of the Qalandar in Pakpattan. The red-robed dervish combined spinning with stamping the ground as well as other dramatic actions mimetically re-enacting the suffering of the fourth Shia Imam Zain ul-Abidin, the only son of Hazrat Imam Husain RA who survived the battle of Karbala in 680 CE. The young Imam is considered to be one of the ancestors of the Qalandar. This re-enacting of his suffering follows a particular dance pattern and musical rhythm called *Sajjādiyyah* because of the saint's honorary name Sajjad which means 'one who bows in adoration'. Qais Ajmi explains: 'Sajjadia *dhamāl* demonstrates the walking of Imam Sajjad Zain ul-Abidin sick, chained and neck braced and whipped too' (2001). *Sajjādīyyah* is also performed by *dhamālī*s, common devotees and understandably the Shias.

During other nightly performances I observed that dervishes occasionally raised their burning hashish pipe in a celebrative mood. A dervish like Amir Husain, the well-known *nāg-wālā-faqīr* from Sehwan, performs entranced with peculiar, almost habitual gestures, presenting the construction of 10 wood-carved snakes (*nāg*) impressively draped around his body, stamping the ground, raising one of the snakes, and now and then blowing his horn.

Dancing dhamālīs

In Sehwan as well as at other Sufi shrines particularly in Punjab experienced dancers called *dhamālī*s perform under a ritual leader (for instance a respected *malang*) and in close coordination with the drummers. At the shrine of Baba Shah Jamal in Lahore, the weekly event of trance music in the lower courtyard is dominated by main *dhōl* player Pappu Sain who directs and controls dancers' movement through the hypnotic strokes of his drum. The dancers follow his rhythmic pattern (*thēkah*), so-to-speak the heartbeat of the drum consisting of four, eight, or sixteen beats. Wolf further explains: '[…] drummers create interest for the dancers by inserting breaks (*torā*) and tripartite cadences (*tiyā*) as well as other patterned gaps in the otherwise thick texture of strokes.'[50] Together with his co-drummer Jhura Sain, Pappu thus creates a pulsing space in which the dancers move ecstatically: whirling, jumping, and stamping their feet on the ground, anticipating and responding to the drummers' rhythmic articulations. Wild movements, caprioles, and abrupt leaps are said to reflect the *jalālī* nature of the saints of the Qalandar tradition, that is to say their majesty and frightening power, reflecting an attribute of God, whereas the body language is gentler in case of saints said to embody the 'beauty of God' (*jamāl*). Wolf aptly emphasizes that 'these forms of musical and kinaesthetic synchronicity, coming together, are critically valued from the artistic perspective of some participants'.[51] Swirling their long hair creates a further aesthetic dimension in addition to the rhythmic patterns of body movements.

The dancers visually dominate the performance and attract the attention of the audience. In addition to musicians, they are the key actors in this nocturnal ritual at Baba Shah Jamal's shrine. The choreography is dramatic not only when the lead drummer starts spinning and rotating in the middle of the dance floor, ceaselessly beating his drum, but especially when a *dhamālī* instinctively reacts to the sound of the *dhōl*, sensually nestles against it as if in intimate embrace and then both dancer and drummer accelerate to an ecstatic run.[52] In comparison to the enraptured dance of the dervishes, *dhamālī*s specifically indulge in the frenzy of ecstasy (*jadhb*) seeking its utmost peak. As I observed at Sehwan and at Shah Jamal in Lahore that their *hāl* is often induced through drugs (hashish). Accomplished *dhamālī*s are brilliant in their individual kinaesthetic style dancing with instinctive assurance. At Sehwan, for instance, I observed a sturdy young woman with a shawl draped around her upper body, eyes almost closed who gyrated for a full hour—at times swirling her long hair and rotating her head at such a speed that I could hardly distinguish between head and hair— virtually like a spinning top. She alternated this gyration with a particular figurative choreography, namely spreading her arms like a cross then bending forwards and moving her arms like a flying bird—obviously mimetically enacting the image of her beloved Qalandar saint miraculously flying like a 'royal falcon' (*shahbāz*).

A particular ecstatic circling movement which I only observed among *dhamālī*s is rotating the head in frenzy virtually like the head of a drill in motion.[53] This is commonly known as *sar kā dhamāl*. At Sehwan one of the most accomplished trance dancers in this respect was the young Abdul Qayyum who was 20 to 25 years old in 2008/2009 (Fig. 85). He told me that he had been dancing since he was six. Born to a Pashtun family in a small town in Balochistan he lived permanently in a Sehwan dervish lodge while his parents stayed in Karachi. While whirling his head, he occasionally performed different habitual gestures, such as raising his arms, pointing his right index finger into the air, and beating his chest with his right hand in the Shia gesture of *mātam*.[54] When I observed him a year later he had added a new movement to his repertoire of bodily actions: explosively shooting his arms in the air to the rapidly whipping rhythm of the drums.[55] Another year later he had further enhanced his performance through an occasional half turn as well as explosively shooting his arms forward. Both movements served as a break to control the trance and complete an ecstatic part of it. In December, 2011 he added several spins of utmost rapidity at the climax of his spectacular performance.

Another example of outstanding individual agency as well as performance art in *dhamāl* is the respected dancer Mohabbat Sain at Shah Jamal in Lahore: dressed in a loincloth and a long black shirt, he remained in a standing position almost like a statue, only his head spinning in frenzy and at times swinging his arms and hands.[56] He stood in the middle of the circle representing the axis, the rest of the dancers rapidly moving around him. In 2009, this magnificent *dhamālī*, whose real name is Haq Nawaz, was around 70 years old, had been married with five children and is long since the caretaker of a small shrine in Qainchi, Lahore. In his youth he acted for some time in Punjabi films. He told me he learned *sar kā dhamāl* at a young age from his elder brother.

The *dhamāl* at Shah Jamal is only partly inclusive in the sense that untrained neophytes in the circle of experienced dancers, who try to mingle with them, quickly realize they are largely unable to dance in the congested space. They might even fall and disturb others; therefore most of them drop out soon, if they dare to step into the arena at all. Staggering dancers, unable to control their dance and align themselves with others, are rudely removed from the circle either by an older *malang* or the leading drummer. The same treatment awaits charlatans who just try to show off or behave improperly.[57] Thus, responsible ritual experts take care that the pattern of performance remains structured and its quality ensured. That means there should be a 'somatic mode of attention' among dancers in relation to other bodies while they form a collective body.[58] In fact, as I frequently observed at Shah Jamal, experienced *dhamālī*s and *malang*s (such as the late Baba Firuz Sain) dance with closed or almost closed eyes, instinctively responding to each other's movements. Firuz was a charismatic, saint-like Pathan with long hair who passed away in 2015 around the age of 70. He was long been respected as the most accomplished dancer at Shah Jamal. When I visited him on March 19, 2010 he told me he had been working for years as an oilman at Lahore's Allama Iqbal International Airport but he had then started to earn his living by transporting vegetables on a donkey cart. Dancing *dhamāl* since his youth, he was also a gifted singer of *qalandarī* songs. Many years ago he became the caretaker of a shrine in Kot Lakhpat, an underdeveloped area on the periphery of Lahore. Although married with one son and a daughter he lived alone in his dervish lodge at a graveyard in the same locality. A couple of years ago he stopped dancing because of age.

Baba Arif Sain (d. 2012) was one of the respected *malang*s with authority to supervise the *dhamāl* (cf. Fig. 90); he also mingled with the dancers and contributed to the aesthetics of the performance not only by blowing his horn at times but also through his sheer presence as a dervish in traditional robe with patchwork cap.[59] Similarly, the long-haired drummer Pappu Sain wears an ankle-length garment and several necklaces, sometimes with a large pendant in the shape of a falcon (symbol of Lal Shahbaz Qalandar) made of German silver (cf. Fig. 37).[60] While mostly playing with his co-drummer at the edge of the circle facing the shrine, at an advanced state of the trance session he himself moves into the centre of the arena and circles around with small toddling steps, followed by the *dhamālī*s reciting *bōl*s invoking God, Hazrat Ali RA, and Lal Shahbaz Qalandar. The audience and dancers alternately respond to these formulas. Pappu himself gradually works himself into the state of *hāl*. His final spinning while steadily and competently playing the heavy *dhōl*, which flies horizontally in front of him through the power of rotation, marks the sonic-visual climax of the event. The dramatic effect can even be increased when a second person puts his arms around the drummer's neck from behind, flying and gyrating on the back of the musician like a counter-weight to the drum. Such an acrobatic and spectacular performance, which I had the chance to observe at the *'urs* of Baba Bullhe Shah on August 26, 2004 in Kasur (performed there by the rather frail Lahore-based drummer Bijli Sain), is part of the drummer's training by his master. Another spectacular effect is when the drummer holds his heavy instrument using his teeth while continuing to play and whirl.

Among *dhamālī*s who perform with drummers at Sehwan and during *mēlā*s at other shrines are mostly young single men (Fig. 86) and young middle-aged women. The latter are usually members of small groups under the leadership of a *malang*. For their performance, these *dhamālī* entertainers receive a share of the donations presented by onlookers to the main drummer or cash showered on them in the traditional gesture of *vel*; at times they are also paid in kind (for example hashish). Similarly, professional *nāch-wālī*s (dancing girls and prostitutes from the Kanjar-caste) and *gharvī-wālī*s (women, often speaking Marwari who belong to peripatetic groups and sing and play on a small metal pot) also perform for money. Offering cash to dancers is considered auspicious for the donor. Drawing on Grimes's modes of ritual sensibilities, the dance of these *dhamālī*s might have a pragmatic component, yet this does not exclude deep feelings of devotion.[61] Those labelled 'true', 'full-time' *dhamālī*s by devotees, however, rarely dance for money but in abandonment for the saints and God. They frequently identify with and become *malangs/malangnī*s or are identified as enraptured *mastānās/mastānī*s. Male *dhamālī*s emphasize that long hair (called *jōg*) is indispensable for real *dhamāl* and dedicated dancers should in any case also wear ankle bells.

Dancing Devotees

Contrary to the gatherings at Shah Jamal, Sehwan vibrates with *dhamāl* performances open for everybody. Particularly during the *'urs*, day and night a unique soundscape is created with the rhythm of drums continuously overlapping. Here *dhamāl* is a collective ritual taking place in various circles of drummers and dancers. Apart from performances in the two courts of the central shrines, dances are arranged spontaneously at any place within the precincts of the holy town. At times, men and women dance alongside within a group of devotees.

While visiting the shrine of Lal Shahbaz Qalandar many times, I was able to study this context of *dhamāl* in detail whereby I could differentiate distinct kinaesthetic styles and 'techniques of the body' among male and female devotees. As to the first, *dhamāl* is predominantly performed by men whose dance in comparison to women appears more conventional, choreographed, and routinized. Often they dance collectively in a group (sometimes of 20 to 40 persons), faces and bodies turned towards the saint's tomb. Men move with 'restrained unrestrained' to quote an expression coined by the German anthropologist W. E. Mühlmann. Usually they dance with their arms raised and elbow-angled—a central gesture attributed to Hazrat Ali RA, venerated as the founding figure of the Sufi tradition.[62] Occasionally, both index fingers are pointed towards the sky, hands placed at earlobes in the traditional gesture of repentance (*taubah*). Further characteristic body movements include swinging the head rapidly from right to left, which can be intensified to whirling and to induce trance, as well as balancing from right to left and toddling backward and forward with short steps in tune with the rhythm of the *dhōl*. There is also room for devotees to differ from this rather structured repetitious pattern of *dhamāl* and to dance individually in a joyful mood (Fig. 87), in spiritual abandonment (Fig. 88) or in a wild, frenzied and feverish way with abrupt leaps (Fig. 89).

As for the second, there are very few shrines in Pakistan where women are traditionally allowed to join the *dhamāl*.[63] During the *'urs* in Sehwan their style of *dhamāl* appears not only more varied and idiosyncratic but also more impulsive and eccentric in comparison to men. Their dance typically starts with one arm akimbo and the other hand opening their long, tied hair. The latter can be interpreted as part of the embodied self which is now presented in public. Overpowered by the presence of Lal Shahbaz Qalandar, women literally 'sweep' the floor of the shrine with their hair swinging in a circle while sitting on the ground, kneeling or standing with their upper body bowed forward. While many whirl their hair, covering themselves after their trance, others are conscious never to let their shawl slip down; thus, there is a dialogue going on between covering (or concealment) and uncovering. In addition to the aforementioned movements for male devotees, women 'go into *hāl*' or 'play *hāl*' (*hāl khēlnā*) by gracefully waving their arms wide and sweepingly, making circling gestures with their hands and fingers, swinging their hips, gradually spinning their entire body (either to the right or to the left). Having thus gone into *hāl*, they may increase their trance by rotating their head, pirouetting, jumping, and other frenetic, spontaneous movements. The intense sensual expression of their body moving in abandonment has a strong erotic appeal for men who magnetically flock around. *Dhamāl*, thus, can at times turn into a sexually explicit performance and overt expression of female sexuality.[64]

During a long performance I observed early morning October 5, 2004 in the southern court of the shrine, female spectators sitting on the ground formed an inner half circle around dancing women (about 8 to 12), protecting and shielding them from the standing male audience. The dancers first moved in an oval, later in a circle. Police frequently pushed back male onlookers threatening them with batons, ensuring 'ordered spatiality'. Ecstatic behaviour is always 'conducted' and controlled in the sense that non-dancing women (often relatives) or dervishes act as custodians preventing improper behaviour by men and indecent exposure by dancers. In contrast to *malangnīs* and female *dhamālīs*, women observing seclusion in daily lives and staying home are called *ghar-wālīs*. The latter usually start their dance with soft and stately movements, getting into *hāl* at a pace slower than experienced *dhamālīs*. Obviously, there is individual variation in trance dance according to each dancer's temperament and state of rapture. Female devotees sometimes try to remain covered and if the veil slips from their head and upper body, a relative will throw it over her if possible. But, as whirling and gyrating are essential for real *hāl*, a shawl for covering is not practical and therefore sooner or later shed to the ground. After their *dhamāl*, however, women immediately cover themselves with a veil when they leave the circle of dancers. Thus, morality seems as much contextual as normative.

The fact that performances of all dancers are spatially oriented towards the tomb of Lal Shahbaz Qalandar creates a particular magical and aesthetic power.[65]

Embodied Ritual Attitudes

In accordance with the variety of its protagonists, dervishes, *dhamālīs*, and devotees, *dhamāl* is multi-functional, referring to different levels and horizons of motivation, activity, and meaning. Insofar as trance dance is a medium of communication with the divine, its dominant theme is individual devotion (*'aqīdat*) expressed by a particular gestural performance. Before investigating this notion of devotionalism in relation to *dhamāl*, I will first apply Grimes's analytical framework of differentiating modes of ritual sensibilities in light of my ethnographic data.

For dervishes, not only the most devoted followers of Lal Shahbaz Qalandar and his disciple Bodlah Bahar, but also those who carry on the antinomian tradition of these saints *lāl phērī* and *dhamāl* are ultimate forms of veneration, expressing praise of their beloved saint and longing to spiritually unite with God—a central theme of the Sufi tradition time and again expressed in poetry. As travellers on the spiritual path to God seeking 'unio mystica', trance dance is for them crossing a threshold between this world and the next and thus a ritual of transcendence. For Lal Shahbaz Qalandar, this whirling dance was a way to unite with God, a 'communal' trance.[66] By imitating the Qalandar's exemplary gyration, the dervish dance bears the character of a mythical movement, re-enacting the saint's union with God. This way, through mimesis in ritual practice, liturgical power is conveyed to dervish dancers.

Habitual dancers, such as those performing at Shah Jamal, are in a sort of intermediate position between mystics and devotees, some living a dervish life, for instance, as custodians of small shrines or as peripatetic *malang*s and *faqīr*s; others do menial jobs and dedicate their life to *dhamāl*, thereby becoming experienced dancers. It seems many seek ecstasy and intoxication for its own sake that they focus on the rapidity of movements, frenzy, and the virtuosity of mastering their ecstatic state acquired through constant practice. Addressing similar contexts, the Islamologist and historian of religion Rudolf Gelpke mentioned 'differences in the extent of rapture' (in German: Gradunterschiede der Entrückung), differentiating between a 'lower' preliminary stage and a 'higher' level,[67] whereby the former would be identified with devotees and in part with *dhamālī*s and the later with dervishes and advanced *dhamālī*s. It should be added that many of the *dhamālī*s habitually drink *bhang*: the green 'spiritual liquid' made of cannabis or smoke hashish. When I talked in Sehwan to dancing girls, prostitutes, and people of the 'third gender', who also receive monetary remuneration for performing *dhamāl*, they explained through trance dance they purified themselves and sought solace from the burden of their sins.[68] Also, several male *dhamālī*s in town, who wished to remain anonymous, confided they would dance out of penance for grave sins they had committed earlier (criminal acts inclusive of even murder). The modes of embodied attitudes expressed by *dhamālī*s are predominantly aesthetic, theatrical, spectacular, playful, and erotic but at the same time often also achievement-oriented. For these dancers in particular, *dhamāl* constitutes their identity.

For common pilgrims, *dhamāl* is a customary, stereotyped, and ritualized but also intense celebrative form of annually expressing their veneration of the saint, receiving a vision of the great Qalandar, communicating with him, and affinity with him. Many devotees and also a number of *dhamālī*s, additionally, explain they perform the devotional dance as an offering in connection with a vow (*mannat*) uttered in prayers of supplication. *Ghar-wālī*s, for instance, expect fertility as a practical outcome of *dhamāl* performed during the *'urs*. They also dance when the men of their family have been imprisoned as *dhamāl* is considered magically effective to free them. Other desires and motivations for vows are healing, prosperity, and seeking to overcome other life challenges. If a petition as been granted with the help of the saint or if the devotee receives dreams and visions of the saint they again express gratitude by dancing. One might say a devotee has struck a 'deal' with the respective saint with dance becoming an offering. Modes of ritual sensibilities enacted in the *dhamāl* of devotees, thus, are magic in tandem with ritualization but deeply impregnated by the overall festive mood of the pilgrimage.

The nodal point of these embodied attitudes expressed in *dhamāl* is a loving kind of devotion to the 'Friend of God' whose blessedness (*barakat*) is transferred to those who venerate him through their trance dance.[69] In the words of a male pilgrim from Lahore: 'Nobody would dare to enter the sacred city of Sehwan and do *dhamāl* without being overwhelmed by love for the Qalandar!' This shows that devotion is a basic attitude, a kind of prerequisite before expressing individual desires at the saint's abode.

Habitual dancers, such as dervishes and *dhamālī*s, mimetically perform the dance in reference to the fettered martyr-mystic Hallaj, who danced in abandonment in chains when led to the gallows (this tradition is also reflected in Persian verses attributed to Lal Shahbaz Qalandar). According to Shia tradition, *dhamāl* is said to symbolize the suffering of Imam Zain ul-Abidin and Hazrat Imam Husain's sister Bibi Zainab, who survived the tragedy of Karbala after the martyrdom of Imam Husain. The explanation posited for movements of *dhamāl* in Sehwan given by devout Shias is, as fleetingly aforementioned, the young Imam had to walk with heavy iron chains bare feet in small steps on scorching desert sand, head bowed by the weight of a heart-shaped stone put around his neck.[70] He raised both his arms to God in a gesture of supplication. His movements are not only imitated by habitual dancers as well as by a number of common devotees but particularly by Sayyids of various Sehwan dervish lodges during the three main days of the 'urs when they dance in a very formalized and disciplined way following the scripted expression of ritual visitation of the saint's tomb. Bibi Zainab, whose arms were bound to her back, is said to have let her hair down in order to avoid the gaze of her male tormentors when they snatched her veil. This distinct style of *Zainabī dhamāl* is a form of ritual mourning similar to the *Sajjādiyyah* dance aforementioned. Both Shia holy figures, Imam Zain ul-Abidin, respectfully called Sajjad, and Bibi Zainab fulfil pivotal roles in collective Shia memory and serve as role models for devotees. Their movements are mimetically enacted by tripping from right to left like the Imam (or even through carrying chains in case of Shia dervishes) and whirling with open hair like Bibi Zainab. For Shia followers of the Qalandar, these dance movements are therefore sanctified representing 'authentic', 'true' *dhamāl*. The evocation of Shia holy figures shows how 'images of the past are conveyed and sustained by (more or less) ritual performances'.[71] For the Shias aware of these traditions, *dhamāl* constantly evokes what Paul Connerton has aptly called a 'bodily social memory' whereby the body is transformed into a site of memory.[72] Drawing both on Pierre Bourdieu's notion of 'habitus' and Marcel Mauss' concept of 'techniques of the body', Connerton further explains that body memory is 'habit-memory'. This analytical category helps to explain the importance of learning and successfully performing a spiritual discipline and technique such as *dhamāl*. For habitual dancers, invoking Imam Zain ul-Abidin and Bibi Zainab is in line with their attachment to Hazrat Ali RA and Lal Shahbaz Qalandar (a descendant of the Shia Imams). Both Hazrat Ali RA and the great Qalandar are essential mediators whose presence is felt through whirling the body in a state of rapture.[73]

Within the Qalandar tradition, this ecstatic rapture is commonly known as *mastī*: the central emotion of *dhamāl* ritual. *Mastī* means the mystic ardour of love to God, 'where analytical thinking is switched off' as formulated by a young, well-educated performer from Lahore.[74] It is a devotional, blissfully experienced divine love (*'ishq*) and absorption in spirituality expressed by all Punjabi and Sindhi Sufi saints in their poetry. To cultivate this *'ishq* is the veritable core of the whirling dance. A female dancer, interviewed by the anthropologist Omar Kasmani in Sehwan, explained she performed *dhamāl* not only following the order of her spiritual guide Lal Shahbaz Qalandar but for Prophet Muhammad PBUH too. When asked how she would do this, she responded: 'That too happens in his *'ishq*, all of this is about *'ishq*. It all depends on *'ishq*. One who has more *'ishq* will do more *dhamāl*.'[75] Concerning the rapture of *mastī*, the same female *dhamālī* described: 'I'm moving in my *mastī*. From one end there is *mastī*, from the other I'm doing *dhamāl*, so I don't know how I appear then, good, bad or whatever. I do not know. But it is fact that everybody tells me that "your *dhamāl* is very pretty." My husband himself says "your *dhamāl* is stunning".'[76]

Part of the formal aesthetic elements of *dhamāl* are specific gestures of devotion, such as touching the ground with the right hand, turning towards the saint's tomb with both hands raised, touching and kissing the drum, raising one's hands above in an imploring way, folding and spreading them as if offering *du'ā*. Ecstatically spinning the head turns into an embodied prayer offered by the 'lover' (*'āshiq*) to his 'beloved' (*ma'shūq*). A striking example of this is Baba Ilmuddin's *dhamāl* at the minor shrine of his forefather Ditta Sain (d. 1991) in Lahore (Miani Sahib Graveyard) when he stands whirling first at the foot of the tomb, then continues supporting himself with both hands on the cenotaph and finally sweeps it with his long hair, almost lying on the tomb. The late Baba Firuz Sain from Lahore, the renowned dervish-cum-*dhamālī*, in one of our conversations (March 19, 2010) referred to such ritual performances when he aptly termed *dhamāl* the 'prayer of the dervish' (*darwēsh kī namāz*). Of course, this also holds true for *dhamālī*s as well as common devotees. Individual ardent devotion is articulated by similar gestures at tombs in the main courtyard of the Qalandar's shrine in Sehwan. Devotees emphasize the heart should have a relation to God; only then can *dhamāl* be considered a form of *'ibādat* (worship of God) and facilitate emotional absorption in Lal Shahbaz Qalandar.

The latter's shrine is a particular example of the diversity of religious denominations, ethnicities, gender, and social statuses. *Dhamāl* there belongs to shared devotional practices typical for shrines in Sindh where Hindus and even Christians join Muslim pilgrims. As far as their performance style is concerned, the only ritual gesture typical for Hindus is worship with folded hands (*añjali-mudrā*) at the beginning of the dance (which at times can also be seen with Muslims); Christians, on the other hand, spread their arms in mimesis of Jesus at the cross.[77]

Dimensions of Experience and Agency

Trance dance creates a space to express emotions through the idiom of rapture and devotion to a Sufi saint. In discourse on rituals the question has been formulated if this is a spontaneous, individual emotion, an articulation of feelings in a raw state, or something Stanley Tambiah has called an 'attitude of feelings'.[78] He thinks of the expression of an emotional-cultural pattern, the performance of conventional gestures of behaviour which refer to feelings. Scholars investigating theatrical performances have critically questioned whether ritual performers are not simply fulfilling the expectations of participants and spectators through a playful 'doing-as-if'.[79] Part of this perspective is the important aspect of mimesis, in our context the re-enactment of the body movements of saints through *dhamāl*, referred to in the previous section. Nevertheless, at the sacred places discussed here, devotional dance appears not as something pretended, deceptive, or inauthentic; it is rather that aesthetic theatrical performativity with mythic connotations marks the scripted expressions[80] of the dervishes (as well as of the Sayyids of Sehwan), spectacular performativity with ludic elements marks the trance of the *dhamālī*s and ritualized performativity with celebrative and sensuous elements marks the dance of common devotees. Thus, as a lived experience, *dhamāl* is both idiosyncratic in the sense of the German 'Erlebnis', which has the connotation of something particular and exceptional, as well as typical, customary, habitual, and pattern-like.[81]

The experience of the divine through the body as 'Leib' constitutes a cultural pattern especially in Sindh and Punjab. Considering how essential metaphors of love are within the mystically-inspired folk religiosity of these regions, this seems in particular true for the 'poetics of movement' typical of female *dhamāl* dancers, which displays not only passion and frenzy, but also sensuousness and eroticism. Basically, Sufism can be characterized as a 'religion of love' where the mystic in ecstasy seeks true love of God, which requires annihilating his or her own ego. *Mastī* is not only a state of spiritual excellence but also rapture, joy and intoxication, a consciousness of paradoxically 'being outside oneself', but 'being with the body';[82] therefore it has erotic connotations which also explain sexual undertones in the movements of dancers. The latter explain that the form of love (*'ishq*) which manifests in *dhamāl* is energetic and 'hot' (*garam*), its seat is supposed to be the heart. This power of love leads to an intoxicating perception and experience of the Qalandar's presence through the 'flow' of *mastī*. The element of divine love and experience of God turns ecstatic dance into a veritable spiritual discipline. In my conversations with dervishes, *dhamālī*s, and devotees, it was unanimously emphasized that both *'ishq* and *mastī* are veritable cornerstones of dance irrespective of the performance style characterizing respective ritual modes. These semiotic terms mark the experience shared by the individual dancers belonging to different groups of performers.

In the course of my research in Sehwan and Lahore, I requested *dhamāl* dancers to describe their concrete bodily experience. A middle-aged male devotee from Lahore, who frequently goes into trance, spontaneously referred to his state of *hāl* as 'sinking' (*dubnā*); another trance-experienced music lover, who spent lengthy periods in Europe, corroborated this view by drawing a comparison to a swimmer who gently rocks himself on the waves lying on a surfboard seeing paradisiacal things in the water. Abdul Ghafar, a devotee in his thirties who performed *dhamāl* over his pilgrimage to Sehwan daily, likened his feelings during the dance to 'drowning in an ocean of love'. He specified: 'When I perform *dhamāl*, I feel my *murshid* Bodlah Bahar places his right hand on my shoulder, sometimes he then even embraces me. And the great Lal Shahbaz Qalandar is all the time standing right behind Bodlah Bahar.'[83] The late Sayyid Asif Ali Zaidi, who I mentioned afore, related his personal experience: 'When I do *dhamāl*, I feel the presence of the Qalandar as a fragrance, warmth. You know, it is as if you feel the breath of a person very close to you in a pitch-dark room. And then the saint's energy "charges" through while one is performing, he takes over' (cf. Fig. 88).[84]

Within all three embodied ritual attitudes, be they mythic-liturgical, theatrical-spectacular, or customary-ritualized in Grimes's terminology, boundaries of the individual body are transcended, dancers experience a 'flow' of sensations and veils between man and the divine temporarily removed. A symbolic gesture associated with this experience in the domain of the unspeakable and subjective is dancing on one leg and pointing the index finger upwards like the letter *alif* towards God, the One, thus indicating unity (*tauhīd*), the ultimate goal of the mystic. Often dancers make this gesture as a habitual attitude using their right or both hands.

In Muslim societies where the body (especially the female one) is controlled, regimented, and disciplined a particularly expressive, eccentric, and frenetic dance such as *dhamāl* represents an alternative emphasizing 'joie de vivre' and exuberance. Following the approach of Nancy Scheper-Hughes and Margaret M. Lock,[85] *dhamāl* allows protagonists to experience the 'individual body', the material body in its subjectivity and its presentation in a public arena. In the *dhamāl* courts at the Qalandar shrine in Sehwan female dancers stage an entrance as 'imposing figures', like a 'work of art' visible by men in public.[86] Genders are often not strictly segregated. This challenging of social norms imposed not only by scriptural Islam (particularly since 1977 in the era of former president Ziaul Haq) but also by rigid local codes of moral behaviour can be read as casting a critical look at social conflict, 'flirting with an alternative', evading male control. Female devotees, and in smaller numbers also men, find catharsis in a ritual allowing them to express emotional needs. Having observed *dhamāl* in Sehwan on many occasions for hours, it seems the dance could also in many cases be interpreted as a vehicle to express suppressed sexuality. Moreover, I think the suffering experienced by underprivileged devotees in their daily lives is reflected in the style of embodiment typical for *dhamāl*. Such questions, however, need to be addressed in greater detail in the future.

To understand the experience of Pakistani dervishes, *dhamālīs*, and devotees during *dhamāl* it is enlightening to take a look at comparative phenomena in North Africa. Ulrike Krasberg has convincingly argued in her study on Moroccan trance dance and possession that in a collective ritual through deep devotion and unconditional love the individual is able to fully concentrate on his or her own self—similarly to a dedicated actor performing on stage.[87]

Experiences are structured and framed through performance: *dhamāl* has extraordinary dynamics and dramatic sequences which unfold through the action of 'aesthetic agents' in the presence of spectators.[88] Particularly, the steady sound of ornamental rhythmic drum patterns creates a solid structure for this performing art. Additionally, there are companions who supervise and assist the dancers if need be. This ritual framework for trance dance can be very open, for instance, during the *'urs* in Sehwan, or less open—more in the sense of an orchestrated improvization where performers follow a kind of 'unwritten script'[89]—for instance at Baba Shah Jamal's shrine and during the daily trance ritual in the inner *dhamāl* court of the central Sehwan shrine. In any case *dhamāl* is not regimented in the sense of a musical score but has various modes of expression as exemplified in the descriptions of the ritual including moments of playfulness. Trance dance is transformative for dervishes, *dhamālīs*, and devotees not only in the sense of 'communitas' uniting the dancers and the captivated audience but also receiving *barakat* and for those afflicted by demons and ghosts through purifying, healing, and thus empowering them.[90] *Barakat* is also received by spectators who share the presence of the divine with performers and are emotionally pulled into *dhamāl*. The wild intensity and power of the dance and sound of drums is simultaneously experienced as a 'mysterium fascinosum' and simultaneously as an entertaining spectacle.

In the frenzy of *dhamāl* the body is all-powerful, breaking limitations through movements of extraordinary form and rapidity which allow enormous individual spontaneity.[91] According to indigenous interpretation, this individual empowerment is God-given. The body is active and the medium to experience ecstatic rapture, to delve into the divine light and be touched by God. This sacred experience is in fact embodied—there is no duality between mind and body. The embodied devotion to Lal Shahbaz Qalandar is of an intensity said to transcend mundane love because it is much purer and subtle. More than that, devotional practice becomes mimesis when dervishes and *dhamālī*s imitate the dancing Qalandar in their respective ritual modes of expression. For underprivileged followers of the saint *dhamāl* also functions as an outlet for the insults and humiliations they suffer daily. Trance dance is thus a transformative practice for them, strengthening self-esteem and helping gain prestige when re-integrated in their respective social environment following the liminal phase of the ritual.

Conclusion

Devotion to Sufi saints in Pakistan is the preserve of a pluralistic indigenous value system shared by both the common and the elite. Its concrete embodiment in the spectacular and vibrant ritual of *dhamāl*, however, is contested by Muslim theologians and followers of scriptural, legalistic Islam who condemn dance (*raqs*) as an 'un-Islamic practice'.[92] As an expression of local ecstatic 'danced religion' in the public sphere, nevertheless, it belongs to the multiple worlds of Sufi shrines and is characteristic of concrete devotional practice of rural people and the urban poor especially in Sindh and Punjab. In these provinces ecstatic dance guided by the hypnotic repetitive sound of drums is theatrically and aesthetically performed with extraordinary emotion and intensity at several shrines in audience-oriented situations creating spontaneous 'communitas'.

Drawing on Grimes' concept of distinguishing various modes of embodied ritual attitudes, one ascertains that scripted expressions and choreographed performance dominate among dervishes, celebration with aesthetic, dramatic, and ludic dimensions among *dhamālī*s (not excluding means-end oriented aspects) and ritualization, magic, and enjoyment among common devotees (also in the special case of possession trance) which at times opens up space for the erotic and playful. These modes of ritual sensibilities coexist and interpenetrate each other, whereby celebration tending towards pure expressivity remains the overall impulse of the ritual. Thus, for all performers, *dhamāl* is a celebrative form of interaction with the beloved saint expressing a temporal coexistence between this world and the divine. For the Shias in particular, it is in addition mythologized as a mnémotechnique connecting them with pivotal figures. This notion of mystical unity expressed through ecstatic rapture (*mastī*) and love (*'ishq*) is the central theme of Sufi poetry and 'Sufi Islam' constituting an essential religious value among the Punjabis and Sindhis participating in *dhamāl*. The performing body is the medium of this transformation which happens in dialogue with bodies of other dancers and the audience. The efficacy of *dhamāl* becomes especially apparent in its function as a 'need-fulfilment-ritual' (fulfilment of vows) and healing rite in the context of spirit possession.

This passionate devotional dance is experienced and performed by most practitioners since youth. As such it is a ritual practice learned through creative processes of direct observation and mimesis. This full-bodied, active experience of mystical devotion belongs to the 'body hexis' and 'social habitus' of the dancers, their 'permanent disposition' as coined by Bourdieu which integrates former experiences like a matrix of action and perception in the body as a subject.[93] Drawing on Bourdieu's concept that the body serves as a store for the most important values of a culture, that the 'Leib' as a symbolic form is in fact one of the basic dimensions of cultural practice, *dhamāl* also has an intrinsic social value in the Dumontian sense, which is inscribed into the body.[94] As with rituals in general, it fulfils basic emotional needs but specifically for the underprivileged it also represents an outlet for frustrations.

Furthermore, this trance dance is an expression and reaffirmation of practically lived religious and cultural identity, which allows the experience of alterity. This holds not only true for *malang*s and *dhamālī*s whose life as 'outwordly individuals' and liminal figures centres on the ecstatic veneration of Lal Shahbaz Qalandar and who have become the very experts of the dance but any devotee. As exemplified by the analysis of two contextualized shrine-events, nevertheless, the key-performers' patterns of body use display distinctive aesthetic qualities, individual ingenuity, artistic creativity, and level of mastery contrasting those of common pilgrims.

Notes

1. This dance is also performed on occasion at a number of other shrines in Sindh and Punjab. For further references, see Shemeem Burney Abbas, *The Female Voice in Sufi Ritual: Devotional Practices of Pakistan and India* (Austin: University of Texas Press, 2002), 33–5; Michel Boivin, 'Le pèlerinage de Sehwan Sharif, Sindh (Pakistan): territoires, protagonistes et rituels,' in *Les pélerinages au Maghreb et au Moyen-Orient*, eds. S. Chiffoleau and A. Madoeuf (Damas: Institut Français du Proche-Orient, 2005), 334–7; and Richard K. Wolf, 'The Poetics of "Sufi" Practice: Drumming, Dancing, and Complex Agency at Madho Lāl Husain (and Beyond),' *American Ethnologist* 33/2 (2006): 246–68. A variation of this ecstatic dance is practiced by the Sikhs in Indian Punjab who call it *thummal*.

2. I. M. Lewis, *Ecstatic Religion: A Study of Shamanism and Spirit Possession* (London and New York: Routledge, 1989).

3. There has been a long, controversial debate reflected in Sufi literature either arguing for the legitimacy of *samā'* and defending it, but nevertheless setting strict rules for the decorum of 'listening' sessions, or rejecting it outright as un-Islamic accretions. Austere theologians and many *sharī'a*-bound Sufi masters objected to *samā'* and ecstatic whirling, being afraid that the performance of love songs would distract the listener from concentrating upon the majesty of God only. For an overview about the permissibility of music in the Sufi tradition, see Kenneth S. Avery, *A Psychology of Early Sufi samā': Listening and Altered States* (London and New York: RoutledgeCurzon, 2004), 10–52. For more detail, Jean During, *Musique et extase: L'audition mystique dans la tradition soufie* (Paris: Albin Michel, 1988), 217–47.

4. Carl W. Ernst and Bruce B. Lawrence, *Sufi Martyrs of Love: The Chishti Order in South Asia and Beyond* (New York: Palgrave Macmillan, 2002), 36. In a masterful study of *qawwālī* Sufi music, Regula Burckhardt Qureshi [*Sufi Music of India and Pakistan: Sound, Context and Meaning in Qawwali*

(Cambridge: Cambridge University Press, 1986)] has described and analyzed this *samā'* of the Chishti tradition.

5. Therefore, also the genre of songs related to this dance and to the veneration of Lal Shahbaz Qalandar is known as *qalandarī dhamālaiñ*.

6. Boivin, 'Reflections on La'l Shahbāz Qalandar,' 48–9 and 62–3; Boivin, 'Note sur la danse dans les cultes musulman du domaine Sindhī,' 160–4; Boivin, 'Le pèlerinage de Sehwan Sharif;' and Boivin, 'Le sama' dans la région du Sindh,' in *Des voies et des voix: Soufisme, culture, musique*, ed. Zaïm Khenchelaoui (Alger: CNPRAH, 2006), 308–11.

7. Rune Selsing, *Without Experience no Knowledge: A Ritual Study of the Ecstatic Sufi Practice dhamāl in Pakistan*' (M. A. thesis, Department of Anthropology, Copenhagen University, 2010).

8. As already mentioned in Chapter 1, I participated six times in the *'urs* (between 2003 and 2011) and, in addition, visited Sehwan another six times (between 2007 and 2011). I reflect about these pilgrimages in my ethnographic narrative: *At the Shrine of the Red Sufi*.

9. Ronald L. Grimes, *Beginnings in Ritual Studies* (Columbia: University of South Carolina Press, 1995).

10. Thus, my main focus is on the dancing performers not so much on ritual functionaries such as drummers. For the important role of the latter, see Wolf, 'The Poetics of "Sufi" Practice' and Selsing, *Without Experience no Knowledge*.

11. Boivin, 'Note sur la danse dans les cultes musulman du domaine Sindhī,'162; and Frembgen, *The Friends of God-Sufi Saints in Islam*, 68.

12. John T. Platts, *A Dictionary of Urdū, Hindī and English* (Oxford: Clarendon Press, 1884; repr. New Delhi: Munshiram Manoharlal, 1997), 546; see also, Wolf, 'The Poetics of "Sufi" Practice,' 254; and Boivin, 'Reflections on La'l Shahbāz Qalandar,' 48.

13. Personal communication by Richard K. Wolf (Munich, July 27, 2009).

14. Boivin, 'Note sur la danse dans les cultes musulman du domaine Sindhī,'160; and Boivin, ed., *Sindh Through History and Representation: French Contributions to Sindhi Studies* (Karachi: Oxford University Press, 2008), 38.

15. On the Qalandar tradition, see for instance: Simon Digby, 'Qalandars and Related Groups: Elements of Social Deviance in the Religious Life of the Delhi Sultanate of the Thirteenth and Fourteenth Centuries,' in *Islam in Asia*, vol. 1, ed. by Yohanan Friedmann (Jerusalem: The Magnes Press, 1984), 60–108; Ahmet Yaşar Ocak, *Osmanlı imparatorluğu'nda marjinal sûfîlik: Kalenderîler, XIV-XVII. Yüzyıllar* (Ankara: Türk Kurumu Basıevi, 1992); Karamustafa, *God's Unruly Friends*; Frembgen, *Journey to God*, 71–2, 83–90, and 96–101; and Frembgen, '"Ich weiß nichts außer Liebe, Rausch und Ekstase". Lal Shahbaz Qalandar (gest. 1274) und die Bewegung der Qalandar-Derwische,' in *Mystik: Die Sehnsucht nach dem Absoluten*, ed. A. Lutz (Zürich: Museum Rietberg and Scheidegger & Spies, 2011b), 157–9.

16. Boivin, 'Reflections on La'l Shahbāz Qalandar,' 42–5; Frembgen, *The Friends of God-Sufi Saints in Islam*, 62–70. According to Kaleem Lashari

(personal communication, September 17, 2005), in Sindh *dhamāl* is only found at Sufi shrines which are influenced by Punjab; see Uzma Rehman, 'Sacred Spaces, Rituals and Practices: The *mazar*s of Saiyid Pir Waris Shah and Shah 'Abdul Latif Bhitai,' in *Sufism Today: Heritage and Tradition in the Global Community*, eds. C. Raudvere and L. Stenberg (New York: I. B. Tauris, 2009), 141 (*dhamāl* at the shrine of Shah Abdul Latif).

17. Hallaj, an extreme lover of God and a saint of intoxication (*sāhw*), is especially known for his ecstatic prayers (*munājāt*) and being gifted by divine speech (*shāth*); see Herbert W. Mason, *Al-Hallaj* (Richmond: Curzon Press, 1995), 27 and 16.

18. Anonymous, 'Qalandar Lal Shahbaz,' 20; and Boivin, 'Reflections on La'l Shahbāz Qalandar,' 45.

19. Ibid., 19–20; and Mohammad, *Hazrat Lal Shahbaz Qalandar of Sehwan-Sharif*, 9–11.

20. In addition, the dance of the Qalandar is explained by different mythic tales, see Selsing, *Without Experience no Knowledge*, 22.

21. Boivin, 'Note sur la danse dans les cultes musulman du domaine Sindhī,' 161; Boivin 'Reflections on La'l Shahbāz Qalandar,' 65; and Boivin, 'Le sama´ dans la région du Sindh.'

22. The problem whether *dhamāl* can still be considered within the framework of *samā'* is discussed in more detail in Boivin, 'Le sama´ dans la région du Sindh.'

23. Lack of space does not allow delving deeper into questions of the origin of *dhamāl* here. Influences or borrowings from the *goma* dance of the local African diasporic community (known as Shidis) or from the Balochi *gwatī* exorcism ritual cannot be ruled out, but in my view, evidence is not yet sufficient to support such hypotheses. On the other hand, musicologists such as Denis Erin Mete do also support the hypothesis that the Qalandar saint might have imported the gyrating dance along with shamanistic drum rhythms from his northwest Iranian place of origin (personal communication; Lahore, March 17, 2010).

24. While until November 2008 there had been only a long aisle between the women and the family space on the one hand and the space for male dancers on the other (whereby male dancers and male spectators were separated by a rope), a year later the aisle had been marked by two long ropes separating both spaces more clearly.

25. Boivin, 'Le pèlerinage de Sehwan Sharif, Sindh (Pakistan),' 320.

26. Differing dates of Shah Jamal's death are found in literary sources, such as 1639, 1650, and 1671.

27. Frembgen, *The Friends of God-Sufi Saints in Islam*, 94–6.

28. Due to the popularity of this *dhamāl* event, in the course of the 1990s not only people from the elite of Lahore (including college girls), but also female expatriates started to attend the ritual. First these 'outsiders' were seated in a separate corner close to the musicians, but some years later a metal cage

was constructed to protect the few female spectators from the frenzy of the otherwise all-male audience.

29. For a general impression of the multi-sensory world of this pilgrimage, see Frembgen, *At the Shrine of the Red Sufi.*

30. Roger Caillois, *Die Spiele und die Menschen. Maske und Rausch* (Munich and Vienna: Albert Langen Georg Müller Verlag, 1965), 97.

31. Boivin, 'Le pèlerinage de Sehwan Sharif, Sindh (Pakistan),' 334–5.

32. See Gilbert Rouget, *Music and Trance: A Theory of the Relations between Music and Possession* (Chicago and London: The University of Chicago Press, 1985), 26 and 284. On the concepts of *hāl* and *wajd* in the Sufi tradition, see Avery, *A Psychology of Early Sufi samā'*, 69–74 and 26–8.

33. See Seyyed Hossein Nasr, *Living Sufism* (Lahore: Suhail Academy, 2005), 60–4.

34. The *dhōl* is made from *shīsham* (rosewood) or mango wood and both skins of this two-headed drum from goatskin.

35. In Punjab, *dhōl-wālā*s usually belong to the caste-like group of Mirasis; in Sindh they belong to the group of hereditary musicians called Manganhar (who perform, for instance, in Sehwan at the shrine of Bodlah Bahar, but not at the main Qalandar shrine). The *naubat* drummers in Sehwan, who are also called *dhamālī*s, are Sindhis belonging to the kinship groups of Channa and Unar. The rhythm they play is: 1-2, 1-2-3, 1-2-3-4-5-6 [see Boivin, 'Le pèlerinage de Sehwan Sharif, Sindh (Pakistan),' 335].

36. Thus, it is unusual and more of an exception when *dhamāl* is performed to the sound of mystical *qawwālī* singing (e.g., at the shrine of Mian Mir in Lahore).

37. In addition to invocations of the saint's honorary names (*yā 'Alī; mast Qalandar*), the following *bōl*s are common: *arē mast, dast bā dast; panjtān pāk haydarī.* For an analysis of the drumming text in *dhamāl*, see Wolf, 'The Poetics of "Sufi" Practice,' 255–6; and Selsing, *Without Experience no Knowledge*, 35–7 and 53–7.

38. Ibid., 56–7 (for additional *dhikr*-formulas used in Lahore, see 54–5).

39. Ibid., 54.

40. Frembgen, *Kleidung und Ausrüstung islamischer Gottsucher*, 174–5 and 186–7.

41. Personal communication (October, 2002).

42. In principle, what I prefer to call a 'field of aesthetics' (including the aesthetic features of a saint's shrine and the dress of dervishes) corresponds to Richard K. Wolf's concept of 'poetics' of music and movement in South Asian Sufi practice ('The Poetics of "Sufi" Practice').

43. Boivin, 'Le sama' dans la région du Sindh,' 308.

44. On the specific groups of world-renouncers in Sehwan Sharif, see Boivin, 'Le pèlerinage de Sehwan Sharif, Sindh (Pakistan),' 328–31.

45. On the spinning of dervishes and other movements in Sufi dance, see During, *Musique et extase*, 125–34.

46. Wolf, 'The Poetics of "Sufi" Practice, '259.

47. Conversation in Sehwan on July 30, 2010.
48. On the ritual initiation among Qalandar dervishes, see Frembgen, *Journey to God*, 89–90.
49. William Dalrymple portrayed her some years ago in a literary essay on Sehwan. See Dalrymple, *Nine Lives: In Search of the Sacred in Modern India* (London: Bloomsbury, 2009), 119–22, 125–32, and 140–45.
50. Wolf, 'The Poetics of "Sufi" Practice,' 255.
51. Ibid., 248.
52. Jürgen Wasim Frembgen, *Nocturnal Music in the Land of the Sufis: Unheard Pakistan* (Karachi: Oxford University Press, 2012b), 78.
53. During comments on this whirling with the head: 'Il est possible que le mouvement rotatoire de la tête, accompagné d'une respiration rythmique créant par sa cadence rapide une hyperventilation, produise des dérèglements de l'oreille interne, qui, se cominant aux effets de la respiration forte, engendrent un état de stupeur ou d'obnubilation' (*Musique et extase*, 159).
54. Observations on November 7 and 8, 2008.
55. Observations on October 15, 16, 17, 19, and 20, 2009. Older Sehwanis tend to denounce such kind of dance movements as 'disco-style'.
56. Observation on March 9, 2006 (Frembgen, *Nocturnal Music in the Land of the Sufis*, 80–1). On November 5, 2009 I met Muhabbat Sain again at the shrine of Shah Kamal (the younger brother of Shah Jamal) in Lahore where he did *sār kā dhamāl* but due to his advanced age he was no longer able to master the whirling movements. The weekly Thursday night event at Shah Kamal, which had been started in spring 2009 for some years, turned out to be a pastiche of drumming, singing *qasīdaiñ*, and *dhamāl*. Trance ritual had thus been transformed into religious entertainment and merriment. Rune Selsing, who selected this ritual space as the basis for his research on *dhamāl*, critically questions the business of *dhamāl* and the 'self-branding' of *dhamālīs* in the context of a discussion of ritual ossification and the decline of ritual as well as the growing new age appeal (*Without Experience no Knowledge*, 74–7 and 89–92).
57. Wolf, 'The Poetics of "Sufi" Practice,' 256–7.
58. Thomas J. Csordas, *Body/ Meaning/ Healing* (New York: Palgrave, 1993), 244–5; see also Christoph Wulf, 'Anthropologische Dimensionen des Tanzes,' in *Tanz als Anthropologie*, eds. Gabriele Brandstetter and Christoph Wulf (Munich: Wilhelm Fink, 2007), 123.
59. See Frembgen, *The Friends of God-Sufi Saints in Islam*, 3 (photograph of Arif Sain); and Frembgen, *At the Shrine of the Red Sufi*, 37–9 and 89–91.
60. For biographic data on Pappu Sain, see Wolf, 'The Poetics of "Sufi" Practice,' 249.
61. Grimes, *Beginnings in Ritual Studies*, 41. Selsing also considers the issues of sincerity and authenticity concluding that '... to the practitioners of dhamāl "belief" cannot be seen as some separate pure realm of the sacred in opposition to something profane; "belief" rather constitutes an activity in

the world. To dhamāl practitioners it is not a matter of belief or unbelief but rather of "doing it right"' (*Without Experience no Knowledge*, 97).

62. During, *Musique et extase*, 126.

63. Women also join, for instance, in *dhamāl* at the shrine of Shah Abdul Latif in Sindh (Rehman, 'Sacred Spaces, Rituals and Practices,' 141).

64. Frembgen, *At the Shrine of the Red Sufi*, 51–7 and 117–24.

65. David Parkin, 'Ritual as Spatial Direction and Bodily Division,' in *Understanding Rituals*, ed. Daniel de Coppet (London and New York: Routledge, 1992), 17.

66. Boivin, 'Note sur la danse dans les cultes musulman du domaine Sindhī,' 161; see also Rouget, *Music and Trance*, 26 and 284.

67. Rudolf Gelpke, *Drogen und Seelenerweiterung* (Munich: Kindler, 1975), 213–14.

68. Without going into further detail, it should be noted that the main features of the *dhamāl* style as performed by *khusrē* are exalted whirling with their long hair and swaying their hips.

69. It should be emphasized that *dhamāl* also functions as a therapeutic ritual particularly for women. The ritual takes place within a regulated, gender-segregated performance in the eastern *dhamāl* court of the shrine. This configuration as religious trance and therapy cult in the field of spirit possession needs detailed field-research in Sehwan as well as at other specialized healing shrines in Sindh. See Boivin, 'Reflections on La'l Shahbāz Qalandar,'62; and Boivin, 'Note sur la danse dans les cultes musulman du domaine Sindhī,' 163–4.

70. This stone, called *gulūband*, in the shape of a heart had later been inherited by Lal Shahbaz Qalandar and is preserved to this day as his most precious relic at his tomb (see Boivin, *Artefacts of Devotion*, 91–6).

71. Paul Connerton, *How Societies Remember* (Cambridge: Cambridge University Press, 1989), 38.

72. Ibid., 71. From the numerous Shia practitioners of *dhamāl* who I asked about the mythological-mimetic background of the dance, I learned only a minority (but see, for instance, Ajmi, *Three Days' Journey*) possessed consistent and coherent knowledge of the ritual tradition.

73. See Abbas, *The Female Voice*, 26 (also famous folk melodies, such as *lāl mērī pat rakhīo*, are addressed both to Hazrat Ali RA and the Qalandar). Concerning the concept of *mastī*, see Frembgen, 'Charisma and the Holy Fool,' 156–8.

74. Conversation with Usman Raja in Sehwan on August 13, 2009.

75. Omar Kasmani, *De-centering Devotion: The Complex Subject of Sehwan Sharif* (M.A. thesis, Institute for the Study of Muslim Civilizations, Aga Khan University, London, 2009), https://sindh.hypotheses.org/290, 114, 116.

76. Ibid., 138.

77. Especially at the 'Easter-*dhamāl*' at the '*urs* of Muslim saint Waris Shah in Jandiala Sher Khan, close to the city of Sheikhupura in Punjab.

78. In Ulrike Krasberg, *Die Ekstasetänzerinnen von Sidi Mustafa* (Berlin: Dietrich Reimer, 2002), 24, 101, and 153.

79. Klaus Peter Köpping, 'Inszenierung und Transgression in Ritual und Theater. Grenzprobleme der performativen Ethnologie,' in *Ethnologie und Inszenierung. Ansätze zur Theaterethnologie*, eds. Bettina E. Schmidt and Mark Münzel (Marburg: Curupira, 1998), 47–8; and see also, Erika Fischer-Lichte, 'Diskurse des Theatralen,' in *Diskurse des Theatralen*, eds. Erika Fischer-Lichte, Christian Horn, Sandra Umathum, and Mathias Warstat (Tübingen and Basel: A. Francke, 2005), 11–32.

80. Grimes used the term liturgy 'liturgy' for such a symbolic action containing motifs that are ceremonious, magical and decorous (*Beginnings in Ritual Studies*, 51–3).

81. See Michael Jackson, *Paths Toward a Clearing: Radical Empiricism and Ethnographic Inquiry* (Bloomington: Indiana University Press, 1989), 13.

82. Göran Ogén, 'Religious Ecstasy in Classical Sufism,' in *Religious Ecstasy. Based on Papers Read at the Symposium on Religious Ecstasy Held at Åbo, Finland, on the 16th-18th of August 198*1, ed. N. G. Holm (Stockholm: Almqvist & Wiksell, 1982), 226–40, esp. 227–9, 232, and 236; Kugle, *Sufis and Saints' Bodies*, 24.

83. Conversation, March 28, 2010.

84. Conversation, July 30, 2010 in Sehwan.

85. Nancy Scheper-Hughes and Margaret M. Lock, 'The Mindful Body: A Prolegomenon to Future Work in Medical Anthropology,' *Medical Anthropology Quarterly* 1/1 (1986): 6–41.

86. See Boivin, 'Le pèlerinage de Sehwan Sharif, Sindh (Pakistan),' 337.

87. Krasberg, *Die Ekstasetänzerinnen*, 78 and 95.

88. See Gell, *Art and Agency*, 66; and Krasberg, *Die Ekstasetänzerinnen*, 22 and 133.

89. Köpping, 'Inszenierung und Transgression in Ritual und Theater,' 47.

90. See Klaus Peter Köpping and Ursula Rao, *Im Rausch des Rituals. Gestaltung und Transformationen der Wirklichkeit in körperlicher Performanz* (Münster: LIT Verlag, 2000), 7–8.

91. Ibid., 21–2.

92. This important question cannot be taken up here, but is addressed in an ethnographic narrative on Sufi music and classical music in Pakistan, see Frembgen, *Nocturnal Music in the Land of the Sufis*, 40–5.

93. Pierre Bourdieu, *Entwurf einer Theorie der Praxis* (Frankfurt a. M.: Suhrkamp, 1976), 165 and 169.

94. Louis Dumont, 'On Value, Modern and Nonmodern,' in *Essays on Individualism: Modern Ideology in Anthropological Perspective* (Chicago and London: The University of Chicago Press, 1986), 234–68 (esp. 240). See also, Kugle, *Sufis and Saints' Bodies*, 13.

AFTERWORD

In the present time, conservative, scriptural, and reformist currents of Sunni Islam have usurped the power of discourse in Pakistan and elsewhere across the Muslim world. Following the import of puritan Wahhabi ideology from Saudi Arabia (since the 1970s also by Pakistani migrant workers in the Middle East), the proponents of these movements propagate strict application of *sharī'a* and oppose what they perceive as 'secularism' (*ladīniyāt*). They use a prescriptive approach saying 'how Islam should be', claiming to follow 'true Islam' and emphasizing Sunni-Shia differences. By proliferating intolerance, which has now infested minds of myriads, small wonder Sufism also became their target. Fundamentalists intend to bomb and raze all saints' shrines. Proponents of 'rigid normative' Islam promote exclusivity, but the faith is by its very nature not exclusive. With their insistence on a single, clear, and unambiguous meaning, typical for the thinking of the modern masculine 'homo rationalis', they aspire to transform Pakistan into a monochromatic society not only by reducing the scope for different interpretations, for instance, in reading the Holy Quran, but above all by eliminating plural social reality. In fact, one may say 'Islam is plural'! The Sufis were always cognisant of that when they proclaimed in Urdu: *Allāh-tālā tak pahuñchne kēlīyē itne rāste haiñ jitne tamām insāniyāt ke sāñse*—'The paths to the Almighty are as varied as mankind's breaths'. As public intellectual Raza Rumi rightly points out, the shrine of Lal Shahbaz Qalandar is representative of Pakistan's plural heritage and the lived faith for millions of its inhabitants.[1]

Across the Muslim world there are 'Islamic ethnographic variations', local forms of Islam rich in mythology, symbol, and ritual. Also, in Pakistan vernacular devotional Islam manifests itself as an emotional, pragmatic, and rather women-friendly 'religion of the shrines' deeply impregnated by Sufism. Unfortunately, today many people look down with contempt on these local traditions as 'superstitious' and 'primitive' (*paīndū*) *Islām*. This neglected facet of Islam is inclusive in the sense that it neither overemphasizes boundaries between sects nor excludes adherents of other religions. On the contrary, this many-faceted jewel of folk Islam allows sharing, a plural ethos. At the shrines of Sufi saints, people often practice 'tolerance' or better non-interference. The attitude of 'letting things happen' (*rawādarī*) as expressed in the popular Urdu saying: *apnā 'aqīdah chōdō nahīñ dusrē kā chēdō nahīñ*— 'To you your faith and to me my faith'.[2] Sufism today carries idealized notions of peace, love, and harmony. But, as aptly marked by literary translator Zahra Sabri concerning the institutionalization of Sufi Islam in Pakistan, these days prominent Pirs and Shaikhs '[...] are often all too well-entrenched in the social and political status quo [...]' some of them rising to become powerful party leaders, ministers and even prime ministers.[3] Nevertheless, only a limited number of those who follow this religion of love, as Sufism has been termed, will respectfully recognize that all faiths teach good things (value-pluralism) or even desire to learn from other religions although appreciation of other faiths has been enjoined on all Muslims in the Holy Quran. Anwar Abbas lucidly writes:

> If God had willed to create a world in which all the men and women were alike in every way, the people would have followed the same religion, spoken the same language and evolved an identical pattern of culture and conduct. He did not do so because it was not His purpose.
>
> The different beliefs and ways of life make for enrichment if believers can live a spirit of tolerance and compete with one another in doing good. It is also extremely important not to impose their will on others by force, at gunpoint or through the explosion of bombs.[4]

Notwithstanding the eminent roles essayed in politics by prominent Sufi leaders over the history of Islam and even preaching of militancy in times of conflict and crisis[5] in past and present saints' shrines offer compassion and solace to the oppressed and extend a lifeline to the underprivileged. It is at shrines where others are cared for as I observed time and again. In everyday religious practice it is heart-warming to experience that many people still cherish this South Asian folk wisdom: *mohabbat sab kēlīyē, nafrat kisī sē nahīñ*—'love for all, hatred for none', a saying not seldom prominently inscribed on Pakistani trucks. In this sense, people could draw from Sufi poetry which contains many such distinct affirmations of love, both to God and to fellow humans and lay the foundation for the acceptance of diversity. Thus, Baba Farid once addressed the following remarkable words to a visitor: 'Don't give me scissors! Give me a needle! I sew together don't cut apart!' Baba Farid's lodge in Pakpattan became a place where Muslims and Hindus met and peacefully exchanged views and where Sufis even discussed questions of spirituality and yoga with Hindu ascetics. The most impressive realization of the dissolution of religious boundaries is found in the ecstatic verses of the great Sufi poet Bullhe Shah whose verse many in Pakistan are acquainted with. He, who confronted ritualistic religion and found himself to some extent on the threshold between being Muslim and Hindu, in a state of 'as well as', wrote and sang: 'We are neither Hindu nor Muslim. We just sit and turn the spinning wheel—we have nothing to do with pride in the religious creed. We are neither Sunni nor Shia. We are non-violent towards everyone.' Inspired by the same spirit, one of the last great Sufi poets of Pakistan Mian Muhammad Bakhsh (d. 1907) from Kashmir crooned, 'If He is my friend, then everyone is my friend, even a stranger.'

This variety of poetry is vivid at shrines of mystics and ascetics till date. Hardliners, however, are strictly opposed to the openness and practiced tolerance in such spaces of 'informal' Sufism, indigenous 'folk' Islam, and Muslim-Hindu religious interface. Music and trance dance as well as the presence of women and Shia devotees particularly irk them. They condemn all this as 'un-Islamic' and brand visitors and pilgrims as 'unbelievers' who deserve to be killed. Indigenous Sufi-inspired Islam is powerless considering repeated attacks on shrines over the last 20 years. On February 16, 2017 a Daesh suicide bomber killed over 90 and left over 300 injured in an attack at the shrine of Lal Shahbaz Qalandar during *dhamāl* following evening prayers.

My intention in writing this book (which puts together results of my long-term fieldwork on the veneration of the Qalandar) is to show what is going to be lost in terms of cultural diversity and religious identity when local Sufi-inspired Islam is stigmatized, threatened, and attacked, when the syncretic religious milieu of Sehwan with its shared faith becomes a target. In the first two chapters we looked at aspects of 'material religion' associated with the visitation of the tomb of Lal Shahbaz Qalandar examining extraordinary rich visual piety. Images of the Qalandar have become powerful icons of love and devotion indicating the presence of the saint. They shape and affirm the religious identity of devotees and reflect their cultural identity. Through its dense iconography this visual art becomes extraordinary meaningful. The analysis of placards and banners announcing the pilgrimage to Sehwan provided important insights into contemporary devotional practices as well as the institutionalization of Punjabi pilgrims' Sufi networks. As far as social structure is concerned, they cut across barriers of ethnicity, caste, brotherhood, and sect. Their collective identity is characterized by a powerful sense of sharing, belonging, comradeship, and spiritual bonding. This also holds true for the 'Sufi lineage' of Mai Kausar from Lahore, a unique 'chain' of devotees centring around three saintly women, investigated in detail through Mai's written life story. As exemplified by portraying three remarkable 'liminal figures' the Dionysian cult of Lal Shahbaz Qalandar is able to accommodate difference and otherness. Both music and dance are integral rituals at the shrine in Sehwan and other shrines associated with the Qalandar. In the study of trance dance various modes of embodied ritual attitudes, performance and aesthetics of this public, predominantly collective dance, differentiating three groups of actors in terms of ritual structure, techniques of the body, gestural grammar, and gender-related kinaesthetic styles were explored. Apart from marked differences between performers, these modes of ritual sensibilities coexist and interpenetrate each other whereby the celebrative form of interaction with the beloved saint Lal Shahbaz Qalandar remains the central theme of this 'danced religion'.

As Raza Rumi emphasized in the aftermath of the bloody attack on the pilgrims at the shrine of Lal Shahbaz Qalandar: 'Sehwan as an expression of counterculture, of allowing human bodies to find expression in a sacred realm, of providing voice to the voiceless, needs to be treasured.'[6]

Notes

1. Raza Rumi, 'The meaning of Sehwan.' *The Friday Times*, March 10, 2017.
2. For this quotation and other verses in this paragraph, see Jürgen Wasim Frembgen, 'Tolerance in the Sufi Tradition: Islamic mysticism is devoted to the promotion of openness and pluralism,' *East-West Affairs* 1 (2013): 94, 97, and 99–100.
3. Zahra Sabri, 'Mystic Power. Why "Sufism" is not what it is made out to be', *Herald* (Karachi), May 28, 2018.
4. Anwar Abbas, 'Religious unity,' *DAWN*, February 13, 2015.
5. See, for instance, Frembgen, *Journey to God*, 57–65; Alix Philippon, *Soufisme et politique au Pakistan*; Nile Green, *Sufism: A Global History* (Chichester: Wiley-Blackwell, 2012); and Sabri, 'Mystic Power.'
6. Rumi, 'The meaning of Sehwan.'

BIBLIOGRAPHY

Abbas, Anwar. 'Religious unity.' *DAWN*. February 13, 2015. https://www. dawn.com/news/1163221.

Abbas, Shemeem Burney. *The Female Voice in Sufi Ritual: Devotional Practices of Pakistan and India*. Austin: University of Texas Press, 2002.

Ahmed, Durre S. *Masculinity, Rationality and Religion: A Feminist Perspective*. Lahore: ASR Publications, 1994.

Aitken, E. H. *Gazetteer of the Province of Sind*. Karachi: 1907. Reprint, Karachi: Indus Publications, 1986.

Ajmi, Qais. *Three Days' Journey into the Wonderland of Sehwan*. Lahore: 2001; unpaginated typed manuscript, 78 pages.

Anonymous. 'Qalandar Lal Shahbaz.' Karachi: Department of Public Relations, Government of Sind, n. d.

Appadurai, Arjun. 'Introduction: commodities and the politics of value.' In *The Social Life of Things: Commodities in Cultural Perspective*, edited by A. Appadurai, 3–63. Cambridge: Cambridge University Press, 1986.

Asghar, Muhammad. *The Sacred and the Secular: Aesthetics in the Domestic Space of Pakistan/Punjab*. Münster: LIT Verlag, 2016.

Avery, Kenneth S. *A Psychology of Early Sufi samā': Listening and Altered States*. London and New York: RoutledgeCurzon, 2004.

Aziz, Hasan. *Kalaam-e-Aarifaan. Poetry of Sufis and Mystics*. Karachi: Kalaam-e-Aarifaan, 2014.

Baldick, Julian. *Imaginary Muslims: The Uwaysi Sufis of Central Asia*. New York: New York University Press, 1993.

Beinhauer-Köhler, Bärbel. *Gelenkte Blicke. Visuelle Kulturen im Islam*. Zürich: Theologischer Verlag Zürich, 2011.

Boivin, Michel. 'Reflections on La'l Shahbāz Qalandar and the Management of his Spiritual Authority in Sehwan Sharif.' *Pakistan Historical Society* 61/4 (2003): 41–72.

_____. 'Note sur la danse dans les cultes musulman du domaine Sindhī.' *Journal of the History of Sufism* 4 (2004): 159–67.

_____. 'Le pèlerinage de Sehwan Sharif, Sindh (Pakistan): territoires, protagonistes et rituels.' In *Les pélerinages au Maghreb et au Moyen-Orient*, edited by S. Chiffoleau and A. Madoeuf, 301–45. Damas: Institut Français du Proche-Orient, 2005.

_____. 'Le sama´ dans la région du Sindh.' In *Des voies et des voix: Soufisme, culture, musique*, edited by Zaïm Khenchelaoui, 293–333. Alger: CNPRAH, 2006.

_____. 'Representations and Symbols in Muharram and Other Rituals: Fragments of Shiite Worlds from Bombay to Karachi.' In *The Other Shiites. From the Mediterranean to Central Asia*, edited by Alessandro Monsutti, Silvia Naef, and Farian Sabahi, 149–72. Bern: Peter Lang, 2007.

_____, ed. *Sindh Through History and Representation: French Contributions to Sindhi Studies*. Karachi: Oxford University Press, 2008.

_____. *Artefacts of Devotion: A Sufi Repertoire of the Qalandariyya in Sehwan Sharif, Sindh, Pakistan*. Karachi: Oxford University Press, 2011.

_____. *Le soufisme antinomien dans le sous-continent indien. La'l Shahbāz Qalandar et son heritage XIIIe – XXe siècle*. Paris: Les Éditions du Cerf, 2012.

Bourdieu, Pierre. *Entwurf einer Theorie der Praxis*. Frankfurt a. M.: Suhrkamp, 1976.

Buck-Morss, Susan. 'Aesthetics and Anaesthetics: Walter Benjamin's Artwork Essays Reconsidered.' *October* 62 (1992): 3–41.

Caillois, Roger. *Die Spiele und die Menschen. Maske und Rausch*. Munich and Vienna: Albert Langen Georg Müller Verlag, 1965.

Centlivres, Pierre, and Micheline Centlivres-Demont. 'Une présence absente: symboles et images populaires du prophète Mahomet.' In *Derrière les images*, edited by Marc-Oliver Gonseth, Jacques Hainard, Roland Kaehr, and François Borel, 139–70. Neuchatel: Musée d'ethnographie, 1998.

Connerton, Paul. *How Societies Remember*. Cambridge: Cambridge University Press, 1989.

Csikszentmihalyi, Mihaly. 'Why we need things.' In *History from Things: Essays on Material Culture*, edited by Steven Lubar and W. David Kingery, 20–9. Washington: Smithsonian Institution Press, 1993.

Csordas, Thomas J. *Body/ Meaning/ Healing*. New York: Palgrave, 1993.

Dalrymple, William. *Nine Lives: In Search of the Sacred in Modern India*. London: Bloomsbury, 2009.

Diamond, Stanley. *Kritik der Zivilisation. Anthropologie und die Wiederentdeckung des Primitiven*. Frankfurt a. M. and New York: Campus, 1976.

Digby, Simon. 'Qalandars and Related Groups: Elements of Social Deviance in the Religious Life of the Delhi Sultanate of the Thirteenth and Fourteenth Centuries.' In *Islam in Asia*, vol. 1, edited by Yohanan Friedmann, 60–108. Jerusalem: The Magnes Press, 1984.

Dumont, Louis. 'On Value, Modern and Nonmodern.' In *Essays on Individualism: Modern Ideology in Anthropological Perspective*, 234–68. Chicago and London: The University of Chicago Press, 1986.

During, Jean. *Musique et extase: L'audition mystique dans la tradition soufie*. Paris: Albin Michel, 1988.

———. 'Sufi Music and Rites in the Era of Mass Reproduction, Techniques and Culture.' In *Sufism, Music and Society in Turkey and the Middle East*, edited by Anders Hammarlund, Tord Olsson, and Elisabeth Özdalga, 149–68. Istanbul: Swedish Research Institute in Istanbul, 2001.

Eck, Diana. *Darśan: Seeing the Divine Image in India*. New York: Columbia University Press, 1998.

Elias, Jamal J. 'Truck Calligraphy in Pakistan.' In *The Aura of Alif: The Art of Writing in Islam*, edited by Jürgen Wasim Frembgen, 211–23. Munich: Prestel, 2010.

———. *Aisha's Cushion: Religious Art, Perception, and Practice in Islam*. Cambridge: Harvard University Press, 2012.

Elkins, James. 'The Concept of Visual Literacy, and its Limitations.' In *Visual Literacy*, edited by James Elkins, 1–9. New York: Routledge, 2008.

Ernst, Carl W. 'An Indo-Persian Guide to Sufi Shrine Pilgrimage.' In *Manifestations of Sainthood in Islam*, edited by Grace M. Smith and Carl W. Ernst, 43–67. Istanbul: The Isis Press, 1993.

———, and Bruce B. Lawrence. *Sufi Martyrs of Love: The Chishti Order in South Asia and Beyond*. New York: Palgrave Macmillan, 2002.

———. 'Ideological and Technological Transformations of Contemporary Sufism.' In *Muslim Networks from Hajj to Hip Hop*, edited by Miriam Crooke and Bruce B. Lawrence, 191–207. Chapel Hill: The University of North Carolina Press, 2005.

Fischer-Lichte, Erika. 'Diskurse des Theatralen.' In *Diskurse des Theatralen*, edited by Erika Fischer-Lichte, Christian Horn, Sandra Umathum, and Mathias Warstat, 11–32. Tübingen and Basel: A. Francke, 2005.

Foucault, Michel. 'Of Other Spaces, Heterotopias.' *Diacritics* 16/1 (Spring 1986): 22–7.

Frembgen, Jürgen Wasim. *Kleidung und Ausrüstung islamischer Gottsucher: Ein Beitrag zur materiellen Kultur des Derwischwesens.* Wiesbaden: Harrassowitz, 1999.

_____. 'Devotional Service at Sufi Shrines: A Punjabi *Charāgwālā* and his Votive Offering of Light.' *Journal of the History of Sufism* 4 (2003–4): 255–62.

_____. 'Assemblage und Devotion: Macht und Aura von Objekten in muslimischen Heiligenschreinen im Punjab.' In *Die Dinge als Zeichen: Kulturelles Wissen und materielle Kultur*, edited by T. L. Kienlin, 171–7. Bonn: Verlag Dr. Rudolf Habelt, 2005.

_____. *The Friends of God-Sufi Saints in Islam: Popular Poster Art from Pakistan.* Karachi: Oxford University Press, 2006.

_____. *Journey to God: Sufis and Dervishes in Islam.* Karachi: Oxford University Press, 2008a.

_____. 'Charisma and the Holy Fool: Gul Mastān Bābā, the Enraptured, Saint of Udaipur.' In *Sufi Traditions and New Departures: Recent Scholarship on Continuity and Change in South Asian Sufism*, edited by Søren Christian Lassen and Hugh van Skyhawk, 151–80. Islamabad: Taxila Institute of Asian Civilization, 2008b.

_____. '*Rehmat ka Sayah*—The Shadow of Mercy: Glimpses of Muslim Saints' Portraits.' In *Mazaar, Bazaar: Design and Visual Culture in Pakistan*, edited by Saima Zaidi, 10–15. Karachi: Oxford University Press, 2009.

_____. 'Calligraphy in the World of Sufi Shrines in Pakistan.' In *The Aura of Alif: The Art of Writing in Islam*, edited by Jürgen Wasim Frembgen, 225–35. Munich: Prestel, 2010a.

_____. 'Icons of Love and Devotion. Sufi Posters from Pakistan depicting Lal Shahbaz Qalandar.' In *Religiöse Blicke – Blicke auf das Religiöse. Visualität und Religion*, edited by Bärbel Beinhauer-Köhler, Daria Pezzoli-Olgiati, and Joachim Valentin, 227–41. Zürich: Theologischer Verlag Zürich, 2010b.

_____. *At the Shrine of the Red Sufi: Five Days and Nights on Pilgrimage in Pakistan.* Karachi: Oxford University Press, 2011a.

_____. '"Ich weiß nichts außer Liebe, Rausch und Ekstase". Lal Shahbaz Qalandar (gest. 1274) und die Bewegung der Qalandar-Derwische.' In *Mystik: Die Sehnsucht nach dem Absoluten*, edited by A. Lutz, 157–9. Zürich: Museum Rietberg and Scheidegger & Spies, 2011b.

_____. '*Dhamāl* and the Performing Body: Trance Dance in the Devotional Sufi Practice of Pakistan.' *Journal of Sufi Studies* 1 (2012a): 77–113.

_____. *Nocturnal Music in the Land of the Sufis: Unheard Pakistan*. Karachi: Oxford University Press, 2012b.

_____. 'Tolerance in the Sufi Tradition: Islamic mysticism is devoted to the promotion of openness and pluralism.' *East-West Affairs* 1 (2013): 93–103.

_____. 'The Symbolism of the Boat in Sufi and Shi'a Imagery of Pakistan and Iran.' *Journal of the History of Sufism* 6 (2015): 85–100.

_____. 'Betwixt and between: Figures of ambiguity in the Sufi cult of Lāl Shāhbāz Qalandar (Pakistan).' In *Pilgrimage and Ambiguity: Sharing the Sacred*, edited by Angela Hobart and Thierry Zarcone, 119–29. Canon Pyon: Sean Kingston Publishing, 2017a.

_____. *Das Rätsel des Pfeils. Begegnungen mit Sufi-Meistern.* Frauenfeld: Waldgut, 2017b.

_____. 'Islamic Stickers from Pakistan and India. Eye-catching, Protective and Carrying a Message.' *Journal Fünf Kontinente* 3 (2018/19a): 152–65.

_____. 'Words and Images in the Muslim Public Space: Placards announcing Sufi Saints' Festivals in the Pakistani Punjab.' *Baessler-Archiv* 65 (2018/19b), 51–66.

Gell, Alfred. *Art and Agency: An Anthropological Theory*. Oxford: Clarendon Press, 1998.

Gelpke, Rudolf. *Drogen und Seelenerweiterung*. Munich: Kindler, 1975.

Ger, Güliz, and Russell W. Belk. 'I'd like to buy the World a Coke: Consumption Scenes of the "Less Affluent World".' *Journal of Consumer Policy* 19 (1996): 271–304.

Ghaffaar, Muzaffar A. *Masterworks of Punjaabi Sufi Poetry: Bulleh Shaah. Vol. 1*. Lahore: Ferozsons, 2005.

Gidwani, Charu J. 'Three *panjrā*s of Udero Lāl.' *Mission Interdisciplinaire Française du Sindh*, *Newsletter* 3 (September 2009): 8–9.

Gilmartin, David. 'Religious Leadership and the Pakistan Movement in the Punjab.' *Modern Asian Studies* 13/3 (1979): 485–517.

_____. 'Biradari and Bureaucracy: The Politics of Muslim Kinship Solidarity in 20th Century Punjab.' *International Journal of Punjab Studies* 1/1 (1994): 1–37.

Gombrich, Ernst H. 'Visual Metaphors of Value in Art.' In *Meditations on a Hobby Horse and other Essays on the Theory of Art*, edited by Ernst H. Gombrich, 12–29. London and New York: Phaidon Press, 1985.

_____. 'Expression and Communication.' In *Meditations on a Hobby Horse and other Essays on the Theory of Art*, edited by Ernst H. Gombrich, 56–69, London and New York: Phaidon Press, 1985.

Green, Nile. *Sufism: A Global History*. Chichester: Wiley-Blackwell, 2012.

Grimes, Ronald L. *Beginnings in Ritual Studies*. Columbia: University of South Carolina Press, 1995.

Gruber, Christiane. 'Between Logos (*Kalima*) and Light (*Nūr*): Representations of the Prophet Muhammad in Islamic Painting.' *Muqarnas* 26 (2009): 229–62.

Gulraj, Jethmal Parsram. *Sind and its Sufis*. Karachi: Culture & Tourism Department, Government of Sindh, 1924. Reprint, 2016.

Habermas, Jürgen. *The Inclusion of the Other: Studies in Political Theory*. Cambridge: MIT Press, 1998.

Jackson, Michael. *Paths Toward a Clearing: Radical Empiricism and Ethnographic Inquiry*. Bloomington: Indiana University Press, 1989.

Kalhoro, Zulfiqar Ali. 'Ashram of Ascetics.' *The Friday Times*. December 28, 2018. https://www.academia.edu/38102736/Ashram_of_Ascetics_pdf?auto=download.

Kapferer, Bruce, *A Celebration of Demons: Exorcism and the Aesthetics of Healing in Sri Lanka*. Bloomington: University Indiana Press, 1983.

Karamustafa, Ahmet T. *God's Unruly Friends: Dervish Groups in the Islamic Later Middle Period 1200-1550*. Salt Lake City: University of Utah Press, 1994.

Kasmani, Omar. *De-centering Devotion: The Complex Subject of Sehwan Sharif*. M.A. thesis, Institute for the Study of Muslim Civilizations, Aga Khan University, London, 2009. https://sindh.hypotheses.org/290.

———. 'Women [un-]like women. The Question of Spiritual Authority among Female Fakirs of Sehwan Sharīf.' In *Devotional Islam in Contemporary South Asia. Shrines, Journeys and Wanderers*, edited by Michel Boivin and Remy Delage, 47–62. London and New York: Routledge, 2016.

Khan, Dominique-Sila. 'Jhulelal and the Identity of Indian Sindhis.' In *Sindh through History and Representation: French Contributions to Sindhi Studies*, edited by Michel Boivin, 72–81. Karachi: Oxford University Press, 2008.

Khosronejad, Pedram. 'Introduction.' In *The Art and Material Culture of Iranian Shi'ism Iconography and Religious Devotion in Shi'i Islam*, edited by Pedram Khosronejad, 1–22. London: I. B. Tauris, 2012.

Knysh, Alexander. *Sufism: A New History of Islamic Mysticism*. Princeton: Princeton University Press, 2017.

Köpping, Klaus Peter. 'Inszenierung und Transgression in Ritual und Theater. Grenzprobleme der performativen Ethnologie.' In *Ethnologie und Inszenierung. Ansätze zur Theaterethnologie,* edited by Bettina E. Schmidt and Mark Münzel, 45–85. Marburg: Curupira, 1998.

————, and Ursula Rao. *Im Rausch des Rituals. Gestaltung und Transformationen der Wirklichkeit in körperlicher Performanz.* Münster: LIT Verlag, 2000.

Korom, Frank J. 'The Presence of Absence: Using Stuff in a South Asian Sufi Movement.' *AAS Working Papers in Social Anthropology/ÖAW Arbeitspapiere zur Sozialanthropologie* 23 (2012): 1–19.

Krasberg, Ulrike. *Die Ekstasetänzerinnen von Sidi Mustafa.* Berlin: Dietrich Reimer, 2002.

Kugle, Scott. *Sufis and Saints' Bodies. Mysticism, Corporeality, and Sacred Power.* Chapel Hill: University of North Carolina Press, 2007.

————. 'Dancing with Khusro: Gender Ambiguities and Poetic Performance in a Delhi *Dargah.*' In *Rethinking Islamic Studies. From Orientalism to Cosmopolitanism,* edited by Carl W. Ernst and Richard C. Martin, 245–65. Columbia: The University of South Carolina Press, 2010.

Kurin, Richard, and Carol Morrow. 'Patterns of Solidarity in a Punjabi Muslim Village.' *Contributions to Indian Sociology* 19/2 (1985): 235–49.

Lewis, I. M. *Ecstatic Religion: A Study of Shamanism and Spirit Possession.* London and New York: Routledge, 1989.

Mason, Herbert W. *Al-Hallaj.* Richmond: Curzon Press, 1995.

Massignon, Louis. *Essai sur les origines du lexique technique de la mystique musulmane.* Paris: Edition du Cerf, 1922.

Mohammad, Inam. *Hazrat Lal Shahbaz Qalandar of Sehwan-Sharif.* Karachi: Royal Book Company, 1978.

Nasr, Seyyed Hossein. *Living Sufism.* Lahore: Suhail Academy, 2005.

Ocak, Ahmet Yaşar. *Osmanlı imparatorluğu'nda marjinal sûfîlik: Kalenderîler, XIV-XVII. Yüzyıllar.* Ankara: Türk Kurumu Basıevi, 1992.

Ogén, Göran. 'Religious Ecstasy in Classical Sufism.' In *Religious Ecstasy. Based on Papers Read at the Symposium on Religious Ecstasy Held at Åbo, Finland, on the 16th-18th of August 1981,* edited by N. G. Holm, 226–40. Stockholm: Almqvist & Wiksell, 1982.

Papas, Alexandre. *Mystiques et vagabonds en Islam. Portraits de trois soufis qalandar.* Paris: Les Éditions du Cerf, 2010.

Parkin, David. 'Ritual as Spatial Direction and Bodily Division.' In *Understanding Rituals,* edited by Daniel de Coppet, 11–25. London and New York: Routledge, 1992.

Parwani, Lata. 'Myths of Jhuley Lal: Deconstructing a Sindhi Cultural Icon.' In *Interpreting the Sindhi World: Essays on Society and History*, edited by Michel Boivin and Matthew A. Cook, 1–27. Karachi: Oxford University Press, 2010.

Petievich, Carla. *When Men Speak as Women: Vocal Masquerade in Indo-Muslim Poetry*. Delhi: Oxford University Press, 2008.

Pfeffer, Georg. 'Manliness in the Punjab: Male Sexuality and the *khusra*.' *Sociologus* 45/1 (1995): 26–39.

Philippon, Alix. *Soufisme et politique au Pakistan*. Paris and Aix-en-Provence: Éditions Karthala & Sciences Po Aix, 2011.

Pinney, Christopher. 'Piercing the Skin of the Idol.' In *Beyond Aesthetics: Art and the Technologies of Enchantment*, edited by Christopher Pinney and Nicholas Thomas. Oxford and New York: Berg, 2001.

Platts, John T. *A Dictionary of Urdū, Hindī and English*. Oxford: Clarendon Press, 1884; Reprint: New Delhi: Munshiram Manoharlal, 1997.

Qureshi, Regula Burckhardt. *Sufi Music of India and Pakistan: Sound, Context and Meaning in Qawwali*. Cambridge: Cambridge University Press, 1986.

Rehman, Uzma. 'Sacred Spaces, Rituals and Practices: The *mazar*s of Saiyid Pir Waris Shah and Shah 'Abdul Latif Bhitai. In *Sufism Today: Heritage and Tradition in the Global Community*, edited by C. Raudvere and L. Stenberg, 137–57. New York: I. B. Tauris, 2009.

———. 'Spiritual Power and "Threshold" Identities: The *Mazārs* of Sayyid Pīr Waris Shāh Abdul Latīf Bhitai.' In *South Asian Sufis: Devotion, Deviation, and Destiny*, edited by Clinton Bennett and Charles M. Ramsey, 61–81. London et al.: Bloomsbury, 2012.

Renard, John. *Friends of God: Islamic Images of Piety, Commitment, and Servanthood*. University of California Press, 2008.

Rouget, Gilbert. *Music and Trance: A Theory of the Relations between Music and Possession*. Chicago and London: The University of Chicago Press, 1985.

Rumi, Raza. 'The meaning of Sehwan.' *The Friday Times*. March 10, 2017. https://www.thefridaytimes.com/the-meaning-of-sehwan/.

Sabri, Zahra. 'Mystic Power. Why "Sufism" is not what it is made out to be.' *Herald* (Karachi). May 28, 2018. https://herald.dawn.com/news/1398514.

Sadiq, Azra. 'Hazrat Lal Shahbaz Qalandar.' *Humsafar* (PIA in-flight-magazine) (February 2012): 60–3.

Scheper-Hughes, Nancy, and Margaret M. Lock. 'The Mindful Body: A Prolegomenon to Future Work in Medical Anthropology.' *Medical Anthropology Quarterly* 1/1 (1986): 6–41.

Selsing, Rune. *Without Experience no Knowledge: A Ritual Study of the Ecstatic Sufi Practice dhamāl in Pakistan*. M. A. thesis, Department of Anthropology, Copenhagen University, 2010.

Starrett, Gregory. 'The Political Economy of Religious Commodities in Cairo.' *American Anthropologist* 97/1 (1995): 51–68.

Strathern, Marilyn. *Property, Substance, and Effect: Anthropological Essays on Persons and Things*. London: Athlone Press, 1999.

Suvorova, Anna. *Muslim Saints of South Asia: The eleventh to fifteenth centuries*. London and New York: RoutledgeCurzon, 2004.

Welch, Stuart Cary. *India: Art and Culture, 1300-1900*. New York: Metropolitan Museum of Art, 1985.

Wolf, Richard K. 'The Poetics of "Sufi" Practice: Drumming, Dancing, and Complex Agency at Madho Lāl Husain (and Beyond).' *American Ethnologist* 33/2 (2006): 246–68.

Wulf, Christoph. 'Anthropologische Dimensionen des Tanzes.' In *Tanz als Anthropologie*, edited by Gabriele Brandstetter and Christoph Wulf, 121–31. Munich: Wilhelm Fink, 2007.

Photography Credit

Aly Philippe Bossin, Figs. 68–69, 77, 82–84.
Jürgen Wasim Frembgen, Figs. 1–67, 70–76, 78–81, 85–90.
Salman Zaidi, Fig. 88.

INDEX